·THE·
Wisconsin
Almanac

·THE·
Wisconsin Almanac

Being a loosely organized compendium of facts, history, lore, remembrances, puzzles, recipes, and both household and gardening advice with which to offer elucidation, assistance, and occasional amusement to the conscientious reader

Jerry Minnich
General Editor

NORTH COUNTRY PRESS

North Country Press
3934 Plymouth Circle
Madison, Wisconsin 53705

First Printing
Manufactured in the United States of America

Library of Congress Cataloging-in-Publication Data

The Wisconsin almanac : being a loosely-organized compendium of
    facts, history, lore, remembrances, puzzles, recipes, and
    both household and gardening advice with which to offer
    elucidation, assistance, and occasional amusement to the
    conscientious reader / Jerry Minnich, general editor.
        p.   cm.
    ISBN 0-944133-06-1 : $8.95
    1. Wisconsin—Miscellanea.   I. Minnich, Jerry
F581.5.W56 1989   977.5--dc20   89-39590
                                                         CIP

Cover illustration by Renée Graef
Designed by Jane Tenenbaum
Manufactured by Edwards Brothers, Inc.

Contributors

Diana Cook is responsible for all the puzzles, trivia teasers, and quizzes in this book, as well as for the "Years Ago" and "Excuses for a Party" items and several major features of unusual interest. As an examination of her work quickly indicates, she is at once inquisitive, insightful, playful, and just very slightly mischievous.

Don Davenport is a veteran Wisconsin travel writer and photographer, the author of both *Shipwreck on Lake Michigan* (NorthWord Press, 1983) and the new *Fodor's Michigan, Wisconsin, Minnesota* (Random House, 1989). He has contributed to a number of magazines, and his work appears frequently in the Chicago *Tribune* and other newspapers. In addition to the historical essays he has contributed to this book, Don is responsible for the monthly "openers" and weather charts.

Tim Eisele is a popular outdoor writer and photographer whose work appears regularly in the *Wisconsin State Journal*. He has also contributed work to a number of outdoor publications. Tim is past president of the Wisconsin Outdoor Communicators Association and is a member of the Outdoor Writers Association of America.

Kristin Visser is a freelance writer who specializes in outdoor subjects, travel, health, medicine, and fitness. Her work has appeared in a number of magazines and newspapers, including *Wisconsin Trails*, *Wisconsin Woman*, the Milwaukee *Journal*, and the Los Angeles *Times*.

Jerry Minnich is the author of five books on plants, gardening, and soil biology, including *The Wisconsin Garden Guide* (NorthWord Press, 2d ed. 1982), *No Time for House Plants* (University of Oklahoma Press, 1977), and *The Earthworm Book* (Rodale Press, 1977). He is a former editor of *Organic Gardening* and has contributed to numerous newspapers and magazines, including *House Beautiful* and *Wisconsin Trails*. He is responsible for all the gardening material and has served as general editor of this book.

Contents

JANUARY, 1
Wind Chill Index, 5
Winter—Wisconsin's Longest Season, 12

FEBRUARY, 19
Some Like It Hot, 22
How to Make Duck Decoys: Aldo Leopold, 25
My Indian Doll: Esther Donnelly, 32
My Norwegian Grandfather: Mabel Longley, 36
Musicians of Note, 39
The Old Man's Garage: George Vukelich, 42

MARCH, 45
Woodcock in the Spring, 52
Stairsteps on the Mississippi, 56
Boys Basketball Championship Games, 61
Girls Basketball Championship Games, 64
Sigurd Olson: George Vukelich, 65

APRIL, 69
Wisconsin's $8 Billion Paper Industry, 72
I Remember a Wilderness: Lydia Doering, 78
Turtle: George Vukelich, 82

MAY, 87
Tornado! 91
Confederate Rest, 95
Wisconsin's Champion Trees, 99
The Sturgeon Bay Ship Canal: George Vukelich, 103

JUNE, 107
Wisconsin's Agricultural Bounty, 111
Wisconsin's State Parks: Wyalusing, 114
Wonderful Wisconsin Water, 122
Site Unseen: Maureen Mecozzi, 125
Wisconsin's State Parks: Copper Falls, 128

JULY, 131
Nearby Places with Strange Sounding Names, 135
Soldier in Ouisconsin, 138

AUGUST, 149
The Chinaberry Tree: Ann C. Haller, 158
Wisconsin Cheddar, 161

SEPTEMBER, 165
The Last Covered Bridge in Wisconsin, 169
Wisconsin's Orient Express, 173
It's a Cow's Life, 174
Famous Cows, 176
Weather, Whether or Not, 177
Canvas-Back Ducks in Wisconsin, 182
The Hardest Working River in the World, 185
Rattlesnake Tom, 187

OCTOBER, 191
Wisconsin's Ghost Towns, 195
They Said It with Cement, 198
The Last Lighthouse, 207

NOVEMBER, 213
The Greatest Storm, 216
Venison Delights, 220
Election for President—1988, 222
Wisconsin Presidential Elections, 1848-1988, 225
A Brush with Death, 231
Wild Turkeys in Wisconsin, 234

DECEMBER, 237
Body Heat: George Vukelich, 240
The Christmas Tree Ship, 244
Wisconsin's 72 Counties, 248
51 Things You Should Know about Wisconsin, 255

·THE·
Wisconsin
Almanac

JANUARY

*A summerish January,
a winterish spring
January warm,
the Lord have mercy!*
—*Old English proverb*

Even though the days grow longer, January is the cold month. The lowest temperature ever recorded in Wisconsin was -54 F. on January 24, 1922, at Danbury in Burnette County. Lake Geneva, in southern Wisconsin's Walworth County, recorded -50 F. on January 9, 1977. But the cold is sometimes broken by the "January thaw," a spell of warm weather that most often occurs between the 20th and 26th. Madison reached a record high of 58 F. on January 6, 1880. According to Indian lore, the January full moon is called the Wolf Moon.

January Weather History

MADISON

Day	Record High		Record Low		Record Precip.		Average High/Low
1	54	1897	-16	1887	1.80	1892	26/9
2	53	1897	-22	1879	1.74	1876	25/8
3	57	1874	-23	1887	0.75	1880	25/8
4	53	1880	-26	1886	1.22	1874	25/8
5	48	1946	-27	1884	1.11	1939	25/8
6	58	1880	-24	1912	1.30	1885	24/7
7	45	1965	-29	1887	0.68	1913	24/7
8	50	1880	-23	1971	1.04	1937	24/7
9	53	1939	-25	1875	0.75	1889	24/7
10	53	1975	-22	1979,82	1.12	1869	24/7
11	53	1880	-28	1979	0.75	1890	24/7
12	55	1871	-25	1912	1.07	1960	24/6
13	53	1961	-22	1916	1.21	1910	24/6
14	48	1952	-26	1963	0.52	1940	24/6
15	54	1953	-30	1963	1.00	1906	24/6
16	52	1933	-28	1979	0.80	1870	24/6
17	54	1894	-26	1982	0.50	1877	24/6
18	52	1894	-26	1971	0.68	1973	24/6
19	47	1933	-24	1985	1.02	1907	24/6
20	53	1906	-26	1985	1.11	1898	24/6
21	52	1964	-29	1888	0.57	1895	24/6
22	53	1964	-26	1936	1.70	1887	24/6
23	50	1909	-27	1963	0.80	1871	24/6
24	55	1981	-24	1936	1.42	1938	24/6
25	53	1973	-26	1904	1.14	1950	25/6
26	56	1944	-21	1963	1.15	1974	25/6
27	48	1919	-19	1915	1.14	1944	25/7
28	52	1914	-23	1915	0.45	1891	25/7
29	53	1914	-26	1951	1.32	1947	25/7
30	47	1974	-37	1951	0.61	1947	26/7
31	56	1989	-22	1985	0.60	1871	26/7

JANUARY

January Weather History

LA CROSSE

Day	Record High		Record Low		Average High/Low
1	57	1897	-27	1947	24/7
2	44	1933	-26	1879	24/7
3	57	1874	-23	1919	23/7
4	50	1880	-28	1884	23/6
5	46	1930	-29	1884	23/6
6	52	1933	-26	1912	23/6
7	47	1880	-34	1912	23/6
8	49	1880	-25	1881	23/5
9	51	1939	-31	1875	23/5
10	50	1928	-30	1881	22/5
11	47	1980	-26	1912	22/5
12	50	1928	-34	1912	22/5
13	50	1894	-28	1965	22/5
14	47	1914	-27	1965	22/4
15	48	1933	-32	1888	22/4
16	51	1913	-39	1888	22/4
17	56	1894	-30	1875	22/4
18	53	1880	-43	1873	22/4
19	48	1921	-32	1970	22/4
20	50	1968	-28	1943	23/4
21	50	1921	-42	1888	23/4
22	51	1964	-28	1936	23/4
23	50	1916	-26	1963	23/4
24	54	1981	-26	1936	23/4
25	57	1981	-27	1904	23/5
26	52	1972	-25	1963	24/5
27	52	1919	-26	1950	24/5
28	49	1914	-28	1950	24/5
29	49	1914	-36	1873	24/5
30	48	1931	-37	1951	25/5
31	52	1989	-27	1985	25/6

The normal average precipitation for La Crosse in January is .94 inches. The wettest January was in 1886 when 3.44 inches was recorded; the driest was in 1981 when only 0.14 inches was received.

Excuses for a January Party

1 Beach Party

On January 1, hundreds of people wearing parkas and carrying picnic baskets and beach umbrellas gather at Bradford Beach in Milwaukee. They are there to watch members of the Polar Bear Club—some in swimsuits, a few still in tuxedos—plunge into the frigid waters of Lake Michigan for their annual New Year's Day swim. A Polar Bear Swim also takes place in Sheboygan. Most participants are costumed, all are crazy.

9 Progressive Party

On January 9, 1909, Robert M. (Fighting Bob) La Follette founded what is now known as *The Progressive* magazine in Madison with the motto "You shall know the truth and the truth shall make you free." La Follette was the first Wisconsin-born governor. He then progressed to the United States Senate, and in 1924 became the first Presidential candidate from Wisconsin, under the Progressive Party. Wisconsin voted for him, but the rest of the country elected Calvin Coolidge.

26 Roy Chapman Andrews Birthday Brunch

The first dinosaur eggs that humans had ever seen were found on an expedition to the Gobi Desert in 1922 led by Roy Chapman Andrews (born January 26, 1884, in Beloit). The eggs were about 70 million years old and looked like loaves of French bread. Some of them contained skeletons of little baby dinosaurs. After graduation from Beloit College, Andrews went to New York and began his career as a naturalist by mopping floors and stuffing birds at the Museum of Natural History, where eventually he became Director.

Janubeary Fun

January can be more than bearable—it can be a creative challenge and an opportunity to enjoy the snow with which Wisconsin is so amply endowed. Inspiration can be found at the International Snow Sculpting Competition, which takes place in Milwaukee every year. Contestants carve out fantastic creatures and structures, or re- create famous statuary. Let it snow!!

WIND CHILL INDEX

How cold is cold? Both air temperature and wind speed determine how fast a warm object cools. But an object left outside will get only as cold as the temperature of the air. Therefore, the wind chill index is a measurement of how quickly the object reaches that temperature. Think of the wind chill as an equivalent temperature. With a wind chill index of minus 10 (F.), the object is losing heat as quickly as if the wind were calm but the temperature was minus 10.

It follows, then, that exposed flesh will lose heat much more rapidly under windy conditions than if the air is calm, increasing the danger of frostbite (the actual freezing of the surface tissues of the skin). ❀

WIND CHILL CHART

		TEMPERATURE												
		35	30	25	20	15	10	5	0	-5	-10	-15	-20	-25	-30
W I N D S P E E D	5	32	27	22	16	11	6	0	-5	-10	-15	-21	-26	-31	-36
	10	21	16	9	2	-2	-9	-15	-27	-31	-35	-38	-45	-52	-58
	15	16	11	1	-6	-11	-18	-25	-33	-40	-45	-51	-60	-65	-70
	20	12	3	-4	-9	-17	-24	-32	-40	-46	-52	-60	-68	-76	-81
	25	7	0	-7	-15	-22	-29	-37	-45	-52	-58	-67	-75	-83	-89
	30	5	-2	-11	-18	-26	-33	-41	-49	-56	-63	-70	-78	-87	-94
	35	3	-4	-13	-20	-27	-35	-43	-52	-60	-67	-72	-83	-90	-98
	40	1	-4	-15	-22	-29	-36	-45	-54	-62	-69	-76	-87	-94	-101

Wind speeds above 40 mph have little additional chilling effect.

Years Ago...

FOND DU LAC—The Fond du Lac Company E basketball team now claims the distinguished title "Champion of the United States." The Fond du Lac team has wrested the championship title from the Yale boys. The honor and distinction is not alone to the credit of Fond du Lac, as it will be shared by the entire state of Wisconsin and will go down in athletic history as an event of more than passing importance. The resulting score Tuesday night was Company E 27, Yale 6.—*The Daily Reporter*, January 3, 1900.

Uncle Woody *Says*

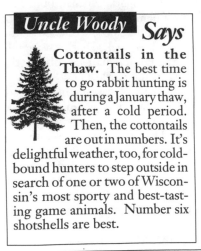

Cottontails in the Thaw. The best time to go rabbit hunting is during a January thaw, after a cold period. Then, the cottontails are out in numbers. It's delightful weather, too, for cold-bound hunters to step outside in search of one or two of Wisconsin's most sporty and best-tasting game animals. Number six shotshells are best.

JANUARY RECIPE

Treasured Potatoes

8-10 medium potatoes (6 cups shredded)	1 tablespoon grated onion
1 cup (4 ounces) shredded Wisconsin Provolone cheese	1 teaspoon seasoned salt
	1/2 teaspoon pepper
	1/4 cup (1/2 stick) butter
	1 cup half and half

Boil potatoes until nearly tender. Drain and cool. Peel and shred. Combine shredded potatoes with cheese and onion. Layer 1/3 of potato mixture in greased 9x9-inch baking dish. Sprinkle with 1/3 of the seasoned salt and pepper. Dot with 1/3 of the butter. Repeat layers twice more. May be covered and refrigerated at this point. When ready to bake, put half and half over all and bake at 375° F. for about one hour or until browned and crispy. Makes 4-6 servings.

Invented Right Here!

The Automobile

John Carhart, Racine physician and Methodist minister, was a tinkerer at heart. While recuperating from an illness in 1871, he spent his time designing a steam-powered buggy.

The Spark, which he built with the financial help of a number of wealthy Racine citizens, was the first self-propelled highway vehicle in the United States, probably the first in the world. The Spark was powered by a two-cylinder steam engine, steered by a lever, and had a cruising speed of five mph.

Though the machine was extremely noisy and otherwise impractical, it did arouse enough interest that the Wisconsin legislature offered a $10,000 prize to anyone who could build a horseless carriage that could run 200 miles, operate in reverse, and get off the road for other vehicles. (The winner of the 1878 Green Bay to Madison race eventually won $5000 of that prize.)

Though Carhart went back to preaching and doctoring, he was remembered by automobile afficionados, and was honored at the 1908 Paris International Automobile Exposition as the "Father of Automobiles." ❧   —K.V.

Uncle Woody Says

Instant Sheaths. No-cost sheaths can be quickly made for axes and hatchets by flattening tin or aluminum cans. Punch holes in one end of the flattened can for attachment of wire or thong, to keep the sheath in place over the sharp edge of your cutting tool.

JANUARY RECIPE

Wisconsin Cheese Sauce

2 tablespoons butter
2 tablespoons flour
1/2 teaspoon salt
1 teaspoon dry mustard
1/8 teaspoon pepper

1 cup milk
1 cup Wisconsin sharp
   Cheddar cheese, grated
1/2 teaspoon Worcestershire
   sauce

Melt butter. Blend in flour, salt, mustard and pepper. Add milk. Cook, stirring constantly, until mixture thickens and bubbles. Add cheese and Worcestershire sauce and stir until melted. Serve over favorite vegetables. Yield: 1-1/2 cups.

Years Ago . . .

MADISON—This morning the National Guard from Eau Claire and Menomonie and the First Regiment Band escorted Governor Rusk to the Northwestern depot to meet the incoming special train bearing Governor-elect Hoard and party. With the bands playing stirring airs, the handsome uniforms of the military, and the carriages filled with dignitaries, the procession to the Capitol was truly attractive. The inaugural ceremony took place in Assembly chambers. The Inauguration ball begins at 10 p.m. in both senate and assembly chambers. On the program are ten old-fashioned quadrilles, two waltz quadrilles, a gallop, a military schottische, and a medley to go home with.—*Wisconsin State Journal*, January 7, 1889.

Wisconsin's Favorite

If you haven't eaten walleye recently, consider yourself deprived. Up to 5,000,000 walleye are caught each year in Wisconsin. Old glassy eye is our most popular game fish. A member of the perch family, its white, flaky meat is a delicacy on any table, whether poached, grilled, or fried. Walleye pike are common in lakes and rivers throughout Wisconsin. The best time to catch them is on cloudy days or at evening, when they move from the deep into the shallows. These fish favor reefs, rocky shores, and sandy bottoms. An effective lure-and-bait combination is a weighted jig, with a minnow or nightcrawler attached to the jig hook. Retrieve baits and lures slowly, near the bottom. When using minnows, three to four inches are the preferred lengths. Walleye travel in schools, so when you catch one, keep fishing hard in that area. You may get into a flurry of rod-bending action. ❀

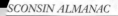

JANUARY IN THE GARDEN

Highlights:
❀ *Bring amaryllis upstairs*
❀ *Order seeds for spring*
❀ *Force forsythia indoors*
❀ *Get tools in shape*

In truth, there is no beginning to the gardening season, just as there is no end. Gardeners know this.

In the garden, the wheel of life is always turning, one season inexorably following the last, and new life continues to spring forth from death, as nonchalantly as if there were no miracle at all.

Even in January, when everything is covered with a white blanket of snow, the garden is not really asleep. Right below your living room window, not ten feet from your favorite TV-watching chair, the strong white roots of tulips are springing forth from bulbs beneath the snow, preparing to thrill you once again in May.

In January, the outdoor garden has work of its own to do, and does not need our help. It is better that we remain inside, close to the fire, there to read and dream with the new garden catalogs. We will plan for the spring planting season, when everything will be better than last year. Already we have forgotten the heat of August, the drought that turned our carrots to wood, the raccoons that got to the sweet corn first. Next year, everything will be perfect—just like the pictures in the seed catalog.

Before ordering seeds and plants for the spring, be sure to make a plan. Use graph paper, sketch in all the perennials and permanent plantings now in your garden, and only then consider which flowering annuals and vegetables you will order.

Unless you have already done so, you

might wrap the trunks of your young trees to prevent sun scald damage. Hardware mesh wrap will also prevent rabbits from girdling the trunks of young fruit trees.

Indoors, now is the time to bring amaryllis plants up from the basement. Give them a bright location and resume watering and fertilizing them. They will reward your slight efforts with spectacular bloom in just a few weeks.

Keep Christmas gift plants well watered, out of drafts, away from heat outlets, and feed them every one to two weeks for long-term performance.

Pay close attention to your houseplants now. The shortest days of the year will occur during the end of January, and low light intensity from cloudy days can place special stress on your indoor plants. If any plants seem to be stretching toward the nearest window, help them by moving them closer to the window.

Heavy snow can damage your prize shrubs and evergreens. Take time to brush the snow off these specimen plants soon after it falls—and before

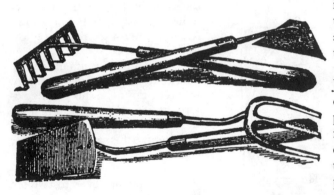

it has a chance to thaw partially and turn to ice.

A fun January project is to experiment with forcing branches of forsythia, crab apple, and other f l o w e r i n g shrubs and trees. Take lively new branches, set them in water, and give them good light indoors.

Now, in the off season, is also a good time to pay some attention to your garden tools. Clean them, sharpen blades, tighten joints, and oil metal surfaces.

During the second week in January, you may start seeds of ageratum and begonia. During the last week, start seeds of fragrant heliotrope and verbena indoors.

You will start seeds of some other annuals next month, so now is the time to clean your flats and trays, and to be sure that you have enough starting medium on hand.

The gardener is never idle—not even in January. ❀   —J.M.

Spotlight on House Plants

Asparagus. Two common kinds of asparagus are suitable for growing as house plants: fern asparagus (*A. plumosus*), with its slender, needlelike, dark green leaves and feathery appearance, and emerald feather (*A. sprengeri*), which has thicker yellow-green leaves and drooping stems. The latter makes a good plant for hanging baskets, and the older plants of this species produce red berries around Christmas. Both like some sun in the summer and full sun in the winter, and both can grow to a height of about two feet. ❀

Growing Herbs Indoors

Start an indoor herb garden now. Not only will it produce fresh herbs for kitchen use, but some of the herbs will impart a delightful fragrance to the room in which they are grown. Some herbs that lend themselves particularly to growing under fluorescent lights include basil, sweet bay, chives, lavender, mint, parsley, rosemary, and sage. ❀

Preventing Sunscald

Young trees are particularly susceptible to winter sunscald, which can produce permanent injury or even cause death to the tree. The problem is explained well by experts at the Stark Brothers Nurseries:

"The sun is lower in the sky during the winter, so its rays hit the tree trunk at nearly a right angle. If there is snow on the ground, the reflection intensifies the glaring of the sunlight, heating the tree bark to dangerously high temperatures. And this can cause premature flow of the tree sap.

"When this occurs in the late afternoon on the southwest side of the tree, it's only a short while before the sun goes down. Then the temperature quickly drops below freezing and this rapid temperature change causes the injury.

"The solution to prevent sunscald is simple, however. Just whiten the dark bark so it heats up less in the sun. A white or light colored tree guard works well and is a practical way to protect young trees.

"On older trees, it's usually easier and more practical to paint the lower trunk with exterior-type, white latex paint. Any brand will do, and usually one paint job is good for two years. Paint from the soil line up to the lowest branch. You only need to paint the southwest side, but most fruit growers prefer to 'whitewash' the entire trunk for a neater appearance." ❀

35 Most Popular Garden Vegetables

Rank	Vegetable	Grown by % of Gardeners
1	Tomatoes	94%
2	Peppers	68%
3	Green Beans	66%
4	Cucumber	64%
5	Onions	62%
6	Lettuce	52%
7	Summer Squash	48%
8	Carrots	45%
9	Radishes	42%
10	Corn	39%
11	Cabbage	39%
12	Peas	39%
13	White Potatoes	36%
14	Beets	33%
15	Melons	27%
16	Rhubarb	23%
17	Broccoli	23%
18	Spinach	21%
19	Turnips	20%
20	Okra	18%
21	Winter Squash	17%
22	Eggplant	17%
23	Pumpkins	16%
24	Asparagus	16%
25	Herbs	16%
26	Sweet Potatoes	10%
27	Swiss Chard	10%
28	Dried Beans	9%
29	Brussels Sprouts	9%
30	Celery	7%
31	Dried Peas	5%
32	Oriental Vegetables	5%
33	Parsnips	5%
34	Leeks	4%
35	Peanuts	3%

—*Gardens for All Survey*

Winter
Wisconsin's Longest Season

DICK KALNICKY
Madison Climatologist

Studies show that season length and climate have changed in Wisconsin over the past 100 years. Whether it's for better or worse is up to you. According to the calendar, there are four seasons a year, each three months long. But anyone who's lived in the state very long knows winter doesn't read the calendar. That unwelcome shot of sub-zero cold that blew in from the arctic early last November is a case in point. And the December 21 calendar date never did make sense to deer hunters. They customarily trudge through knee-high snow in frostbite temperatures just about every season. Cold-nosed snow shovelers braving deep-freeze windchills are an accepted part of Wisconsin's November lifestyle. The winters here definitely arrive ahead of the calendar.

Every year all of us have to live through this real "meteorological" winter, but sometimes wish it could be the "astronomical" one. A meteorological season is a period of several weeks or months in which a few distinct weather patterns dominate. The winter meteorological season in Wisconsin includes frequent cold air masses from Canada with snowfalls coming in between air masses.

My studies show that in Wisconsin, winter averages four and a half months and extends from early November to mid-March. Its temperatures are below freezing, and the storm track dividing cold and warm air masses is usually far south of Wisconsin.

And, as we all suspected, summer lasts only two and a half months, from mid-June through the end of August. Moist tropical and mild dry Pacific air masses dominate. The storm track that separates these warm air masses from the cooler Canadian air is north of us near the Canadian border.

Spring, from mid-March through mid-June, really is three months long and pretty much goes by the calendar. This is a period of transition from winter to summer. Warm air masses expand northward and cold ones retreat ahead of them. The mean storm track passes northward over Wisconsin in late May and early June.

Autumn in Wisconsin, on the other hand, is only two months long. We have it in September and October. The opposite of springtime, in fall the transition to winter finds warm air masses retreating southward and the cold air following close behind. The mean storm track passes southward over Wisconsin in September.

Winter is definitely Wisconsin's longest season of the year!

The average duration of ice cover on Wisconsin lakes lasts as long as winter—four and a half months. However, the timing is delayed by two to three weeks because of the slow response time of water temperature to air temperature. For Wisconsin as a whole, the average lake freeze date is late November and the average thaw date is early April.

In some winters (1985-1986, for example) a January thaw occurs. During the thaw, Wisconsin's cold air masses are temporarily replaced by mild air of Pacific origin. Thaws can melt snow and ice off roofs and provide wildlife with warm and dry conditions to replenish food supplies. Thaws in Wisconsin occur most frequently near January 5th to 10th or 18th to 23rd.

In many years, it doesn't feel like spring in Wisconsin until mid-to-late April, even though spring weather patterns begin in March. At this time much of Canada is still snow-covered. Cold air masses continue to form over the Canadian snow and move down to Wisconsin as often as they do in December and January. However, in March and April they're less intense and don't travel as far south as they do in December and January. This lets the southern states experience spring by the calendar while Wisconsin still shivers.

Winter is Wisconsin's driest season in terms of water equivalent precipitation. Rainfall gradually increases until a peak is reached in late May and June, drops off in July and early August, reaches a secondary peak in late August and September, then decreases the rest of the year. Rainfall peaks occur when the storm track is over Wisconsin, usually at the spring-summer and summer-autumn transitions. The summer rainfall deficit causes our lawns to turn brown, stream flows to decrease, and ground water and lake levels to fall. For the Department of Natural Resources, the summer dry spells of July and early August are the most appropriate times to schedule surveys on low flow streams to develop wasteload allocations.

In most years, one or more spells of Indian summer occur during the last half of autumn. Indian summer is a quiet, mild, dry period with warm days and cool nights which occurs after the first killing frosts. Indian summer weather patterns peak during the second and third weeks of October, but can occur several times from late September to mid-November. Mild, dry high pressure brings Indian summer, which often coincides with the fall foliage peak. However, if the high pressure system circulation is especially stagnant, air pollution conditions can be aggravated during Indian summer and at other times of the year with similar weather patterns.

If we know so much about these seasons and weather events, why can't meteorologists do a better job of forecasting what will happen months in advance? Part of the answer is that studies can describe long-term averages (my data is for 1899 to 1969) but each specific weather event of the past may or may not occur in any given year or group of years in the future. Meteorologists have not been able to find consistent associations between weather anomalies in one season and events several months in advance. The probabilities of a repeat are only about 60 percent, claims of the Old Farmers' Almanac notwithstanding. Even flipping a coin gives a 50 percent chance of being right. The intricate workings of atmospheric circulation are not completely understood. Its complex relationships and feedback mechanisms in association with the differential heating and cooling among the variety of earth's surfaces make long-term predictions chancy.

My own investigations have found changes in climate as well as different timing and intensity of seasons during various climatic episodes. The mean temperature of the Northern Hemisphere increased about one-degree Fahrenheit (0.6 Celcius) from the late 1800s to 1950 and then decreased during the period from 1950 to 1970. In some locations near the transition zones between air masses, the temperature change was greater. For example, in Wisconsin the change was about two degrees Fahrenheit.

There were three climatic episodes during my 70-year study period:
* 1899 to 1919—the coldest

✳ 1920 to 1952— the warmest—there is considerable evidence that this was the warmest in the last 1000 years.

✳ 1953 to 1969 —a cooling episode.

More recent evidence indicates that the cooling trend continued into the 1970s. Some climatologists believe we are now in a cold climatic period similar to the one from 1899 to 1919.

The facts about climate change reveal what appears to be significant influence on all our lives, economically, socially, politically, and environmentally. Note that the northern part of the United States grew the fastest and achieved economic prominence during the warming episode. As temperatures cooled during the 1960s and 1980s and winters became more severe in the North, industries and "Snowbirds" headed south permanently (or until the next climatic change?). Are these trends related or just a coincidence?   If 1920-1952 was the warmest period in the last 1000 years, can Wisconsin and the rest of the upper Midwest ever regain economic supremacy? Consider that in 1985, manufacturers of the Saturn automobile chose a southern state for their plant rather than Wisconsin, partly because of our cold winters. And more recently Sony turned down Milwaukee for the same reason.

When Madison's average temperature dropped two degrees, there was about a 10 percent increase in the annual total of heating degree days. Degree days closely correlate to the use of energy to heat homes and other buildings. Colder winters mean extra cost and more taxes for snow removal, heating public buildings, and other necessary government activity.

The specific climatic changes that occurred in Wisconsin during the period from 1899 to 1969 are especially interesting. Summer from 1899 to 1919 lasted two months, mid-June to mid-August. From 1920 to 1952, it lasted three months, early June to early September. But from 1953 to 1969, there were only three weeks of summer scattered through late June and July. The rest of the time in those years, June, July, and August had spring or autumn-like weather patterns. During the period from 1961 to 1970, July and August temperatures in Wisconsin were two degrees cooler than they were from 1931 through 1960.

Indian summer happened most frequently in the 1920 through 1952 period. During 1920-'52 and '53-'69 they occasionally occurred as late as mid-November, but in 1899-1919 they were finished by the first week in November. Likewise, the earliest winters came between 1899 and 1919, usually before the end of October. During 1920-'52 and '53-'69, winter most often began the second week of November.

Winters from 1920 through 1952 had more west to east flow, which brings Wisconsin milder temperatures. The other two climatic episodes had more north-south flow which usually brings cold, variable weather.

The average length of ice cover on Wisconsin lakes is associated with the temperature trend. For example, on Lake Mendota in Madison, average ice cover per winter season was over 130 days in the cold late 1800s. This decreased to a minimum of 97 days in the warm spell from 1931 through 1940, then went up to 112 days as temperatures cooled between 1956 and '65.

Why have these changes in climate occurred during the last 100 years? Why did we have the great ice ages, which were much more dramatic climatic changes? No one definitely knows. However, there are two popular theories to explain the recent changes. One theory is that growing levels of carbon dioxide in the atmosphere increase the "greenhouse effect," thereby warming the earth's atmosphere. This has been a popular way to explain the warming trend from 1900 through 1950. The second theory is that increased amounts of dust in the atmosphere, particularly from volcanic eruptions and to some extent from agricultural and industrial activity, reflect more sunlight and lead to cooler temperatures. Proponents of this theory show that volcanic eruptions were greatest around 1900 and again after the 1950s, which were the cooler episodes. Emissions of dust from agriculture and industry are also up dramatically since World War II.

My own opinion is that dust in the atmosphere is currently more significant than carbon dioxide. While levels of both have increased since 1950, my analysis shows mean temperature has decreased. This indicated dust has had the major influence, at least since 1950.

I believe EPA's recent pronouncement of an impending warmup and consequent melting of the ice caps because of increased carbon dioxide is unfounded and misleadingly alarmist. Too many unknowns make their prediction highly suspect. Decreases in air pollution are occurring in some industrial nations even while the trend toward more carbon dioxide in the atmosphere continues. Either one could contribute to a warmup, but both could be more than offset by increased agricultural and industrial dust from the developing Third World. Furthermore, the frequency and intensity of future volcanic eruptions and associated dust in the atmosphere are unpredictable. In addition, the climatic episode from 1930 through 1960, which was the warmest in the Northern Hemisphere in the past 1,000 years, did not feature massive ice melting.

Meteorologists still have much to learn about weather and climate before accurate, long-term predictions can be made. One thing we do know is that our climate has changed significantly in the past—even in the last 100 years—and will continue to do so in the future. In making climatic assessments, we need to consider far more than 30-year averages described as "normal" by the U.S. Weather Service. Although these averages correctly describe the recent past, climatic history teaches us that such averages may not accurately describe the next 30 years. The climate may instead more closely resemble that of 60 to 90 years previous, or some other episode. A long-term perspective is required.

In the meantime, however, everyone who likes snow, cold, and frigid wind-chills can rejoice. Studies confirm that the average Wisconsin winter drags on for four and a half months. It doesn't just seem like a long time, it really is—despite those dates on the calendar. Not only that, our winters may be growing even longer! So the best advice for those who love Wisconsin is to just "warm up" to it all and participate. Dig out the ski mask, turn off the TV, put on those skis, ice skates, or snowshoes, jump on the snowmobile, and get into it.

Did anybody say, "Florida"? ❀

Reprinted with permission of <u>Wisconsin Natural Resources</u>

The Weather-lore of the Greeks

Many shooting stars are a sign of rain or wind, and the wind or rain will come from that quarter from which they appear.

Again, if the wind is from the south, the snuff of the lampwick indicates rain; it also indicates wind in proportion to its bulk or size: while if the snuff is small, like millet seed, and of bright colour, it indicates rain as well as wind. Again, when in winter the lamp rejects the flame but catches, as it were, here and there in spurts, it is a sign of rain: so also is it, if the rays of light leap up on the lamp, or if there are sparks.

It is a sign of rain or storm when birds which are not aquatic take a bath. It is a sign of rain when a toad takes a bath, and still more so when frogs are vocal.

It is a sign of rain when a crow puts back its head on a rock which is washed by waves, or when it often dives or hovers over the water.

Again it is a sign of rain when a tame duck gets under the eaves and flaps its wings. Also it is a sign of rain when jackdaws and fowls flap their wings whether on a lake or on the sea—like a duck. It is a sign of wind or rain when a heron utters his note at early morning: if, as he flies towards the sea, he utters his cry, it is a sign of rain rather than wind, and in general, if he makes a loud cry, it portends wind. ❀

Theophrastus (c. 370-285 B.C)
<u>Enquiry Into Plants and Minor Works</u>

FEBRUARY

All sorts of things and weather
Must be taken in together,
To make up a year
And a Sphere.

—*Ralph Waldo Emerson.*
"The Mountain and the Squirrel"

While February's full moon is called the
Snow Moon, the month is Wisconsin's driest
since the storm patterns tend to track south of
the state. On the 2nd, Groundhog Day in folk
lore, Sun Prairie's Jimmy the Groundhog draws
attention as he emerges from his den at dawn.
Tradition holds that there will be six more
weeks of winter if Jimmy sees his shadow. Scientific investigation shows the lore to have no
basis in fact, but Jimmy's annual emergence
always draws attention. The shortest month,
February brings an increase in the amount of
daylight by about an hour and 15 minutes from
the beginning to the end of the month.❁

February Weather History

MADISON

Day	Record High		Record Low		Record Precip.		Average High/Low
1	47	1968	-28	1985	0.46	1915	26/7
2	47	1987	-28	1959	1.48	1983	26/8
3	48	1882	-21	1886	1.20	1875	27/8
4	55	1890	-23	1965	1.47	1986	27/8
5	54	1946	-21	1895	0.64	1953	27/8
6	54	1882	-19	1977	0.94	1904	28/9
7	50	1987	-21	1875	0.63	1892	28/9
8	55	1925	-22	1899	0.93	1900	28/9
9	50	1966	-28	1899	0.61	1925	28/9
10	53	1876	-25	1899	0.57	1959	29/10
11	54	1932	-22	1885	1.00	1880	29/10
12	63	1882	-23	1899	0.71	1938	29/10
13	51	1921	-24	1905	1.11	1950	30/10
14	55	1954	-18	1862	1.30	1869	30/11
15	63	1921	-14	1920	0.25	1967	30/11
16	57	1981	-18	1936	1.28	1911	30/11
17	61	1981	-19	1864	1.30	1887	31/12
18	57	1981	-19	1936	0.69	1882	31/12
19	60	1981	-15	1979	0.73	1898	31/12
20	57	1930	-21	1929	0.98	1953	32/12
21	60	1930	-15	1873	1.54	1922	32/13
22	60	1930,84	-15	1873	1.64	1922	32/13
23	58	1984	-20	1889	1.15	1977	32/13
24	56	1957	-13	1889	0.64	1892	33/14
25	58	1932	-15	1967	1.03	1929	33/14
26	57	1932	-8	1963	1.16	1881	33/15
27	58	1976	-12	1879	1.65	1948	34/15
28	56	1895	-20	1962	1.04	1876	34/15
29	53	1964	-13	1884	0.10	1904	

February Weather History

LA CROSSE

Day	Record High		Record Low		Average High/Low
1	48	1931	-28	1918	25/6
2	48	1987	-32	1873	26/6
3	51	1928	-28	1886	26/6
4	53	1890	-26	1893	26/7
5	54	1878	-24	1895	26/7
6	59	1878	-22	1982	27/7
7	54	1878	-34	1875	27/7
8	48	1966	-36	1971	27/8
9	51	1966	-32	1899	28/8
10	51	1886	-32	1899	28/8
11	60	1882	-24	1899	28/9
12	65	1882	-27	1875	29/9
13	53	1921	-21	1965	29/9
14	56	1954	-16	1881	29/10
15	65	1921	-16	1905	30/10
16	60	1981	-23	1936	30/10
17	64	1981	-26	1979	30/10
18	64	1981	-18	1903	31/11
19	59	1930	-20	1929	31/11
20	61	1930	-27	1873	31/12
21	64	1930	-25	1873	31/12
22	62	1984	-22	1873	32/12
23	56	1930	-29	1873	32/13
24	59	1931	-19	1950	32/13
25	58	1876	-21	1967	33/13
26	61	1976	-17	1950	33/14
27	60	1976	-21	1879	33/14
28	61	1878	-17	1962	33/15
29	58	1964	-3	1884	

The normal average precipitation for La Crosse in February is .89 inches. The wettest February was in 1922 when 4.04 inches was recorded; the driest was in 1969 when only 0.05 inches was received.

Some Like It Hot

If you travel the backroads of northern Wisconsin, you may see small log buildings hidden behind some houses. The uninitiated assume them to be tool sheds, guest cabins, or perhaps the original family home. Natives know them for what they are — a cultural centerpiece of Wisconsin's Finnish immigrants. Those small log buildings are saunas. Real saunas, not the electrically-controlled, pine-paneled closets that pass for saunas in health clubs and suburban homes.

A real sauna is a separate structure, made of hand-hewn logs, warmed by a wood fire that heats rocks turned up while clearing the land. It is designed to simultaneously hold the entire family and a group of neighbors.

My first northern Wisconsin Finnish sauna happened on a frigid February night in Ashland County. Our hosts built a fire late Saturday afternoon, so by the time the five of us arrived, the rocks were nearly glowing hot.

The log sauna had two rooms. We removed our clothes in the outer room and gingerly stepped into the 200-plus-degree heat of the sauna room. Sitting companionably on the upper (and hotter, since warm air rises) benches were several neighborhood residents. We joined them to discuss skiing, snow depth, and other crucial questions.

Occasionally, one or more naked, beet-red, sweating bodies would race outside, to return a few minutes later with bits of ice and snow tangled in their hair, body temperature (and color) back to normal. After about 20 minutes, I was close to dropping from the heat, and had obviously stalled

the snow jump as long as possible. I ran out the door, hitting a wall of sub-zero air. One of my companions headed down a well-trod path 25 yards to the lake, where the sauna's owners had kindly cut a hole in the ice. I opted for what I believed to be a lovely pile of fluffy snow conveniently located three steps outside the sauna door. Taking a deep breath, I threw myself in. The snow pile was a bush. I wore the scratches from that encounter on my backside for several weeks. Another companion made snow angels next to my bush.

As we were rapidly approaching the icicles-in-the-blood stage, we raced back into the sauna and lunged for the upper benches. Within minutes, we were turning bright red again. One of our hosts strolled in with a sheaf of small birch branches, with which he proceeded to gently flagellate each of us.

The sauna stayed cranked up all evening, as neighbors came and went, taking a sauna (and occasional run outside) for an hour or so, then, relaxed and dehydrated, repairing to the kitchen for beer and conversation.

No, the sauna did not originate as a way to torture enemies to extract information about rival troop movements. The sauna and its high-humidity cousin the steam bath have been part of virtually every known culture since before recorded history. There is archeological evidence of saunas and steam baths dating back 6000 years. Babylonians, Egyptians, Greeks and Romans had steam baths. American Indians built sweat lodges. All were used for ritual purification in religious activities. The Romans eventually built steam baths for everyday use, and public baths became a center of social life.

It was the Finns, however, who developed the sauna, with its dryer air and much higher temperatures. The Finnish sauna also began as a means of religious purification, and though it has become a part of everyday life, it still has a special role in Finnish culture.

When Finns immigrated to North America, they invariably built a sauna first, and lived in it while building a house. The sauna was not only a center for weekly socializing (traditionally, Finns took a sauna only once a week), it was used for drying laundry, crops, and fishing nets, sheltering animals during blizzards, and curing meat. Because its heat relaxes muscles, many Finnish immigrants' children were born in the family sauna.

With urbanization and electricity, the sauna has lost much of its cultural significance as it has spread far beyond its Finnish origins. But fortunately, the central purpose of the sauna has not been lost. It is still the most physically relaxing and emotionally calming thing to do after a tough day. And if you stick to a cold shower instead of jumping into snow-covered bushes, you'll emerge without a scratch.❧ —*K.V.*

Years Ago...

HOLLAND—Twenty-five children spent the night in the Catholic school building of Holland, Brown County, during a recent blizzard, the teacher fearing to permit the little ones to start for home in the storm.—*Wisconsin State Journal*, February 11, 1889.

Excuses for a February Party

2 Groundhog Day

At Sun Prairie, the Groundhog Capital of the World, all eyes are on Jimmy when he pokes his furry little bucktoothed head out of his burrow at dawn. If he sees his shadow, winter weather will continue for another six weeks. No shadow means an early spring. Jimmy's high degree of accuracy—he's right about 80 percent of the time—permits wise planning of travel, recreation, and planting.

5 Founder's Day

On February 5, 1849, seventeen young men from Madison and environs were the first students to enroll at the University of Wisconsin. Three more (there have always been late registrants) soon joined them, and with those twenty students the first registration was complete. Women weren't admitted until 1866.

22 Skating Party

On February 22, 1980, Mark Johnson of Madison scored two goals as the U.S. hockey team defeated the Soviet Union 4-3 in the medal round of the Winter Olympics at Lake Placid, New York. The following morning Eric Heiden of Madison won the 10,000-meter event to sweep all five men's gold medals in speed skating. On those 29-inch thighs, he broke the world record by 6.2 seconds.

14 Valentine's Day

The song "I Love You Truly," once de rigueur at weddings, was written by Carrie Jacobs-Bond of Janesville. More than two hundred of her songs of sentiment were published, the first of which she called "Is My Dolly Dead?"

18 Elm Farm Ollie Day

On February 18 the Elm Farm Ollie Fan Club of Madison honors the anniversary of the first time a cow flew in an airplane. As part of the celebration of the St. Louis International Air Exposition in 1930, Elm Farm Ollie was milked in flight, then little containers of her milk were parachuted over the city.

How to Make Duck Decoys
ALDO LEOPOLD

During the early 1900s, before he wrote *Sand County Almanac,* Wisconsin conservationist Aldo Leopold published these plans for building duck decoys in the old *Forest and Stream* magazine:

"These are hollow built-up pine decoys. They weigh 2-1/4 pounds—the same as is the mallard. The bodies are built extra wide, and the heads have an extra wide, long bill shaped with an extra 'scoop,' and extra thick cheeks. It is my opinion that in these respects a caricature of an actual mallard pulls in the big red-legged drakes just a little better than a perfect imitation of an actual mallard would do it.   Moreover, this pattern calls for *two degrees of inclination of the heads, and each head is set on the body at a different horizontal angle*—in other words, no two heads have the same posture. This is the biggest single advantage to be gained from home-made decoys. In my opinion, the monotonous uniformity of posture of ordinary decoys sometimes drives away ducks that might otherwise come in, as uniformity of posture is assumed by ducks *when they are scared.*

"How are they made? First of all go to your lumber dealer and tell him you want him to select for you some 8-inch boards, 1/2 inch and 1 inch thick, plus a 2x4, and that you wan*t the lightest, softest, driest stuff to be had for love or mone*y. Give him a week to select your lumber if by so doing you can get anything lighter, softer, or drier. Few people—until they have made a set of decoys—realize what a difference there is between ordinary finishing lumber, pulled at random off the racks, and the choicest finish of the same species. Get the best. You will gain in the end. I used selected western yellow pine sapwood for my set. White pine would probably be better, where available.

"Next draw your patterns on stiff paper, cut them out, and trace off the body boards on your lumber. The diagram will give an idea of the exterior shapes, with exact maximum dimensions; also the shape and location of the hollows. Draw a center line on each pattern and each board. This will help when the time comes to put the boards together.

"Next saw up into sections and go to work with a good sharp keyhole saw. A keyhole saw is much faster than chiseling for the exterior lines and faster than boring for the hollows. Dip your keyhole into a can of water when it gets hot and then wipe dry. You will be surprised to see how fast it cuts the wood.

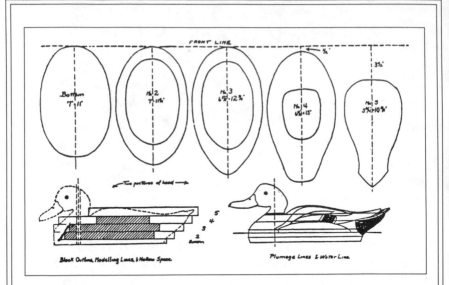

"Now get a box of inch screws, some waterproof casein glue (or white lead if not available), and a pair of hand clamps and build up your bodies. The diagram shows how far each piece is set back from the front of the bottom piece, and the center lines will help you build straight. Start, of course, by gluing and screwing No. 4 to No. 5, then add 3 to 4, then 2 to 3, then 1 to 2. Countersink the screws 1/4 inch; not more, or you will 'meet' them with your chisel in the exterior modeling. Use from 4 to 8 screws to each joint, drawing the vicinity of each screw hole tight with the hand clamp before inserting the screw. Your bodies are now ready to go on the rack to dry.

"Now for the heads. Outline the whole set on both sides of the 2x4, using your small square freely to keep them opposite. Then bore a bunch of holes of various sizes to facilitate the vertical profiling, and go to work with a wide chisel, a woodrasp, and a rat-tail file, and work your profiles complete, except for just enough wood to hold the set together. Then bore 3/8 -inch holes for your neck-dowels before sawing the heads apart. Next comes the modeling of the individual heads. Advice is useless here. It is simply a case of a sharp knife, a tame duck for a model, and the will to succeed. Leave the cheeks the full thickness of the 2x4 and make bill a full inch wide.

"Your bodies are now dry and ready for remodeling. The requisites are a good vise, a wide, sharp chisel, and two rasps, one coarse and one fine. Here also a live model would be a great help. Tilt your tails at various angles, to give still further variety of posture to your flock. With practice a body can be modeled out and sand-papered in an hour. Leave a little extra wood around the neck joint for remodeling after the heads are on.

"Now bore your dowel holes through the bodies. Use the head, which has been already bored, as a guide to keep your bit vertical. Glue up your dowels (first sand-papering both tips to insure against sticking), also glue up your neck joint, put on the heads tight, not forgetting to give each head a slightly different angle. Put away to dry.

"Now comes the finish. Trim off the protruding dowels, and trim the neck joint so that descending curves flow smoothly from the head to the body. Countersink a small screw eye at the front of each bottom board for tying on the strings and weights. Carve your initials on each bottom board, or, still better, do this before the bottoms are put on. Presto; your decoys are complete, except for painting and glass eyes, but these seem little, little bits of jobs as you wade out of your chip pile to carry a sample of your new flock to be inspected by your wife.

"If you have wrought carefully and thoughtfully, you now have a set of stool that any sportsman, especially yourself, should be proud of. And surely those big mallards next fall will appreciate the fact that *your* decoys are no common hand-me-down blocks, but real ducks whose society they should enjoy."❦

Fom Stephen Miller's Early American Waterfowling, published by Winchester Press, Piscataway, NJ.

The American Water Spaniel

There are plenty of reasons that this merry breed has received official status as Wisconsin's state dog. The breed was developed in Wisconsin for waterfowling from small skiffs (these dogs generally weigh from 25 to 45 pounds) and for all-around hunting. As practical as an old-time farmer, the water spaniel performs well on grouse, quail, pheasant, and rabbit. It's been the choice of many Wisconsin game wardens and rural hunters for over 100 years. Two kennels which help to ensure that the American water spaniel remains a living tradition are: Swan Lake Kennels, John and Mary Barth,

Uncle Woody *Says*

Decoys. An excellent source of material for the bodies of duck decoys is old cork that's been used for insulation in freezer plants or meat lockers. It's often available for a moderate price when such buildings are being ripped down. For heads, use pine or cedar.

W6892 Breneman Rd., Pardeeville, WI 53954; and Paul Bovie, Plainfield, WI 54966.❦

Invented Right Here!

The Snowmobile

Trapping was an important winter occupation for young men in the Vilas County community of Sayner in the 1920s. Carl Eliason had trouble running his trap lines because of a deformed foot that made wearing snowshoes or skis difficult. Looking for an easier way to get through the snow to his traps, in the winter of 1924, Carl mounted skis on the front of a toboggan, put a single endless tractor tread under the rear, and hooked the tread to a small gasoline-powered marine engine.

Though others had pieced together various contraptions for getting around in the winter, ranging from steam-powered sleighs to Model T Fords modified with rear tractor treads and skis where the front wheels used to be — Carl's machine turned out to have the right stuff for reliable winter transportation. He patented his invention in 1927, produced 40 snowmobiles himself, then, faced with an order for 200 of the marvelous machines from Finnish customers, he sold the patent to FWD Company of Clintonville.❀   —K.V.

Years Ago . . .

EAGLE RIVER—Wolves are still numerous in northern Wisconsin. Recently a log-teamster at Eagle River, while coming home alone from the landing, was overtaken by three wolves, which followed him hungrily all the way home. The faster he drove the faster they came upon him. They kept within five feet of the sleigh and had he not overtaken two men working on the road and another teamster they would probably have set upon him. An ox and a horse are lying in the wood dead and partly eaten, and two deer have been found in the same condition.—*Wisconsin State Journal*, February 12, 1889.

Uncle Woody *Says*

Sharpening Outdoor Tools.
To sharpen tools such as spades, shovels, and hoes, clamp the tool in a vice and sharpen the edges with a metal file. Take care to duplicate the original line of the tool's bevel.

Apple Raspberry-Ripple Coffee Cake

2/3 cups sugar
1/2 cup butter, softened
2 eggs
2 tablespoons apple cider
2 cups all-purpose flour
2 teaspoons baking powder
1/4 teaspoon salt
1/4 cup raspberry preserves
4 apples (3-1/2 cups) peeled,
    thinly sliced

Topping
1 cup ground almonds
2 eggs, beaten
2 tablespoons flour
1/2 cup sugar
1/2 cup dairy sour cream
1 teaspoon lemon peel
Glaze
1/4 cup powdered sugar
1 to 2 teaspoons apple cider

Heat oven to 350°F. Grease and flour a 9- or 10-inch springform pan. In large bowl, combine 2/3 cup sugar and butter; beat until light and fluffy. Add 2 eggs and 2 tablespoons apple cider; beat until well blended. Lightly spoon flour into measuring cup; level off. In small bowl, combine 2 cups flour, baking powder and salt; blend well. Add to egg mixture; beat at low speed until well blended. Spread in prepared pan. Spoon preserves over batter; carefully spread to cover. Top with apple slices; slightly press into batter. In medium bowl, combine all topping ingredients. Pour over apples. Bake at 350° F. for 55 to 60 minutes. Cool 10 minutes. Carefully remove sides of pan. In small bowl, blend glaze ingredients until smooth; drizzle over cake. Serve warm or cool. Serves 16.

—Bernice V. Janowski, Stevens Point

Easy-going Badgers

According to a 1984 study by the University of New Hampshire, Wisconsin ranks 46 among the 50 states on the "stress index" (with number 1 being the most stressful), as determined by 15 statistical indicators. Our neighbor Illinois, however, ranks 17, which may explain why traffic is heavy in the northbound lane of I-90 on Friday nights and in the southbound lane on Sunday nights. ❊

FEBRUARY IN THE GARDEN

Highlights:
❀ *Start begonias indoors*
❀ *Start slow-growing annuals*
❀ *Prune grapes*
❀ *Order strawberry plants*

February is still largely a month of planning and dreaming for the Wisconsin gardener, although there are plenty of chores, both indoors and out, to keep us busy and out of trouble. Snow does not buy us idleness!

If the winter has been a cold one, count your blessings. All farmers—and especially those who depend on orchard crops—want to see a solidly cold winter, not one with sudden thaws that can send false signals to fruit trees. Generally, the coldest part of winter is from the middle of January to the middle of February. So as soon as Valentine's Day comes along, you can take heart in the knowledge that the worst of winter is over! And indeed, the days are now growing longer with each turn of the clock, and spring is surely on its way.

This is a good time to repair and repaint window boxes—or to build new ones. Be sure to keep a good coat of white paint on the outside of the boxes, to reflect the strong summer sun. Roots of windowbox plants can easily become stressed during hot weather, and the white paint will help to mitigate the effects of the summer sun.

Some gardening books, written for the national market, tell us to plant peas on Washington's Birthday. In Wisconsin, we laugh at such advice, as we continue to brush heavy snows off our prize evergreen shrubs to prevent them from breaking.

Every two weeks, now, check the stored gladi-olus corms, dahlia tubers, begonia tubers, and other stored roots and bulbs for signs of rot (too wet) or desiccation (too dry).

During the first week of February, start seeds of lobelia, petunias, verbena, and vinca—all slow-starters. By the third week, start seeds of geraniums, aster, annual chrysanthemum, godetia (satin flower), annual hollyhock, lantana, forget-me-not, statice (sea lavender), and impatiens. The keys to success are (1) good fluorescent lighting, 12-14 hours a day; (2) cool temperatures after seeds have germinated; (3) a sterile starting medium to prevent damping-off disease; and (4) constant soil moisture and humidity.

During the last week of the month, start seeds of onions, leeks, and chives. If they grow too tall and spindly, you may trim back their tops as they grow. You may also start seeds of bell peppers now, if you can offer proper light and humidity.

Choose a mild day in late February to prune grapes, apples, plums, and cherries. Check for overwintering fire blight cankers and remove these by pruning or minor surgery.

Keep an eye on houseplants. Remember that the leaves of all plants breathe, even when they seem to be dormant in winter. Mist plants occasionally to remove dust that may clog the stomata. Some houseplants will show signs of new growth late in the month, as the days grow longer. Cooperate by gradually increasing water and fertilizer. ❀   *—J.M.*

My Indian Doll
ESTHER DONNELLY

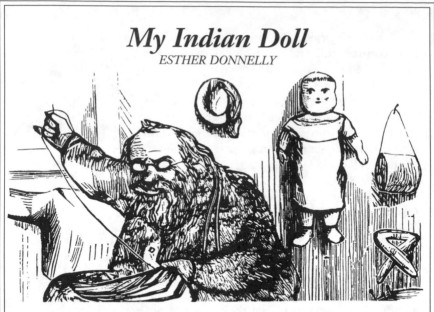

My Indian doll is my oldest possession. She was made for me by Alice Short Bull, a friend of our family, and was given to me when I was four years old. The occasion was a Christmas Eve celebration at a mission church on the Pine Ridge Indian Reservation.

We were the only non-Indian family attending the service and had been seated in a pew not far from the big Christmas tree. From my perch on Mama's lap, I could see laden branches stretching out in every direction. Tall candles flickered on the altar. The delightful fragrance of the newly cut pine tree permeated the air, hiding the kerosene odor of the lanterns which hung from the ceiling.

My little sister, Rose, sat next to me on Papa's lap. We whispered to each other during the singing of the hymns, calling attention to the many unwrapped gifts hanging on the tree. Yards of calico and glistening hair ribbons were draped in graceful fashion on the branches. Bags of tobacco hung suspended at the tips of the branches, and moccasins, made by the Indian mothers, hung closer to the tree's trunk.

"Look up high," I whispered. "There's the doll we asked Santa to bring!"

I was trembling with anticipation. The doll was even more beautiful than her picture, which we had circled in the catalog. Her hair was blonde and curly. Her sheer pink dress had a border of lace. Mama had explained that we would get our presents later at home. But apparently Santa Claus had decided to surprise us by putting the beauty on the church Christmas tree.

It seemed that the songs and prayers, most in the Dacotah Indian language, went on for a very long time. At last came the final carol, "Silent Night," sung in English by the pupils of the day school where Papa and Mama taught.

Suddenly there was a blast of cold air across our faces, and Rose and I were instantly awake. There was a jingling of bells, and Santa himself came running down the church aisle. He had on a red suit and a stocking cap with a bell at the very end.

With almost uncontainable excitement, we watched while Santa and his helpers handed out gifts from the tree. Finally, Santa took the big doll out of the branches and lifted it high for everyone to see. Then, still holding the doll he walked on past our pews and called out the name of Victoria Red Bird, a blind girl who lived in a log hut near Buckle Creek. The congregation, which had been silent for a moment, took up a low humming sound of approval as Santa placed the doll in her arms.

I buried my face in the soft folds of Mama's blouse so my tears wouldn't show. Mama patted my back and said, "Look, Esther, here is a present for you." Ellis Poor Bear, one of Santa's helpers, stood in the aisle with an Indian doll in each hand—one for me and one for Rose.

The doll was dressed in buckskin, heavily fringed on the sleeves and hem. She wore amber beads at her throat. I looked under her skirt hoping to find her tiny moccasins. To my horror, she had no legs or feet at all— and neither did she have arms and hands. How could she look so happy without hands and feet?

As we went out into the cold night, I held her close to keep her warm and wrapped her in my own wool scarf. With my free hand I clung to Mama's coat as our family walked slowly home.

In the childhood days that followed I tried to fit the little doll into my playhouse family. But somehow she didn't seem to fit in. I didn't even give her a name. Finally, I put her in a box on the closet shelf and brought her out only to show off her peculiarities.

All of this happened more than half a century ago.

The other day I brought her into the light again. Her face, made of a soft expanse of unbleached muslin with a few ink-drawn lines for features, still bears an expression of peaceful tranquility. And her black horsehair braids are still tied with leather strings.

She has outwaited my childish disappointments—waited until I am old enough to realize that pity, no matter in what degree of concern, is a pathetic substitute for acceptance. Perhaps I, not she, had been the orphan, shutting off the flow of understanding I might have shared earlier of her people's traditions and virtues of acceptance. ❈

From: We Were Children Then, Volume II, published by NorthWord Press, Inc., Minocqua, WI.

Probable Dates of Spring and Fall Freeze (32°F.) and Freeze-Free Period

Location	Spring freeze dates (mo/day)			Fall freeze dates (mo/day)			Freeze-free period (days)		
	Probability of later date			Probability of earlier date			Prob. of longer period		
	80%	50%	20%	20%	50%	80%	20%	50%	80%
Antigo	5/13	5/23	6/03	9/07	9/17	9/28	132	116	100
Appleton	4/23	5/02	5/10	10/04	10/13	10/22	178	164	150
Ashland	5/21	6/01	6/13	9/10	9/19	9/27	123	109	94
Blair	5/11	5/19	5/27	9/14	9/22	9/29	135	125	116
Crivitz	5/13	5/23	6/02	9/10	9/20	9/29	136	119	103
Darlington	5/02	5/12	5/22	9/21	9/28	10/06	147	138	129
Fond du Lac	4/25	5/04	5/14	9/27	10/07	10/18	172	155	138
Grantsburg	5/07	5/20	6/02	9/12	9/20	9/28	138	122	106
Hillsboro	5/04	5/15	5/26	9/18	9/26	10/05	147	134	120
Janesville	4/20	4/28	5/06	10/01	10/10	10/20	177	164	151
Kenosha	4/19	4/28	5/07	10/05	10/16	10/27	185	170	155
Ladysmith	5/13	5/22	6/01	9/14	9/22	9/29	134	122	109
Lancaster	4/24	5/04	5/15	9/29	10/09	10/18	170	157	143
Montello	4/28	5/09	5/20	9/20	9/29	10/08	155	143	131
Oconto	5/07	5/16	5/24	9/20	9/28	10/05	146	134	123
Oshkosh	4/28	5/08	5/19	9/24	10/04	10/13	160	147	135
Park Falls	5/12	5/19	5/27	9/14	9/23	10/01	139	126	112
Prairie du Chien	4/22	5/03	5/13	9/29	10/07	10/15	169	157	144
Rhinelander	5/12	5/19	5/25	9/15	9/23	10/01	138	127	115
River Falls	4/29	5/08	5/17	9/21	9/30	10/08	157	144	132
Sheboygan	4/19	4/25	5/02	10/10	10/21	11/01	190	178	165
Spooner	5/17	5/28	6/08	9/07	9/17	9/28	128	112	96
Stoughton	4/22	4/30	5/09	9/30	10/09	10/19	175	161	148
Sturgeon Bay	5/08	5/17	5/26	9/27	10/08	10/19	156	143	130
Watertown	4/24	5/04	5/15	9/28	10/06	10/15	167	154	142
Wausau	4/30	5/08	5/17	9/20	9/28	10/06	156	142	128
West Allis	4/16	4/23	5/01	10/14	10/23	11/02	194	183	171
Wis. Rapids	5/09	5/18	5/26	9/14	9/23	10/01	140	127	115

Years Ago...

WATERTOWN—An extraordinary case of childbirth occurred in this city last Saturday morning. The wife of Mr. Edward M. Kanouse gave birth to *five* well-developed children, all boys, whose aggregate weight was ten pounds and two ounces. Two of the children were dead when born and three of them lived about two hours. Four members of the juvenile colony were about equal in size but one of the little waifs weighed only one pound, truly a miniature piece of humanity. Their bodies were taken to Sun Prairie, the former home of Mr. Kanouse, and the clods of the valley cover the five little brothers in one grave.—*Watertown Republican*, February 17, 1875.

Average Monthly Temperatures, 1951-1980

District

	NW	NC	NE	WC	C	EC	SW	SC	SE	State
January	9.1	9.9	13.0	12.2	13.5	16.7	15.6	16.8	18.6	13.9
February	14.7	14.3	16.7	18.0	18.3	20.5	20.9	21.6	23.0	18.7
March	26.3	25.3	27.1	29.4	29.0	30.1	31.8	32.1	32.6	29.3
April	42.3	41.1	42.1	45.7	44.8	43.7	46.9	47.0	45.9	44.4
May	54.3	53.5	54.2	57.9	56.7	54.7	58.7	58.5	56.8	56.1
June	63.3	62.3	63.3	66.9	65.6	64.2	67.6	67.6	66.4	65.2
July	68.5	67.0	68.0	71.4	70.0	69.7	71.9	71.9	71.4	70.0
August	66.3	64.8	65.8	69.1	67.9	68.4	69.9	69.9	70.0	68.0
September	57.2	56.0	57.2	60.0	59.3	60.4	61.5	61.9	62.4	59.5
October	47.0	46.2	47.2	49.5	48.9	49.9	50.8	51.2	51.5	49.1
November	31.1	30.7	32.5	33.7	33.9	36.1	35.8	36.6	37.6	34.2
December	16.8	16.9	19.4	19.9	20.4	23.4	22.5	23.5	25.0	20.9
Annual avg.	41.4	40.7	42.2	44.5	44.0	44.8	46.2	46.5	46.8	44.1

Average Monthly Precipitation, in Inches, 1951-1980

District

	NW	NC	NE	WC	C	EC	SW	SC	SE	State
January	0.99	1.08	1.19	0.91	1.00	1.23	0.96	1.16	1.42	1.10
February	0.77	0.90	1.04	0.80	1.02	1.12	1.01	1.03	1.09	0.98
March	1.65	1.72	1.91	1.91	2.03	2.03	2.06	2.14	2.27	1.97
April	2.43	3.48	2.82	2.90	2.99	2.88	3.32	3.24	3.30	2.93
May	3.65	3.64	3.50	3.88	3.77	3.13	3.62	3.21	2.95	3.48
June	4.39	4.16	3.77	4.42	3.67	3.33	4.13	3.93	3.79	3.95
July	4.20	4.04	3.62	4.03	3.57	3.38	3.98	3.93	3.85	3.84
August	4.58	4.56	3.91	4.11	3.77	3.33	3.98	3.84	3.58	3.96
September	3.54	3.80	3.67	3.58	3.71	3.23	3.50	3.44	3.21	3.52
October	2.23	2.30	2.24	2.25	2.36	2.34	2.27	2.37	2.40	2.31
November	1.67	1.89	1.89	1.61	1.77	1.90	1.80	1.92	2.06	1.83
December	1.17	1.32	1.47	1.10	1.31	1.63	1.28	1.54	1.79	1.40
Annual total	31.27	31.89	31.03	31.50	30.97	29.53	31.91	31.75	31.71	31.28

FEBRUARY RECIPE

Cream of Watercress Soup

Sauté until just wilted:
1 cup fresh chopped water cress
Add and cook gently about 3 minutes:
Salt, white pepper and paprika

1/2 cup white wine.
Remove from heat and add:
4 cups light cream.
Heat but do not boil.
Serve at once.
Makes 4 cups.

My Norwegian Grandfather

MABEL LONGLEY

In the early 1800s my great-grandfather, Christopher Oleson, sold his small farm near Oslo, Norway, and purchased tickets to Palmyra, Wisconsin. Relatives who had preceded him to Wisconsin had written him that here was not only a land of freedom but a country that would provide him and his family a wonderful living. These Norwegians had built not only their homes but a Lutheran church and school.

Christopher had sewn enough money into his woolen underwear to make the down payment on what he hoped would be their future home in the Wisconsin territory. Before they reached the port of sailing, his wife died. After burying his wife in Norway, brokenhearted Christopher and his son, Chris, and daughter, Ann, proceeded on their journey to America.

On the boat a woman made friends with Chris and Ann and convinced Christopher that she would take care of the two children and him. Christopher, who knew little about the care of children, married her. Before they reached the American shore, Christopher died and was buried at sea.

The stepmother took the money that Christopher had sewn in his underwear and continued the journey to Palmyra. When they reached Palmyra, she took them to the town pump, gave them a drink, and told them to wait until she returned. They never saw her again.

Mr. Wilson, the hotel owner, found them. He went home and said to his wife, "There are two children out at the town pump. They are frightened and can't understand English." Mrs. Wilson, a kindhearted woman, went out and brought Chris and Ann into her warm kitchen where she fed them and gave them her love. Soon the children began to love and trust her.

Mrs. Wilson bought new clothes for them, taught them to speak English, and sent them to school. Chris became adept at learning and at making friends.

Mrs. Wilson was not a Lutheran, but she knew the people who lived in the Lutheran settlement, and Chris grew up in that faith. By the time he was eighteen, he had grown from an undersized boy to a six-foot tall, broad-shouldered man.

Though very strong, he was always gentle. The person who said, "Nothing is so strong as gentleness; nothing is so gentle as real strength," must have had people like Chris Oleson in mind.

At twenty-two, he married a Lutheran girl and together they purchased a farm. It had hills and a lovely stream near the house. It reminded them of Norway. Together they raised eight children, all of whom went to high school, and those who wanted it had college training.

Time passed and many grandchildren joined the clan. We were a close-knit family, and at all holidays and in between we gathered at Grandfather's house for a sumptuous dinner where Mrs. Wilson was the guest of honor. It was a Norwegian custom that all men and boys be served first, but Grandfather insisted that Mrs. Wilson sit at his right and be the first one served. She was the spirit of goodness and his first love.

At one of those early Easter dinners, someone remarked, "Father, you certainly have a tall family," so Chris, my mother, and her three younger brothers stood up, and two other sons stood on chairs and held a board just six feet from the floor. All five heads touched the board.

Chris was a fast-working man and he always wanted a fast-traveling road horse. When his wife or daughters wanted to go into town, he would harness Nora to the buggy and bring her to the door for them. He would give Nora a pat on the hip and say, "Don't let anyone pass you on the road." Nora had been well trained. She went off at a brisk trot. If anyone tried to pass her, she broke into a gallop and the driver had to hold a tight rein.

Chris Oleson enjoyed life, God, his family, and all people. They made his life complete. The kindness of Mrs. Wilson was always on his mind. We, of the third generation, called her Grandma Wilson. She was a much-loved guest at my wedding, and when each of our two sons was born she came to see that all was well.

As Chris grew older, it was his delight, after a family dinner, to gather the children about him and throw pennies to them. If a small child didn't get his share, he would throw a handful directly at his feet.

He never forgot how people had helped him when he was in need. Although his purse was often nearly empty, he never refused a few coins to someone who had less than he had. Often, if a hungry man came to his farm, he would go to the kitchen door and say, "Put on an extra plate, Mother. There is a hungry man here who will eat with us."

Chris Oleson was not only a thrifty man but a devout one. Each day began with Bible readings, and before each meal he gave thanks to God for His continued care and guidance.

Goethe once said, "We are shaped and fashioned by what we love." Chris Oleson loved God and his fellow man. If Abou Ben Adhem's vision comes true, the Angel writing in the Book of Gold will write Chris Oleson's name, with Abou's, as "one who loved his fellow man." ❀

From: *We Were Children Then, Volume II*, published by NorthWord Press, Inc., Minocqua, WI.

Seed Germination Made Easy

In order to germinate quickly and successfully, most seeds need a temperature of 70 to 85 degrees F. In Wisconsin's energy-conscious homes, however, winter rooms are kept much cooler. The perfect answer is one or more heating cables made just for the purpose. Looped over the bottom of the planting flat and covered with the planting medium, the cables will keep the seed-growing medium between 70 and 75. If you don't have heating cables, however, an electric blanket will serve as a good substitute. Drape it over a table, cover it with a vinyl tablecloth or other waterproof sheet, and set the temperature to 70. Set the planting flats on it until 80% germination is reached, then remove the young seedlings to a cooler spot for their subsequent growth. ❀

The Gentleman in the Garden

I may perhaps be reckoned an Enthusiast, when I assert, that I am really surprized that Men of Fortune do not employ their Time in this manner. I am very certain that the other Amusements they run into are so far from being able to stand in Competition with that more profitable one of raising Nurseries and planting Trees, that the very naming of them with it would be sufficient Invective: Let each Gentleman consider them, in his own Mind; He will see the Force of what I say: Let him reflect upon Horses and Dogs, Wine and Women, Cards and Folly, &c. and then upon Planting. Will not the last engross his *Whole* Mind, and appear worthy of employing all his Attention? Can there be a more genteel, a more rational Amusement? Can any thing tend more to the preserving of Health, and the prolonging of Life? Can any thing be more innocent, or productive of greater Pleasure? Does not a Man's Planting appear like a Creation of his own, arising round him, defending him from the churlish Winds, and promising to enrich his Posterity? Nay, if he has had an early Taste for it, even in his own Days, he will find the Sweets and Profit of it.

Rev. Wm. Hanbury, An Essay on Planting and a Scheme for Making it Conducive to the Glory of God, 1758

Musicians of Note

Mitchell Ayres born in Milwaukee, 1910; one of TV's busiest conductors in the fifties and sixties, best known as Perry Como's orchestra leader on radio, TV and records (*The Chesterfield Supper Club, The Perry Como Show*).

Bunny Berigan born in Hilbert,1908; trumpeter, with a distinctive, uninhibited style, who played with Paul Whiteman, Benny Goodman, and Dorsey Brothers bands; started own successful big band in 1937.

Ole Bull nineteenth-century concert violinist in Europe; first appeared in concert in Milwaukee in 1853 and in Madison in 1856; married the daughter of an Eau Claire lumber baron in 1870; popular symbol of Norwegian culture.

The Chordettes formed in 1946 as a girls' barbershop quartet in Sheboygan; won *Arthur Godfrey's Talent Scouts* competition; 1954 recording of "Mr. Sandman" established them as top recording artists.

Richard Davis international career as bassist includes playing both jazz and classical gigs, as well as teaching bass, jazz history and improvisation at University of Wisconsin-Madison.

John Harbison composer who has done much of his work at rural retreat near Token Creek, including cantata "The Flight Into Egypt," which won the 1987 Pulitzer Prize for composition.

Gunnar Johansen prodigious pianist, composer, and scholar; in 1969, on 30 hours' notice, learned and triumphantly performed with the Philadelphia Orchestra the piano version of a Beethoven violin concerto; at Blue Mounds home-studio, has recorded the complete works for keyboard of Bach, Busoni, and Liszt.

Thor Johnson born in Wisconsin Rapids, 1913; as one of the first native conductors to direct an American orchestra (Cincinnati Symphony Orchestra, for 20 years), did much to popularize orchestral music.

Liberace born in West Allis, 1919; semiclassical pianist first billed as Walter Busterkeys, whose flamboyant style, candelabrum, and sequins earned him title of Mr. Showmanship; acknowledged his Wisconsin roots by ending concerts with "Beer Barrel Polka."

Ben Sidran born in Racine, 1943; jazz pianist and Madison resident who has recorded 18 albums and conducts the nationally syndicated radio program "Sidran on Record" and the weekly TV show "New Visions."

Ralph Votapek born in Milwaukee, 1939; won a piano in a statewide contest sponsored by Liberace; won Van Cliburn International Competition in 1962, which offered prize money, concert tours, recording contracts, and a one-year army deferment.❧   —D.C.

CROSSWORD PUZZLE

ACROSS

1 State bird
6 Cries noisily
10 "To every one ___ gives a share/Of work to do, sometime, somewhere." —E.E. Rexford.
13 Expunge
14 Spoken
15 Inventor ___ Evinrude
16 Maxims
17 U.W. President, 1986-
19 Long-Delayed Echoes (init.)
20 "His" Town was Madison
24 "Do you think what the end of a Perfect Day/Can _____ to a tired heart." —C. Jacobs-Bond
25 Meadow
26 Lady ___
28 Miners' quest in southwestern Wisconsin
29 ___ in terris

31 Shiocton poet ____ E. Rexford
33 Ecologist ____ Leopold
34 Decline
37 Retired five-term U.S. Senator
42 Designer initials
43 Cable network (abbrev.)
44 Algerian seaport
45 Human guinea pig Alexis ___ Martin
47 ___ facto
50 Sunday afternoon purpose in Green Bay (abbrev.)
51 Lombardi fixation
52 Groove
53 Sun Prairie - born artist
60 Swiss river
61 Seeded
62 Pepin's ___ Ingalls Wilder
64 Is (Ger.)
65 ___ violet, state flower
67 Restricted number, of muskie catch, e.g .

68 Utmost
69 Agriculture Prof. L.F.Graber: "Mr. _____lfa"
70 ___ in Dairyland

DOWN
1 State rock, ___ granite
2 Order of Rock Island Transit (init.)
3 Baroque composer
4 "Every person ___ entitled ___ a certain remedy in the laws." Wis. Const. Art. I, sec. 9.
5 Close to myself
6 Edna Ferber's ___ Big
7 Kenosha's ___ Welles
8 Auto___, Germany's fast track
9 Cabbage dish
10 Israeli Prime Minister, formerly of Milwaukee
11 Ye ___ Booke Shoppe
12 White-tailed ___
18 Westport's Ella Wheeler ___
21 National Education Association (init.)
22 Small child
23 Governor ___ Dreyfus
26 Moist
27 Wading bird
28 Lake Nebagamon News (init.)

29 Pelican Lake Reporter (init.)
30 Busy activity
32 County seat of Pierce Co.
33 Spring Green's Shakespeare theater (init.)
35 The wurst of Wisconsin
36 West ___, Washington Co.
38 Cake coverings
39 La Follette's Mary ___ Law of 1914
40 Encountered
41 Pasture sound
46 Billy Mitchell's type of force
47 Class or kind
48 "Raven" poet
49 Stanley Kowalski's cry
51 Triumph
52 Hamlin Garland's ____ The Middle Border (2 wds.)
53 Benefit
54 ___ Troy, Walworth Co.
55 County of state's oldest courthouse
56 Military desertion
57 Fall short of success
58 Fumes (lt.)
59 Speed skater ___ Heiden
63 Consumed
66 District Attorney (init.)

See back of book for answers.

Saving Last Year's Seeds

Should you throw away last year's packaged seeds? Probably not. If they have been kept in a spot free from excessive heat, there is every chance that they are still viable and capable of producing good crops. Here are the reasonable viability periods of some common garden vegetable seeds:

❀ **Two Years:** Corn, onion, parsnip, soybean, salsify.
❀ **Three Years**: Bean, leek, parsley, pea.
❀ **Four Years:** Carrot, mustard, pepper, tomato.
❀ **Five Years:** Broccoli, cabbage, cauliflower, kohlrabi, lettuce, okra, pumpkin, radish, spinach, turnip.
❀ **Six Years:** Beet, eggplant, melon, squash.
❀ **Eight Years**: Celery.
❀ **Ten Years:** Cucumber, endive.

Some seeds live considerably longer. Michigan State scientists began to bury an assortment of weed seeds in 1879 to test their longevity. Ever since, a portion of the seeds has been unearthed periodically and tested. After 39 years in the ground, 84 percent of the plantain seeds germinated, and 83 percent of the black nightshade seeds. Every year, some of the original 1879 seeds sprout successfully. More astounding, archaeologists have found viable plant seeds that had been sealed in the tombs of the pharaohs of ancient Egypt!❀

The Old Man's Garage

GEORGE VUKELICH

I got to thinking just now about the deer head hanging in The Old Man's garage. Actually, it's my mother's garage, but habit dies hard. I still call it his because it was always packed with his stuff.

He always had so much stuff in there, the car often sat outside under the pines. Even when he put an addition onto the garage, his stuff just sort of accumulated and expanded to fit the space and the car was a real tight squeeze again.

It was your typical North Country inventory: a workbench that ran the length of one wall, overflowing with pails of nails and screws, nuts and bolts, pliers, hammers, chisels, wrenches, and all the tools you ever needed to drill a well or put in plumbing or wire a house or pour concrete or saw up logs or weld or paint or catch fish or butcher deer.

It was The Old Man's garage and not the big house next to it that contained The Old Man's lifestyle, that contained his essence, that contained his spirit.

From canepoles to Coleman lanterns, from outboard motors to shotgun shells, from icefishing tipups to rain ponchos, that endless clutter drew me like a magnet. I spent countless hours poking around in there, amazed at what I discovered, because what I discovered was The Old Man.

He's gone now, and his clutter is gone, too—most of it to friends and neighbors who could use it, some of it squirreled away in my den at home—and the garage is so neat and unlived-in that he wouldn't recognize it.

The deer head is still there, though—it even got to hang in the summer porch of the big house for a time—and it watches over the cold, lifeless garage with its cold, lifeless eyes.

A trophy, Aldo Leopold tried to teach us in *A Sand County Almanac*, whether it be a bird's egg, a mess of trout, a basket of mushrooms, the photograph of a bear, the pressed specimen of a wildflower or a note tucked into the cairn on a mountain peak, is a certificate.

"It attests," Aldo said, "that its owner has been somewhere and done something—exercised skill, persistence or discrimination in the age-old feat of overcoming, outwitting or reducing-to possession. These connotations which attach to the trophy usually far exceed its physical value."

I have only to close my eyes and here I am, up there in The Old Man's garage, the concrete clean-swept, the workbench neat and empty because no one works there anymore, the car gone to Florida for the winter.

There we are, just the two of us in this place.

I stare up at the trophy buck.

The trophy buck stares down at me.

Do we comprehend each other? We are each of us strange artifacts of another time, another life.

I remember driving the cedar swamp with The Old Man in that other time, in that other life.

> Across the snow filled valley land
> our father watches from his stand.
> Here, our big buck cleared the stream.
> The damning prints in the frozen sand.
>
> Upwind, we work as a combat team.
> An army of cedars waits in the steam
> between us now and our father's place.
> Through 7X glasses, he sees an old dream.
>
> Remember the flush on a young man's face
> the first time he opened his rifle case?
> In this swamp, one great last deer.
> Listening for drivers, gauging our pace.
>
> He knows again that we are near.
> It is the terrible time of year.
> The others hope we find him here.
> I hope we do not find him here.

In Dostoevski's *The Brothers Karamazov* , the monk, on his deathbed, admonishes his followers: "Love all the earth, every ray of God's light, every grain of sand or blade of grass, every living thing. If you love the earth enough, you will know the divine mystery."

Amen. The rest is taxidermy. ✾

Reprinted from <u>North Country Notebook</u>.
Published by North Country Press.

MARCH

The stormy March has come at last.
With wind, and cloud, and
*   changing skies;*
I hear the rushing of the blast,
That through the snowy valley flies

—William Cullen Bryant, "March"

March is a transition month, part winter, part spring. Geese fly north and summer birds return during this month named after the Roman god of war. Heavy snows, rain, even thunderstorms are frequent in March, and major ice storms occur on the average of once every four years. One of the worst in south-central Wisconsin occurred on March 3-5, 1976, leaving a four-inch-thick coating of ice that caused more than 50 million dollars damage. The big event for the month is the vernal equinox, on or about the 21st, which marks the first day of spring, when the day and night are of equal length everywhere on earth.❀

March Weather History

MADISON

Day	Record High		Record Low		Record Precip.		Average High/Low
1	62	1882	-29	1962	0.95	1932	34/16
2	67	1964	-13	1913	0.75	1872	35/16
3	70	1983	-8	1884	1.95	1881	35/16
4	69	1983	-9	1884	0.58	1882	35/17
5	67	1983	-12	1890	1.02	1959	36/17
6	66	1983	-14	1960	1.86	1973	36/17
7	70	1987	-7	1920	0.80	1872	37/18
8	71	1987	-10	1960	1.24	1893	37/18
9	66	1977	-8	1975	0.84	1918	37/19
10	66	1894	-4	1948	0.66	1986	38/19
11	65	1977	-9	1948	0.89	1898	38/19
12	68	1977	-5	1948	0.81	1923	39/20
13	65	1957	-6	1975	0.83	1917	39/20
14	68	1973	-4	1960	1.19	1944	39/21
15	65	1935	3	1900	1.49	1943	40/21
16	75	1945	-8	1870	1.28	1889	40/21
17	73	1966	-8	1941	0.77	1965	41/22
18	70	1918	-2	1959	0.80	1923	41/22
19	76	1976	-8	1923	1.09	1897	42/23
20	77	1921	-7	1965	1.00	1886	42/23
21	75	1911	-1	1965	1.50	1886	43/23
22	73	1938	-5	1888	1.00	1916	43/24
23	78	1938	-6	1888	0.72	1913	44/24
24	76	1939	-6	1888	0.91	1904	45/25
25	73	1939	-4	1960	1.41	1920	45/25
26	76	1907	-9	1960	1.12	1925	46/26
27	78	1945	2	1965	1.13	1880	46/26
28	76	1946,86	2	1923	0.90	1977	47/26
29	82	1910,86	1	1887	1.07	1960	48/27
30	78	1967	2	1969	1.15	1891	48/27
31	82	1981	5	1969	1.34	1929	49/28

MARCH

March Weather History

LA CROSSE

Day	Record High		Record Low		Average High/Low
1	59	1878	-28	1962	34/15
2	65	1913	-18	1950	34/15
3	66	1894	-13	1875	34/16
4	62	1983	-26	1873	35/16
5	58	1983	-18	1890	35/17
6	65	1974	-16	1890	35/17
7	74	1987	-10	1945	36/17
8	64	1878	-8	1943	36/18
9	67	1878	-5	1877	36/18
10	67	1894	-10	1949	37/19
11	61	1878	-17	1948	37/19
12	66	1877	-8	1948	38/20
13	66	1922	-5	1975	38/20
14	67	1973	-10	1975	38/21
15	68	1935	-3	1956	39/21
16	75	1930	-8	1956	39/22
17	78	1894	-7	1941	40/22
18	71	1903	-3	1923	40/23
19	76	1921	-12	1923	41/23
20	71	1918	-13	1965	42/23
21	75	1911	-3	1965	42/24
22	70	1945	-10	1888	43/25
23	83	1910	-4	1965	43/25
24	75	1924	-5	1965	44/26
25	76	1928	3	1940	44/26
26	74	1910	-2	1965	45/27
27	77	1910	7	1874	46/27
28	80	1986	4	1923	46/28
29	84	1986	1	1969	47/28
30	80	1967	2	1969	48/29
31	83	1986	5	1969	48/29

The normal average precipitation for La Crosse in March is 1.96 inches. The wettest March was in 1876 when 4.23 inches was recorded; the driest was in 1910 when only 0.03 inches was received.

Excuses for a March Party

Pasta Party

Mountains of spaghetti are consumed the night before the Birkebeiner, as skiers carbo-load in preparation for North America's largest cross-country ski race. In the morning several thousand skiers from all over the world push off from the starting line on Hayward's Main Street for the 34-mile race that ends in Cable.

14 My-Finest-Hour Party

Hank Aaron hit his first home run in professional baseball on March 14, 1954, in spring training with the Milwaukee Braves. About twenty years later (at 2:40 p.m. on April 4, 1974, to be precise) he sent historic homer No. 714 over the stadium wall, tying the record Babe Ruth had set in 1935. Aaron began his career with a farm team in Eau Claire, and went on to rewrite the record books: most professional games played (3,298), most RBIs (2,297), most plate appearances (13,940), most times at bat (12,364), and most home runs (755).

16 St. Urho's Day

Finish writing your St. Urho's Day cards, then celebrate the day that St. Urho saved Finland's grape crop by ridding the country of a grasshopper plague. Wisconsin Finns who are weary of St. Patrick's Day wear purple, parade down Main Street, have parties, and persuade governors with a sense of humor to proclaim March 16 as St. Urho's Day.

21 Vernal Equinox

Winter is officially over! Soon the *turdus migratorius* and the *viola papilionacea* (robin and wood violet, official state bird and flower) will be seen across the land. The realistic people of Black River Falls have another way of determining the end of winter. They push an old car out onto the frozen river; when the ice melts and the car disappears underwater, spring is really here.

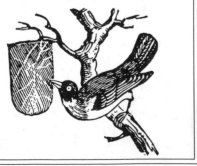

Highlights:
❀ *Start annual seeds*
❀ *Start vegetable seeds*
❀ *Apply dormant oil spray*
❀ *Divide dahlias*

This is a month of trembling anticipation for Wisconsin gardeners. After five months of tending houseplants, of sharpening and cleaning tools, of planning and dreaming and scheming, we know that it is nearly time to move our garden operations to the outdoors.

Nearly—but not quite. We are taunted by national magazines that tell us, "Yes, now you may plant your onions!"—but we know they are talking to gardeners in the broad middle section of the country, and not to us hardy gardeners here in winter wonderland. And to make matters worse, Mother Nature sends us a March thaw, when the temperatures on a Saturday afternoon may reach a tantalizing 60 degrees—only to be followed by six inches of snow the following day.

Experienced Wisconsin gardeners have learned to ignore these temptations. They have been hurt too many times in the past, and now they know that true spring does not come in March but in April—or perhaps May or June.

Still, March is not a month for sloth. Early in the month, you may begin seeds, indoors, of the slower-to-start flowering annuals, including ageratum, anchusa, African daisy, balsam, bells of Ireland, browallia, candytuft, carnation, coleus, dianthus, globe amaranth, larkspur, annual lupine, moonflower, nicotiana, annual phlox, salvia, snapdragon, snow on the mountain, stocks, sweet william, and black-eyed susan vine.

In the second week, begin seeds of anise, basil, lavender, perennial mint and spearmint, rosemary, and thyme.

Then, anytime after the 15th, start seeds of sweet alyssum, bachelor button, calendula, celosia, sweet sultan, cleome, dahlia, four o'clock, rudbeckia, baby's breath, sunflower, strawflower, money plant, marigold, kochia, fragrant mignonette, morning glory, nemesia, annual poppy, portulaca (moss rose), pincushion flower, sweet pea, and zinnia.

This is also the time to start vegetable seeds indoors—broccoli, celery, tomatoes, early cabbage, eggplant, cauliflower, peppers, head lettuce, leeks, and parsley.

You may apply dormant sprays on fruit and ornamental trees for insect and disease control, but wait until the temperature has been above freezing for 24 hours.

Remove the mulch from beds of tulips and other spring-flowering bulbs after the 15th—but be ready to replace the mulch if frigid weather returns. You may also remove rose cones at this time.

By the fourth week in March, you may divide dahlia clumps in preparation for resetting them into the open garden, and you can set out new asparagus beds if the soil is dry enough to be worked. Fertilize established asparagus beds with well-rotted manure.

Last, choose a mild day to rake the garden clean of any remaining debris from winter—and get ready for April. ❀   —*J.M.*

Chocolate Cherry Creme Pie

18 Oreo cookies
2 tablespoons butter or
   margarine, melted
1 4-3/4-ounce package
   vanilla pudding and pie
   filling mix

2 cups frozen (thawed)
   or canned red cherries,
   including juice
1 cup milk
1 pint whipping cream
   (or 12-ounce container
   of whipped topping)

Crush 12 of the cookies into crumbs (either in blender, or put in plastic bag and roll with rolling pin). Sprinkle crumbs on bottom of 9" pie plate; mix with melted butter, pressing to bottom to form crust. Separate other 6 cookies, standing halves around edges of pie plate. In medium size kettle (or microwavable dish) stir together the pudding mix, cherries, and milk. Cook over medium heat until thick, stirring constantly (or microwave approximately 5 minutes until thick, stirring frequently). Cool. Whip cream, reserve 3/4-cup for top of pie; fold remaining cream into cherry mixture. Refrigerate several hours. Decorate top of pie with scoops of cream. (Curls from chocolate bar make an attractive topping to this also.)
—*Mariette Deutsch of Cedarburg.*

Muskellunge Facts

The first muskellunge stocking efforts in Wisconsin took place in 1899.

The muskie was made official state fish in 1955.

Estimates place the state's harvest of legal muskies at about 50,000 per year.

Wisconsin has more than 700 muskie lakes and forty-some muskie streams.

A muskie will prey on objects as large as muskrats, ducks, and even other muskie.

The record Wisconsin fish was 69 pounds 11 ounces, taken from the Chippewa Flowage in October of 1949. There are reports of larger muskellunge that have been netted and released by lake survey crews.

Of fish the same age, it's the female which is usually the heavier.❈

Woodcock in the Spring

Along with the arrival of spring comes the arrival of the "bog sucker," alias timberdoodle or woodcock.

Best described as a bird designed by a committee, the American woodcock is a small shorebird that lives in the woods, especially aspen stands and alder marshes. It resembles a puffball of beige and black feathers from which protrudes its distinctive two-and-a-half-inch bill.

The bill is long and thin, allowing the bird to probe damp soil for earthworms. The upper bill is flexible at the tip, so that it can grab earthworms while probing in the mud.

The bird's ears are located near the base of the bill, to help locate worms, and the large eyes are set far back on the head allowing the bird to see danger above while feeding.

The six-ounce bird is supported by long Ichabod Crane-type slender legs, and when it walks it seems to bob and weave as if to an imaginary beat.

Woodcocks are migratory birds, nesting in the north central and northeastern states and wintering where the earth is warm, allowing easy access to worms. Most of the woodcocks that nest in Wisconsin winter in Arkansas, Louisiana, and Mississippi.

In early spring this usually reclusive bird begins its migration north and, as a harbinger of spring, arrives in southern Wisconsin in early to mid-March. Upon arriving the male woodcock perform daily courtship displays at dawn and dusk in small open territories called singing grounds. These are usually open fields or forest clearings.

Each male announces his presence with a buzzing call, or "peent." It continues peenting, sounding much like the buzz of a nighthawk, while bobbing its head and strutting around the singing ground.

Suddenly, the male spirals upward to a height of 200 to 300 feet, high above the surrounding forest canopy. In less than a minute it dives back down to earth, zig-zagging and swooping and all the while making a musical chirping sound.

As the bird glides to a landing close to where flight originated, it continues to "peent," and if a female has been attracted the birds will mate. The male may make a dozen or more flights in a single evening, and being polygamous, he may breed with several females.

The female woodcock lays four buff-colored eggs and incubates the eggs for 20 to 22 days, during which time she is very reluctant to abandon her nest. When the young chicks hatch they are fluffy and active, and can fly within 14 days. ❀   —T.E.

Planting Sugar Maples

All good citizens, who are desirous of doing good deeds, and of being remembered by posterity hereafter, we would recommend to transplant a goodly number of sugar maples round their dwellings. We think all will see the propriety of giving their immediate attention to the growing of this most valuable tree, not only for adorning our dwellings, but also, a large number may be set in a suitable place on every farm. They, in a few years, will afford the pure juice for sugar, and the best of timber for cabinet and other kinds of work, and all poor trees may be worked up for fuel. Our soil is rich and well adapted for the sugar maple.

This tree, beside or around a dwelling is an ornament, and also by the road-side. How pleasant and beautiful would be the scenery, if this tree, in its full growth and splendor, were along each side of our roads! We have seen the maple tree no taller than a walking-staff, become, in fifteen years, so large as to afford sap and sugar. Be not discouraged by looking forward, and say it will be a long time before you can have any benefit by sugar. You must remember the timber is growing every year, and wait with patience, and be assured the other part will not fail.❧

—The Farmer's and Emigrant's Hand Book, 1845

Then It's Spring by Hamlin Garland

When the hens begin a-squawkin'
   An' a-rollin' in the dust;
When the rooster takes to talkin',
   An' a-crowin' fit to bust;
When the crows are cawin', flockin',
   An' the chickuns boom and sing,
     Then it's spring!

When the roads are jest one mud-hole
   And the worter tricklin' round
Makes the barn-yard like a puddle,
   An' softens up the ground
Till y'r ankle-deep in worter,
Sayin' words y'r hadn't orter —
   When the jay-birds swear an' sing,
     Then it's spring!

(Hamlin Garland was born in West Salem on September 14, 1860, and spent his childhood near Onalaska. His autobiographical A Daughter of the Middle Border *was awarded the Pulitzer Prize in 1922.)*

Matching Quiz

A number of television actors and actresses were born in Wisconsin. Can you match the performer to his or her television role? (Birthplace is shown in parentheses.)

1. **Dan Travanti** (Kenosha)

2. **Tyne Daly** (Madison)

3. **Jory Husain** (Milwaukee)

4. **Charlotte Rae** (Milwaukee)

5. **Allen Ludden** (Mineral Point)

6. **John Fiedler** (Platteville)

7. **Tom Wopat** (Lodi)

8. **Charles Siebert** (Kenosha)

9. **Ellen Corby** (Racine)

10. **Al Molinaro** (Kenosha)

A. Luke Duke, *Dukes of Hazard*

B. Mr. Peterson, *The Bob Newhart Show*

C. Esther (Grandma) Walton, *The Waltons*

D. Frank Furillo, *Hill Street Blues*

E. Dr. Stanley Riverside II, *Trapper John M.D.*

F. Det. Mary Beth Lacey, *Cagney and Lacey*

G. Alfred Delvecchio, *Happy Days* and *Joanie Loves Chachi*

H. Jawaharlal, *Head of the Class*

I. Host, *Password*

J. Edna Garrett, *Diff'rent Strokes* and *The Facts of Life*

For answers, see back of book.

These six Wisconsin-born entertainers changed their names after they left America's Dairyland for Tinseltown. Can you match the well-known names on the left to the original names on the right?

1. Gene Wilder (Milwaukee)
2. Dennis Morgan (Prentice)
3. Don Ameche (Kenosha)
4. Harry Houdini (Appleton)
5. Liberace (West Allis)
6. Fredric March (Racine)

A. Dominic Felix Amici
B. Frederick McIntyre Bickel
C. Wladziu Valentino Liberace
D. Gerry Silberman
E. Stanley Morner
F. Ehrich Weiss

For answers, see back of book.

17th Century Compost

"Have always ready prepar'd several Composts, mixed with natural pasture earth, a little loamy; skreene the mould, and mingle it discreetly with rotten cowdung; not suffering it to abide in heaps too long, but be frequently turning and stirring it, nor let weeds grow on it; and that it may be moist and sweete, and not wash away the salts, it were best kept and prepared in some large pit, or hollow place which has a hard bottom and in the shade." ✤

—John Evelyn's *Direction for the Gardiner* (1687)

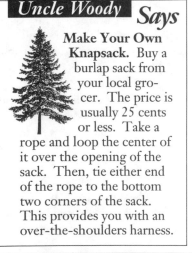

Uncle Woody *Says*

Make Your Own Knapsack. Buy a burlap sack from your local grocer. The price is usually 25 cents or less. Take a rope and loop the center of it over the opening of the sack. Then, tie either end of the rope to the bottom two corners of the sack. This provides you with an over-the-shoulders harness.

Years Ago . . .

MADISON—Today, Deputy U.S. Marshal Ansley brought from the Flambeau reservation Oge-Ma Go-Zek, the Chippewa Indian who when a youth captured Old Abe, the noted war eagle, when he was a nestling, cutting down the pine tree in the top of which the mud and sticks residence of the noble bird was located. The young Chippewa was the son of the chief of the Flambeau band and with his people went down the Chippewa River with his prize and sold it to Dan McCann of Eagle Point for a bushel of corn. The latter carried the eagle to Eau Claire and gave him to Company C of the 8th Wisconsin volunteers. He came through the war unscathed and died in the winter of 1881. His body was embalmed and mounted and now is to be seen in the office of the quartermaster general in the Capitol. His young captor was given permission to go and see him.—*Wisconsin State Journal*, March 14, 1889.

Stairsteps on the Mississippi

The Mississippi River paddlewheelers of Mark Twain's day may be long gone, but the squat, snub-nosed, towboats that replaced them still command attention. It's a rare day when a towboat pushing a string of barges through one of the upper Mississippi's locks doesn't draw onlookers.

Incidentally, towboats don't pull, they push. And each year they push hundreds of millions of tons of cargo up and down the river between St. Paul and New Orleans.

The glory days of paddlewheel steamers began their decline with the Civil War and were virtually over by the turn of the century. Railroads, which were faster, became the new form of commercial transportation.

But the demands of World War I exceeded the capacity of the railroads and revitalized river traffic. Long-forgotten sternwheelers and ancient barges were rescued from dank backwater graveyards and once-retired river pilots were hired to steer whatever would float. New diesel-powered towboats and snub-nosed steel barges were turned out in shipyards that once built speedy river packets. Millions of tons of goods moved by river, and continued to move when the war was over.

By the end of the 1920s, the river trade — now specializing in bulk cargos like coal, petroleum products, and grain —had made a remarkable resurgence. But as it had been since the first steamer moved up the Mississippi in 1823, river traffic came to a standstill in times of low water.

To provide a constant level for navigation, the Army Corps of Engineers built 27 locks and dams on the Upper Mississippi between 1930 and 1940, and added two more in the 1960s. The water stored behind each dam forms a 10 to 50-mile-long lake, called a pool. Each pool is one step in a watery stairway that descends 420 feet in the 669 miles of river between

Minneapolis/St. Paul and St. Louis. By regulating the flow of water through each individual dam, the Corps maintains a minimum depth of nine feet in the river's marked navigation channel. The locks provide a means for boats to safely bypass the dams.

Five locks and dams are located in Wisconsin — at Alma, Trempealeau, La Crosse, Genoa, and Lynxville. The dams at Red Wing and Winona, Minnesota, and at Guttenberg and Dubuque, Iowa, touch the Wisconsin shore, but the locks are located on the west bank of the river.

Two locks and dams — the Upper and Lower St. Anthony Falls at Minneapolis — are named. The rest are numbered, one through 27, downstream from St. Paul to Granite City, Illinois. There is a No. 5, at Fountain City, Wisconsin, and a No. 5A, at Winona, but no number 23. There are no locks or dams on the river below St. Louis.

Most locks are 600 feet long and 110 feet wide, but those at Minneapolis/St. Paul are only 400 feet long and 56 feet wide. No. 19 at Keokuk, Iowa, and No. 27 at Granite City are 1200 feet long — the largest on the river.

Lock No. 27 is actually located in the Chain of Rocks Canal adjoining the river, which was built in 1945 to bypass an obstruction at the confluence of the Mississippi and the Missouri rivers.

The locks are filled and emptied by gravity. No power is required, except to open and close the lock gates and control valves. The vertical lift varies widely from lock to lock. The Upper and Lower Falls of St.

Anthony raise and lower boats a whopping 49 feet, while No. 5A at Winona, Minnesota, has a lift of only five and one-half feet.

Petroleum products from the oil fields of Texas and Louisiana are the largest single commodity moved on the river. Vast quantities of coal are also shipped upriver from southern Illinois and western Kentucky. Grain from the prairie states and Canada is the principal downbound cargo, with much of it going to New Orleans where it is loaded on ocean vessels for overseas destinations.

A huge amount of cargo can be carried in an assembled river tow. One single barge carries 1,500 tons, compared to 100 tons for a jumbo hopper railway car and 25 tons for a large semi-truck.

Fifteen-barge tows — rigged five barges long and three wide, and stretching for a quarter-mile — are common on the Upper Mississippi and have a capacity of 22,500 tons, or 787,500 bushels, or 6,804,000 gallons. A 225-car train or 900 trucks would be required to carry the same amount of cargo.

Such tows are too long to pass through the locks and require a double locking. The tow is "cut," with the first nine barges unfastened from the rest and locked through as a separate unit. A single tow may lock through in 20 to 30 minutes, but a double locking can take up to two hours.

Pleasure boats also use the locks, without charge. At busy times, such as holidays, 30 or 40 pleasure boats are often locked through together. Pleasure boats have the same rights on the river as towboats, but wise recreational boaters give commercial tows plenty of room. The bow wake from a large tow can easily swamp a small boat, and it can take nearly a mile to stop a 15-barge tow.

The creature comforts aboard today's riverboats would astound Mark Twain. Towboats are equipped with hydraulic steering, radar, echo sounders, air conditioning, refrigeration, TV, and radiotelephone. Still, the work is hard and not without danger. Crewmen stand six-hour watches—six on and six off around the clock for 30 days, then leave the boat for about two weeks.

Visitors are welcome at all locks and dams from early morning to late evening; some offer free guided tours, usually on weekends.

Lockages are part of the workaday world of the river and are usually accomplished without fanfare. But not always. At No. 15, located in the heart of Rock Island, Illinois, each vessel passage requires a swing bridge to be opened. Bells ring, whistles sound, safety gates drop, traffic grinds to a halt, and, in rush hour, backs up for blocks.

Mark Twain would have loved it! ❀ —D.D.

LOCKS AND DAMS ON THE MISSISSIPPI

Upper St. Anthony Falls, Minneapolis, MN
Lower St. Anthony Falls, Minneapolis, MN
No. 1 — St. Paul, MN
No. 2 — Hastings, MN
No. 3 — Red Wing, MN
No. 4 — Alma, WI
No. 5 — Fountain City, WI
No. 5A— Winona, MN
No. 6 — Trempealeau, WI
No. 7 — La Crosse, WI
No. 8 — Genoa, WI
No. 9 — Lynxville, WI
No. 10 — Guttenberg, IA
No. 11 — Dubuque, IA
No. 12 — Bellevue, IA
No. 13 — Clinton, IA
No. 14 — Le Claire, IA
No. 15 — Rock Island, IL
No. 16 — Muscatine, IA
No. 17 — New Boston, IL
No. 18 — Burlington, IA
No. 19 — Keokuk, IA
No. 20 — Canton, MO
No. 21 — Quincy, IL
No. 22 — Saverton, MO
No. 24 — Clarksville, MO
No. 25 — Cap au Gris, MO
No. 26 — Alton, IL
No. 27 — Granite City, IL
(Note: no lock and dam No. 23)

Soil Temperature Conditions for Vegetable Seed Germination

Vegetable	Minimum (° F.)	Optimum Range (° F.)	Optimum (° F.)	Maximum (° F.)
Asparagus	50	60-85	75	95
Bean	60	60-85	80	95
Bean, Lima	60	60-85	85	85
Beet	40	50-85	85	95
Cabbage	40	45-95	85	100
Carrot	40	45-85	80	95
Cauliflower	40	45-85	80	100
Celery	40	60-70	70*	85*
Chard, Swiss	40	50-85	85	95
Corn	50	60-95	95	105
Cucumber	60	60-95	95	105
Eggplant	60	75-90	85	95
Lettuce	35	40-80	75	85
Muskmelon	60	75-95	90	100
Okra	60	70-95	95	105
Onion	35	50-95	75	95
Parsley	40	50-85	75	90
Parsnip	35	50-70	65	85
Pea	40	40-75	75	85
Pepper	60	65-95	85	95
Pumpkin	60	70-90	95	100
Radish	40	45-90	85	95
Spinach	35	45-75	70	85
Squash	60	70-95	95	100
Tomato	50	60-85	85	95
Turnip	40	60-105	85	105
Watermelon	60	70-95	95	105

* Daily fluctuation to 60° or lower at night is essential.

Boys Basketball Championship Games

Year	Winner	Runner-Up	Score
1916	Fond du Lac	Grand Rapids	22-7
1917	Eau Claire	Waukesha	15-3
1918	Madison Central	Watertown	37-17
1919	Fond du Lac	Eau Claire	27-19
1920	Superior	Neenah	19-9
1921	Appleton	Menomonie	14-12
1922	Fond du Lac	New Richmond	22-19
1923	Wisconsin High	Oshkosh	26-13
1924	Fond du Lac	Superior Central	32-21
1925	La Crosse Central	Shawano	10-4
1926	Stevens Point	River Falls	9-7
1927	Eau Claire	Madison Central	18-13
1928	Watertown	Madison Central	27-14
1929	Wausau	Kenosha	22-17
1930	Neenah	Racine Horlick	28-5
1931	Wisconsin High	Racine Park	20-19
1932	Beloit	Kenosha	13-11
1933	Beloit	Wausau	15-14
1934	A - Beloit	Wisconsin Rapids	32-18
	B - De Pere	New Lisbon	22-19
1935	A - Superior Cent.	Beloit	34-26
	B - Mayville	Weyauwega	36-22
1936	A - Superior Cent.	Wis. Rapids	22-21
	B - Port Wash.	Niagara	24-20
	C - Pardeeville	Middleton	29-27
1937	A - Beloit	Rhinelander	28-17
	B - Beaver Dam	South Milwaukee	35-22
	C - Fall Creek	Minocqua	32-19
1938	A - Wausau	Wauwatosa	24-16
	B - Shawano	Beaver Dam	33-20
	C - Marion	Cuba City	33-19
1939	A - Rhinelander	Wausau	46-28
	B - Watertown	Neenah	33-28
	C - Altoona	Port Edwards	44-33
1940	Shawano	Marshfield	23-22
1941	Two Rivers	Shawano	35-28
1942	Shorewood	Marinette	34-17
1943	Racine Park	Shawano	40-23
1944	Waukesha	Eau Claire	23-18
1945	Madison West	Lena	44-35
1946	Reedsville	Eau Claire	48-39
1947	Beloit	Hurley	56-37
1948	Wauwatosa	Eau Claire	41-35
1949	Hurley	La Crosse Logan	37-36
1950	St. Croix Falls	Eau Claire	59-35
1951	Wisconsin Rapids	Madison West	64-55
1952	South Milwaukee	Stevens Point	61-54
1953	Menasha	Sheboyg. Central	61-57
1954	Stevens Point	Superior Central	70-65

TRIVIA TEASERS

Q. Who gave a forgettable speech about agriculture, labor, invention, education, and opportunity at the State Fair in Milwaukee in 1859?

A. Abraham Lincoln.

Q. Which seven counties are named for U.S. Presidents?

A. Adams, Jackson, Jefferson, Lincoln, Monroe, Polk, and Washington. (Yes, there is a Grant County, but it's not named for *that* Grant.)

Q. What chance does a person have to find happiness in Wisconsin?

A. Pretty good—and getting better. The Bluebird Restoration Association of Wisconsin is putting up more than a thousand nesting boxes all over the state to encourage the bluebird population. Once common here, the bluebird has all but disappeared.

TRIVIA TEASERS

Q. What important studies did Dr. William Beaumont make at Fort Howard and Fort Crawford in the 1820s?

A. After conducting experiments on a young *voyageur* named Alexis St. Martin, who suffered a gunshot wound in the stomach that never closed, Dr. Beaumont published his findings in a famous book on digestion.

Q. What traditional holiday food has been described as resembling "aged, warm jello," "warm cotton batting," "a translucent food product with a profound odor"?

A. Lutefisk.

Q. The Hideout, in Sawyer County, was formerly the private retreat of a Chicago gangland leader. Name him . . . or *else!*

A. Al Capone.

BOY'S BASKETBALL, continued

Year	Winner	Runner-Up	Score
1955	Eau Claire	Superior Central	81-71
1956	Shawano	Appleton	74-68
1957	Shawano	Madison West	66-61
1958	Madison East	Mwke North	62-59
1959	Milwaukee Lincoln	Mwke North	65-56
1960	Wausau	Menomonie	74-65
1961	Milwaukee Lincoln	Rice Lake	77-75
1962	Milwaukee Lincoln	Eau Claire	93-80
1963	Manitowoc	Dodgeville	74-52
1964	Dodgeville	Mwke North	59-45
1965	Monroe	EauClaire Memorial	74-71
1966	Milwaukee Lincoln	Wis. Rapids	75-62
1967	Milwaukee Lincoln	Wausau	61-56
1968	Manitowoc	Beloit	63-51
1969	Beloit	Neenah	80-79
1970	Appleton West	Neenah	58-57
1971	Janesville Parker	Milwaukee King	79-68
1972	A - Mwke Hamilton	Neenah	58-52
	B - Bloomington	Crivitz	78-56
1973	A - Beloit	Fond du Lac	60-59
	B - McFarland	Luck	51-49
1974	A - Superior	Mwke Lincoln	74-67
	B - Sheboygan Falls	Kiel	53-50
	C - McFarland	Mineral Point	65-43
1975	A - Neenah	Mwke Marshall	64-55
	B - Sheboygan Falls	Wittenberg-Birnamwood	78-60
	C - Marathon	Pardeeville	65-57
1976	A - South Mwke	Eau Claire Memorial	45-43
	B - St. Francis	Clintonville	68-66
	C - Marathon	Kohler	78-59
1977	A - Madison La Follette	Eau Claire Memorial	65-48
	B - Clintonville	Prairie du Chien	91-70
	C - Marathon	Oostburg	53-52
1978	A - Neenah	Beloit	58-49
	B - Elkhorn	Park Falls	81-53
	C - Colfax	Pardeeville	75-61
1979	A - Mwke Technical	La Crosse Cent.	67-65
	B - Elkhorn	Prairie du Chien	79-66
	C - Niagara	Melrose-Mindoro	62-55
1980	A - MwkeNorth	Janesville Craig	65-63
	B - Wautoma	Elkhorn	56-46
	C - Kohler	Edgar	68-58
1981	A - No Champion*	Wausau West	—
	B - Cuba City	Ladysmith	52-47
	C - Iowa-Grant	Wausaukee	59-51

BOYS BASKETBALL, continued

Year	Winner	Runner-Up	Score
1982	A - Madison LaFollette	Stevens Point	62-61
	B - Portage	Valders	58-39
	C - Kohler	Thorp	61-56
1983	A - Mwke Tech.	Watertown	62-54
	B - Mayville	Valders	55-53
	C - Kohler	Fall Creek	70-57
1984	A - Milwaukee King	Janesville Craig	80-72
	B - Wilmot	Valders	67-54
	C - Fall Creek	Washburn	57-46
1985	A - Mwke Wash.	Racine Horlick	56-54
	B - Denmark	Prairie du Chien	63-59
	C - Fall Creek	Oakfield	78-54
1986	A - Sheboy. North	Appleton East	47-38
	B - Chilton	Prairie du Chien	45-44
	C - Oostburg	Whitehall	67-62
1987	A - Mwke Wash.	Fond du Lac	44-41
	B - Wisconsin Dells	Clintonville	62-50
	C - Oostburg	Elk Mound	72-69
1988	A - Onalaska	Neenah	70-62
	B - Whitnall	Clintonville	74-67
	C - Greenwood	Southwestern	41-40
1989	A - Wauwatosa East	Eau Claire N.	49-48
	B - Clintonville	Bloomer	78-53
	C - Florence	Glenwood City	60-54

* Milwaukee Madison defeated Wausau West, 77-60, in final game but championship was declared vacant because Milwaukee Madison used an ineligible player.

Approximately 425 schools are eligible for tournaments. The largest 128 schools comprise Class A. Of the remaining schools, the next largest schools up to a total of 40 percent of them comprise Class B. All others comprise Class C.

TRIVIA TEASERS

Q. Which U.S. President had a summer White House in Wisconsin?

A. President Calvin Coolidge spent the summer of 1928 in the Superior area, entertained presidential nominee Herbert Hoover, and fished in the Brule.

Q. For what is the town of Bloomer famous?

A. It is the Jump Rope Capital of the World. The championship contests held there emphasize speed jumping.

Q. What world record do challengers seek to surpass at an annual event in Door County?

A. Contestants try to better the record of 77 feet, 6 inches in the Wisconsin State Championship Cherry Pit Spit.

TRIVIA TEASERS

Q. Why did the Medford Chamber of Commerce purchase 4,000 little yellow rubber ducks?

A. It provides them for contestants in the annual Great Black River Rubber Duck Race.

Q. In the 1989 annual survey by the national Centers for Disease Control in Atlanta, which 2 states were tied for the highest percentage of overweight people?

A. N. Dakota and Wisconsin, with 23% of each state's residents admitting that they weigh too much.

Q. Who popularized the slogan, "Speak to a cow as you would a lady"?

A. William Dempster Hoard, champion of the dairy farmer and Governor from 1881 to 1891.

Girls Basketball Championship Games

Year	Winner	Runner-up	Score
1976	A - Madison West	Neenah	59-46
	B - Lancaster	Clinton	49-41
	C - Marshall	Bloomington	40-36
1977	A - Watertown	Green Bay West	44-37
	B - Cuba City	Omro	50-41
	C - Marshall	Iola-Scandinavia	47-39
1978	A - Neenah	Beloit	49-38
	B - Lomira	Omro	37-28
	C - Iola-Scandinav.	Oakfield	58-55
1979	A - Mwke Wash.	Greendale	66-40
	B - Lancaster	Sheboygan Falls	36-29
	C - Oakfield	Abbotsford	49-48
1980	A - Stevens Point	Neenah	38-32
	B - Cuba City	Northland Pines	48-40
	C - Lena	Oakfield	70-34
1981	A - Wauwatosa E.	Watertown	36-25
	B - Algoma	Northland Pines	60-44
	C - Prentice	Hilbert	49-47
1982	A - Madison West	Kimberly	49-45
	B - Portage	Kewaskum	52-36
	C - Kohler	Prentice	47-40
1983	A - De Pere	Oak Creek	52-45
	B - McFarland	Portage	59-38
	C - Gilman	Johnson Creek	56-54
1984	A - West Bend E.	Brookfield East	63-62
	B - Platteville	Ashland	41-28
	C - Johnson Creek	West Grant	52-50
1985	A - Brookfld Cent.	South Mwke	47-44
	B - Waterford	Algoma	64-45
	C - Fall Creek	Turtle Lake	63-30
1986	A - D.C. Everest	Whitefish Bay	50-35
	B - Durand	Waterford	56-54
	C - Algoma	Fall Creek	49-48
1987	A - Kimberly	Racine Horlick	69-54
	B - Durand	Brown Deer	65-26
	C - Fall Creek	Marathon	61-58
1988	A - Hartland Arrowhead	Monroe	56-32
	B - Luxemburg-Casco	Horicon	71-60
	C - Fall Creek	Owen-Withee	56-51
1989	A - Monroe	Madison East	62-50
	B - Kimberly	Mauston	56-54
	C - Prentice	Wrightstown	52-30

Source: Wisconsin Interscholastic Athletic Association

Sigurd Olson
GEORGE VUKELICH

When I was with the *Capital Times* back in 1977, Miles McMillin decided the paper could justify a trip up to Ely, Minnesota, to interview Sigurd Olson. Then in his late seventies, Sigurd was again involved in a fight to preserve the Boundary Waters Canoe Area.

We did a three-part series with Sigurd, and I regard the experience as one of the most illuminating of my life. He was the spiritual father of us all, including our daughter Marty, who accompanied me on that memorable trip and who also recalled it when the radio announced the other morning that Sigurd F. Olson had died at age eighty-two in his beloved North Country while trying out a new pair of snowshoes.

Hugh Percy, Steady Eddy, and everyone who loved Sigurd Olson agree with the words spoken by Sig's friend Les Blacklock, the wilderness photographer and writer who collaborated with Sigurd on the book *The Hidden Forest*.

"Any sorrowing we do is not for Sig," Les said. "It is for us."

Of Sigurd's death on snowshoes, Les observed: "He wouldn't have wanted to slow down and spend a lot of time in bed."

When we were up with Sigurd, he had spoken of death in that measured, matter-of-fact way he had. He told of the old Indian legend that said you knew you were going to die when you head the owl call your name.

He said he hadn't heard it yet, but he was still listening.

Marty says she remembers it the same way.

Sigurd had a profound influence on her. She probably would have discovered the Boundary Waters eventually, as so many young people do, but being in his house and hearing his voice may have hastened the process.

"The many young people who come through here," Sigurd said, "they're going into the wilderness now trying to find something bigger than themselves—something sacred. Something the Indians sensed long before we came here.

"They had the sacred places where they didn't speak, just as we have it in our great cathedrals and in our places of worship.

"They had it on the Kawashaway, the land they called 'No Place Between.' They had it on Darkey Lake. They had it on LaCroix. They tried to epitomize in such places that there were values which they felt deeply about. They tried to put those values into words long before there was such a thing as a written language. And the legends have come down."

He discussed the early caves of France and Spain in which the early people had painted pictures, sacred pictures, legends. The early people were all animists at heart, he said. The spirit world was in everything.

"So when people go into the wilderness today," he continued, "where there's any left unravished by noise, by mechanical motors, they are looking for the same spiritual inspiration the early people found. And many of them today, more than ever before, are finding it again.

"They find it in the sense of harmony and oneness with all living things. They find it in a feeling of communion and meditation. And, as I said in one of my books, one doesn't have to be a Buddhist to meditate, or get into any special position. Just looking at any natural thing is, in a sense, meditation. It is communion with God, or the Spirit. I think that's what people are looking for in the wilderness today, spiritual values. And they are almost impossible to define."

Sigurd said it was this feeling, this sense of harmony, that the Boundary Waters Canoe Area represented, along with other wilderness areas. He also admitted that the problem with saving wilderness was that not all people absorbed the wilderness values.

"Some people go into the bush," he allowed, "and come out and never get the spiritual at all. *Intangible* values," he said, "are difficult to explain."

Once in Germany, he recalled, during World War II, along a stretch of the River Main—"ruined buildings all around—the stench of death everywhere"—he saw a flock of mallard ducks come flying down the river as they had always done.

"That flock of mallards," Sig smiled, "was an intangible value. And all of a sudden I was back in the North Country."

He insisted that the whole business of conservation and preservation was based on those intangible values.

"You must understand," Sigurd Olson said that springtime morning in northern Minnesota, "that in saving the Boundary Waters Canoe Area—in saving any wilderness area—you are saving more than rocks and trees and mountains and lakes and rivers.

"What you are really saving is the human spirit.

"What you are really saving is the human soul."

I look at the photograph of Sigurd Olson and he gazes at me like some guru—wise, benign, his very Being full of the knowledge that waits for us beyond the cities where the bush begins. I close my eyes and he is still there, dressed now for the Northern Winter, standing on the new snowshoes in the quiet drifted valley. And in the dazzling stillness the brilliant bundle of feathers is calling his name. ❧

Reprinted from <u>North Country Notebook.</u> *Published by North Country Press.*

APRIL

April's anger is swift to fall
April's wonder is worth it all.

—*Sir Henry Newbolt, "The Adventurers"*

The April showers of the old weather adage are a reality on the meteorological calendar as the increased heating of the earth causes rainshowers to become more frequent. More than three inches of rainfall is the average in Wisconsin during April, while the chance for wet, heavy snow remains. Indeed, the opening day of the baseball season may well see Milwaukee County Stadium covered with snow. April also marks the start of the tornado season in Wisconsin. On Palm Sunday, April 11, 1965, 37 tornadoes touched down in Wisconsin, Iowa, Illinois, Michigan, Indiana, and Ohio, killing 271, injuring 3,000, and causing damage in excess of $500 million.❀

April Weather History

MADISON

Day	Record High		Record Low		Record	Precip.	Average High/Low
1	80	1946	11	1881	1.57	1959	49/28
2	81	1981	10	1886	0.90	1983	50/29
3	76	1956	8	1886	1.35	1982	51/29
4	77	1929	10	1886	1.37	1892	51/30
5	80	1873	14	1886	1.63	1947	52/30
6	79	1929	4	1982	1.09	1929	53/30
7	82	1871	0	1982	1.19	1907	53/31
8	77	1971	9	1972	1.04	1981	54/31
9	75	1955	17	1982	1.29	1882	54/32
10	89	1930	18	1960	2.34	1879	55/32
11	84	1977	12	1973	0.72	1935	55/33
12	87	1887	17	1939	1.36	1971	56/33
13	78	1936	20	1950	1.53	1876	57/33
14	79	1941	22	1957	0.97	1914	57/34
15	83	1977	18	1928	1.35	1884	58/34
16	85	1977	12	1875	1.10	1880	58/34
17	86	1977	11	1875	1.10	1969	59/35
18	87	1977	18	1983	2.15	1880	59/35
19	84	1985	16	1983	0.81	1970	60/36
20	85	1987	21	1962	1.36	1973	60/36
21	84	1980	21	1981	1.22	1972	61/36
22	94	1980	19	1986	1.21	1987	61/37
23	83	1960	19	1978	1.23	1944	61/37
24	82	1939	21	1910	1.56	1955	62/37
25	82	1948	21	1972	1.25	1951	62/38
26	84	1962	25	1980	0.95	1908	63/38
27	85	1952	24	1976	1.79	1956	63/38
28	90	1952	27	1966,82,88	1.91	1975	63/39
29	87	1952	22	1977	1.74	1984	64/39
30	90	1922	21	1956	1.38	1916	64/39

APRIL

April Weather History

LA CROSSE

Day	Record High		Record Low		Average High/Low
1	77	1946	7	1924	49/30
2	80	1981	14	1954	50/30
3	80	1921	10	1954	50/31
4	80	1920	12	1887	51/31
5	80	1921	12	1887	52/32
6	78	1954	7	1982	52/33
7	77	1900	13	1936	53/33
8	84	1931	11	1972	54/34
9	87	1931	17	1928	54/34
10	91	1930	19	1909	55/35
11	85	1977	20	1940	55/35
12	81	1931	19	1957	56/35
13	80	1941	18	1950	56/36
14	80	1954	20	1950	57/36
15	84	1896	17	1928	58/37
16	87	1964	13	1875	58/37
17	82	1985	15	1875	59/38
18	89	1985	20	1983	59/38
19	87	1985	20	1983	60/39
20	89	1987	23	1897	60/39
21	91	1980	26	1988	61/40
22	93	1980	23	1986	61/40
23	86	1960	20	1910	62/40
24	86	1939	24	1956	62/41
25	84	1962	25	1934	62/41
26	86	1962	27	1926	63/42
27	88	1977	25	1946	63/42
28	89	1952	28	1976	64/42
29	93	1910	26	1956	64/43
30	90	1952	17	1956	65/43

The normal average precipitation for La Crosse in April is 3.05 inches. The wettest April was in 1973 when 7.31 inches was recorded; the driest was in 1879 when only 0.42 inches was received.

From the Folks Who Brought You Kleenex
Wisconsin's $8 Billion Paper Industry

Kleenex (and those other brands). Cardboard boxes. Tea bag paper. Napkins. Pipe wrap insulation. Waterproof paper. Cellophane. Concrete molds. And, of course, writing paper and all that paper on which books and magazines (such as *National Geographic, Playboy* and *Time)* are printed.

These are a few of the nearly 200 products manufactured by Wisconsin's paper industry. The average person uses 633 pounds of paper products annually for everything from serving a hamburger to wiping away tears of joy at a Badger football victory to insulating the water pipes.

For over three decades, Wisconsin has been the nation's number one papermaking state, in both volume of paper produced and in diversity of paper products manufactured. Our 35 pulping, paper making and converting (turning huge rolls of paper into finished products) facilities employ nearly 48,000 Wisconsinites.

Wisconsin's paper industry began inauspiciously in 1848, with a small paper mill in Milwaukee that produced newsprint (paper used for newspapers) from cotton rags. Other ventures soon began in Beloit and Whitewater. But difficulty obtaining rags and lack of adequate water power to turn the mills' machines doomed the paper industry in southern Wisconsin.

In the period following the Civil War, the Fox River valley between Lake Winnebago and Green Bay became a major center for flour milling because of the availability of water power. By the 1880s, wheat production was moving west, and the flour mill owners began to look around for another use for their mills. They chose paper making.

The first Fox River mill opened at Neenah-Menasha in 1865. Paper mills spread down the Fox, and, as wood replaced rags as the raw material in paper making, paper mills were built along the upper Wisconsin River, close to the remaining logging areas. By 1910, the output of Wisconsin's 57 paper mills put the state in third place among all states manufacturing wood pulp and paper.

Most Wisconsin mills produced newsprint. But by the 1920s, the industry was forced to diversify its products when cheaper newsprint was imported from Canada and low-priced paper began to be produced in the southern states.

The result is Kleenex, coated paper for fancy magazines, and hundreds of other products that came from the test tubes of Wisconsin paper researchers.

Today Wisconsin's paper industry annually converts 2.3 million cords of wood into 4.2 million tons of paper. In addition, every year the industry recycles 1.5 million tons of paper into new paper products. All this paper is worth more than $8 billion and totals nearly 12 percent of national paper production.

That's a lot of paper. Wisconsin produces enough tissue every year to make a roll of paper towels that would circle the equator more than eight times. Think about that the next time you wipe up a spill.✤   — *K.V.*

When Spring Comes to Wisconsin

An old Wisconsin saying holds that spring advances at the rate of 100 miles a week. In 1918, the American scientist A. D. Hopkins developed his "bioclimatic law," which states that the advance of spring is delayed by four days for each degree of latitude north, for every 400 feet of elevation upward, and for every five degrees of longitude eastward from the Rocky Mountains. That works out, incidentally, to about 100 miles a week. And studies in the 1960s showed that leaf and blossom dates for the Persian lilac advanced 14 miles a day. That's 98 miles a week.✤

1 Fabulous Firsts

The first submarine to be constructed on the Great Lakes was the 312-foot long *Peto*. It was constructed by the Manitowoc Shipbuilding Company from prefabricated parts and launched sideways into the Manitowoc River on April 30, 1942.

Excuses for an April Party

Ethnic Dinner

Students in the cooking classes at Settlement House in Milwaukee, where immigrant women learned American ways, and noted Milwaukee hostesses all contributed to the *Settlement Cookbook: The Way to Man's Heart*, which was first published in April 1901. It has undergone numerous reprintings and revisions, sold more than two million copies, and become one of America's basic cookbooks.

14 Card Party

In response to a call by Cassius M. Paine, president of the Milwaukee Whist Club, the American Whist League convened for the first time on April 14, 1891, in Milwaukee, for a four-day conference. The 83 delegates representing 36 clubs from around the country standardized the rules of whist and adopted a 61-section code.

20 Salute to Miss Forward Day

April 20, 1850, is the birth date of sculptor Daniel Chester French, whose statue "Wisconsin" (also known as Miss Forward) stands atop the Capitol in Madison. French didn't discover his talent until age 19, when he carved a frog, wearing clothes, out of a turnip. He progressed to much larger projects, such as the Lincoln Memorial in Washington.

Academy Awards Trivia Party

For example: Two of the three men ever to twice win the Best Actor award were born in Wisconsin. Who are the actors? What cities are they from? What years did they win and for what pictures? What trivial details can you add?

(1) **Spencer Tracy**, Milwaukee: 1937, *Captains Courageous* (on Oscar night he was in Good Samaritan Hospital, recovering from an appendectomy); 1938, *Boys Town* (the Oscar was mistakenly inscribed to "Dick Tracy").

(2) **Frederic March**, Racine: 1931-32, *Dr. Jekyll and Mr. Hyde* (tied for Best Actor with Wallace Beery, *The Champ*); 1946, *Best Years of Our Lives* (a supporting player accepted the Oscar for March, who was in New York that night).

❀ *The Date for Easter* ❀

Although it has been official for more than 16 centuries, the method used to set the date for Easter still causes confusion.

Easter is celebrated on the first Sunday following the full moon that occurs on, or following, March 21 (the first day of spring). If the full moon happens on a Sunday, Easter Day is the Sunday after. The great Council of Nicaea, a gathering of astronomers called by the archbishop of Alexandria in A.D. 325, officially sanctioned this method of calculating Easter, along with setting the dates of the seasonal year.

But using the moon to determine religious celebrations dates back before the birth of Christ. The Jewish festival of the Passover is determined by the phase of the moon. Early Christians borrowed the method to establish Easter some three centuries before the Council of Nicaea.

Since the calculation for Easter uses the lunar month, the solar equinox, and the seven-day week, Easter becomes a movable feast. It can occur anywhere within a 35-day period — as early as March 22 or as late as April 25. All the Christian observances involving Easter, including Ash Wednesday, Lent, Palm Sunday, and Good Friday, are determined by the date of Easter. ❀

—*D.D.*

Watching Waterfowl

Millions of wild ducks, geese, and swans migrate through Wisconsin each spring. To make sure that you see them, do your bird watching during peak migration periods. Waterfowl migrate by the calendar. The first birds arrive in late February. These include swans, geese, and hardy black-and-white-diving ducks such as goldeneye, mergansers, and scaup. The highest waterfowl populations are seen in April. By May 10, most of the birds have gone northward into Canada.

In autumn, the first migrants begin returning through our state as early as August. These are the warm-weather bluewing teal. The most noticeable flocks of ducks and geese, however, arrive between mid-October and early November. By November, tens of thousands of Canada geese are common on Horicon National Wildlife Refuge and other marshes. Most of the birds head south with December's cold storms, although old squaw, scaup, and other diving ducks stay all winter long when there's open water on Lake Michigan. ❀

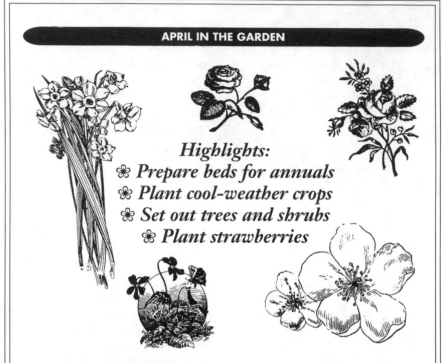

APRIL IN THE GARDEN

Highlights:
❀ *Prepare beds for annuals*
❀ *Plant cool-weather crops*
❀ *Set out trees and shrubs*
❀ *Plant strawberries*

Now there is no doubt that spring, if not actually here, is definitely coming to Wisconsin. A walk in the country removes all doubt. The raucous honking of Canada geese returning from the south, the breathtaking sight of a flock of whistling swans flying across the setting sun, the green splash of skunk cabbage pushing through the last banks of snow, the sudden appearance of silver pussy willows, the soft yellow-green of weeping willows—spring is everywhere.

April marks the end of snow and the start of the outdoor garden season in all but the farthest northern reaches of Wisconsin. The spring advances slowly up the midsection of the country, and while our neighbors in states to the south have been tending the earth for the past month, we have been patiently awaiting our turn to do the same.

Our turn is now here.

Early April is the time to set out pansy plants, as soon as the ground can be worked. We can uncover strawberries now, too, and anticipate the harvest of those luscious red berries in only two more months. On a mild afternoon, take time to prune bush fruits, grapes, and roses.

Indoors, you may start seeds of eggplants, okra, peppers, and tomatoes, if you have not done so earlier. You may also start seeds of cucumbers, melons, and squash, to give them a head start (although these seeds may be planted directly in garden hills, as well).

In the second week of the month, rake the lawn thoroughly, removing as much old thatch as you can. Mow the lawn if it is two inches or higher, and fertilize it with a high-nitrogen formula. Add lime if a soil test shows it is needed.

You may plant fruit trees now, as well as deciduous ornamental trees and shrubs. Established deciduous trees and summer-flowering shrubs may now be pruned.

When daytime temperatures reach into the high 50s and low 60s, remove mulch from perennial beds to allow the soil to warm. Work soil in the vegetable garden when it is dry enough to do so (when a clump crumbles in your closed fist, instead of forming a claylike lump).

During the third week, you may plant these seeds into the open garden: parsley, onion seed (and sets), carrots, kohlrabi, chard, peas, leaf lettuce, early potatoes, radishes, spinach, beets, turnips, Jerusalem artichoke, and parsnip. All remaining flowering annuals may now be started from seed indoors.

During the last week of April, begin to plant gladiolus corms, and plant more every week through June 15th for continuous bloom later in the year. Dig and divide chrysanthemums and other fall-blooming perennials before plants get too tall. Prune and fertilize roses. Plant lilies and strawberries.

Last, prepare the beds for flowering annuals, if the soil is dry enough to be worked. But do not set out the annuals until the first and second weeks of May.❀   —J.M.

SPRING

1885

I Remember a Wilderness

LYDIA DOERING

When I first came to Athens in April of 1883, everything was all woods. I was only five years old at the time, but I remember it well. My family took the train from Milwaukee to Dorchester, which was as close to Athens as the Wisconsin Central could take us. Keel, the land agent for Rietbrock, took us by horse and wagon to Brookerville. We had to walk the rest of the way to Athens. I remember that it was getting dark and we were tired. We finally came to Victor Stremer's shanty, where we spent the night.

The next day we walked on to our land, where my father had built a shanty for us. You see, my father came here first. We had originally come from Saxony, Germany, to Milwaukee. Once in Milwaukee my father contacted the Rietbrock Land Office. He bought 107 acres from Rietbrock for nine hundred dollars and began to clear it before we came. And, oh, that shanty! It wasn't made so sound, and it leaked water. We had to set pots all around inside to catch the water.

There was such fine timber on the land, but we were here to farm the land, so we had to clear it. There was no market yet for timber, so we had to burn it. The logs were pushed together and a big fire was started. The green wood did not burn well, so my father had to get up during the night to make sure that it was still burning.

After the trees were cut down, we had to dig out the stumps. We used a lot of dynamite for this. We had to pick stones and pull roots, too. When the land was cleared we could plant such crops as rye. Everything was hard work then; we had no machines. Do you know how we harvested grain then? The wheat was first cut by a scythe and put into bundles. Then the wheat was beaten with a flail to separate the grain from the stalk. Finally, the grain was thrown up into the air to separate the wheat from the chaff. The chaff would blow away.

We did have oxen right away. We had bought them in Poniatowski. There were no fences or pastures then, so the oxen ran loose in the woods. They were a lot of trouble. When you needed them, you had to go and look for them. Sometimes they would get into a turnip field and dig up the turnips. A little later we bought two cows. They too ran loose in the woods. The cows wore bells; you could recognize your cow by the sound of its bell. We had a house and a barn by this time.

My mother planted a garden right away so that we would have food to eat. She fixed sweet and sour pumpkins and dill pickles. Oh, they were so good! We tapped the trees and made maple syrup. We also got our "gum" off the trees—we chewed the hardened pitch. We picked berries in the woods and dried them for the winter. People also shot deer for meat. At first, we didn't have cows or pigs, but when we did we had veal and pork to eat. My mother fried the pork with lard on a wood stove that had been ours in Milwaukee. After we got more land cleared, we planted potatoes. They grew so well that we sold them for ten cents a bushel to the lumber camps.

Oh, everything grew so well then! I remember that bull thistles grew well, too. They were huge. It was my job to dig them out of the ground and to take the soft white part and stamp it fine. It was then mixed with bran and fed to the pigs.

Ladd School was the first school in the area. It was taught by Mr. White, who came from Manitowoc. All of our teachers were men then. The teachers and the children walked to school. If the teacher wasn't there on time, Frank Stremer and Charles Behrendt taught the classes. The school was heated by a big wooden stove. In the winter we would put our mittens and other clothing underneath it to dry. These school days were good days. I went there until I was twelve years old.

We worked hard, and before we knew it, Athens began to change. Rietbrock built a sawmill, which brought many people here. Pine logs were cut because they could float down the creek to the sawmill. The train ran farther now—in 1887 there were stations named Athens, Corinth, and Milan. More churches were started. By the early 1900s we had electricity to replace kerosene lanterns. In 1906 or 1907 we had a telephone put in.

We worked hard, and before we knew it much of the land was cleared. I often think of all the big and beautiful trees. Oh, that was a long time ago.✿

From We Were Children Then, Volume II, published by NorthWord Press, Inc., Minocqua, WI.

Uncle Woody *Says*

Wilderness Tweezers. If you're in the back country and in need of tweezers to pull a splinter or other small object, look along the sandbars or sandy edges of rivers for a small clamshell with its hinge intact. It does the job, just fine.

APRIL RECIPE

Carrot Cake

1-1/3 cups whole wheat flour	2 eggs
1 cup all-purpose flour	1-1/2 teaspoons vanilla
2 teaspoons baking soda	1-1/3 cups finely
1-1/2 teaspoons ground	shredded carrots
cinnamon	1 3-ounce package
1/4 teaspoon salt	cream cheese
3/4 cup butter	1/4 cup butter
1 cup honey	1 teaspoon vanilla
2/3 cup plain yogurt	2 cups sifted powdered sugar

In a mixing bowl combine the whole wheat flour, all-purpose flour, baking soda, cinnamon, and salt. Set aside. In a large mixer bowl beat 3/4 cup butter with an electric mixer on high speed for 30 seconds. Gradually beat in honey. Beat in yogurt, eggs and 1-1/2 teaspoons vanilla. Beat in carrots. Add flour mixture; beat on medium speed for 2 minutes. Spread in a greased and floured 13x9x2-inch baking dish. Bake in a 350° oven for about 35 minutes or till done. Cool on wire rack. Make Cream Cheese Frosting; spread over top of cake. Store, covered, in the refrigerator. Makes 12 to 15 servings.

Cream Cheese Frosting: In small mixer bowl combine cream cheese, 1/4 cup butter, and 1 teaspoon vanilla. Beat with an electric mixer on low speed till fluffy. Gradually beat in powdered sugar.

Preparation time: 1 hour.

—*Wisconsin Dairy Country Recipes*, compiled by Wisconsin Milk Marketing Board

Uncle Woody Says

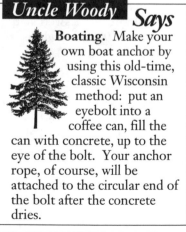

Boating. Make your own boat anchor by using this old-time, classic Wisconsin method: put an eyebolt into a coffee can, fill the can with concrete, up to the eye of the bolt. Your anchor rope, of course, will be attached to the circular end of the bolt after the concrete dries.

Plants for a Shady Window Box

Brighten a shade-covered window box with flaming impatiens. New varieties are available in brilliant reds and orange, through salmon and soft pinks, and all the way to white. Then let asparagus fern, English ivy, or vinca spill over the front of the box and trail to the ground. Boston fern, dracaena, or other houseplants can spend the summer in a shaded outdoor box, and coleus and wax begonias can add colorful accents. With a little planning and experimentation, the shady window box can be just as attractive as any in a sunny location. ❧

Years Ago . . .

MONROE—Enoch Evans is over 100 years of age. His memory is very good, carrying him back to the death of Washington. He has vivid recollection of events all along the stream of time since that event. Mr. Evans has always taken an active interest in policies, casting his first vote for James Madison and has never missed a presidential election since that time.—*Wisconsin State Journal*, April 16, 1889.

Invented Right Here!

The First Typewriter

The first practical writing machine was developed in Milwaukee between 1867 and 1873. Several men took part in its development, but the two who had the most to do with it were Christopher Latham Sholes and James Densmore. (Sholes had been a newspaperman in Kenosha, and Densmore founded the first newspaper in Oshkosh, *The True Democrat.*) The first model looked like a box-shaped frame filled with a maze of wires, letter bars, and hinges. It jumped and wobbled and wrote in wavy lines, some letters above and others below the line. But it *did* write. Sholes and Densmore experimented with positioning the keys and finally arranged them according to convenience and frequency of use. Their final arrangement of keys became the "universal" keyboard that is still used today. The Remington company refined the machine and manufactured the world's first typewriters. ❧

Turtle

GEORGE VUKELICH

We had just come off the Flats with two fair-sized catfish and were carrying the gear up to the car where Dyna-Ann waited.

Steady Eddy had called her to come get us because the big lake was still boiling with white caps and the trip home in the little boat would have been a white-knuckler.

All day long we had bounced around like a cork in the rolling waters of North Bay and watched the rich blueblooded sloops parade down the channel like leashed greyhounds straining to chase rabbits.

We stood at the car trunk. Sunburnt. Windblown. Beaten.

It was hard to tell what Dyna-Ann's eyes were doing behind the sunglasses.

"Never a dull moment," she said, "with Steady Eddy."

A couple of fisherpersons came over to get a closer look at the catfish. After all, one weighed eight pounds, the other a little over thirteen.

One of the men standing there had that tanned, neatly groomed small-town look that always makes me think of forest rangers and the Highway Patrol. Crisp. The name patch over his shirt pocket said "John."

"Nice fish," he said. "One about thirteen?"

Steady went to open the trunk and Dyna-Ann leaned out of the window.

"Don't forget about Oscar," she warned. "He's still in there."

Steady opened the trunk. And there was Oscar. The near-thirty pound snapping turtle that Stenlund and Parisi had caught and given Steady to clean. Steady lifted the turtle by the tail and set it down on the asphalt.

John stuck his boot toe down and the snake-head struck, the jaws clinging to the leather.

The little knot of fisherpersons oohed appropriately. "Geez," somebody said.

"Whattaya take for it?" John asked Steady.

"It ain't for sale," Steady told John.

John stared at the turtle for a long time and then at Steady.

"My father used to be a turtle hunter," he said. "I figure this one's pretty old. I figure about fifty years."

"That's what I figured," Steady said.

The turtle sat immobile as some great weathered stone. It had a dark, greenish, yellowish cast. There was an aura, an ambience of moss, of age, of alien mudbanks and river bottoms. It was something primal, something powerful. And at this age no longer had any natural enemies in the water. Except one.

"My son and I," John said, "came across one about this size and I was ready to kill it. He asked me if I realized how old that turtle was. I did. And that turned me around on killing. My son turned me around on killing. If you sell me this one, I'll put it back in the river."

John and Steady looked at each other and then at the turtle.

"I've killed a lot of turtles," Steady said. "I was having trouble bringing myself to kill this one."

John nodded, kind of smiled, and plucked the turtle up by the tail. The little knot of witnesses followed them down to the water's edge.

"I must be getting old," Steady sighed. "And that wasn't even my turtle."

Dyna-Ann and I looked at each other and I felt we were thinking the exact same thing. We were thinking *that turtle was everybody's turtle.*

What she said out loud was: "Never a dull moment with Steady Eddy." ❀

Reprinted from North Country Notebook. *Published by North Country Press.*

Years Ago . . .

DePere—A spark from a smoke-stack started a fire at the Meinwinkel Wooden-ware company Saturday afternoon. A strong south wind was blowing and the flames soon spread. The West DePere and DePere steamers did good work for an hour, when the DePere engine broke down. A telegram was sent to Green Bay for help and two engines were hurried forward, one by team and one by rail. Appleton and Oshkosh were asked for assistance, each sending a steamer and hose cart, which arrived about 11. Everything about the extensive plant was leveled to the ground.—*Wisconsin State Journal*, April 22, 1889.

APRIL RECIPE

Granny's Wild Rice Hot Dish

1 cup wild rice
1/2 lb. bacon cut in small pieces
1 cup celery
1 medium onion, chopped
1 can cream of mushroom soup
1 can mushrooms

Place wild rice in 2 quarts boiling water. Boil 20 minutes and drain. Fry bacon until crisp but do not overcook. Retain enough grease to sauté celery and onion. Combine all ingredients plus one cup of water in covered casserole dish. Bake in 350° oven for one hour. Add more water as necessary.

—*Olga Schmidt, Middleton*

Years Ago . . .

PALMYRA—While cutting down an old oak tree on his grounds near Palmyra, John Muldeen found, deeply embedded in its trunk, a musket ball that, judging from the tree rings, each representing a year, must have been fired into it as long ago as the Black Hawk war. The Black Hawk warriors traversed that section on their way to Whitewater, where they were mustered out of service.—*Wisconsin State Journal*, April 13, 1889.

GERMINATION TIME FOR GARDEN FLOWERS

Plant	Days
Ageratum	5-8
Alyssum	4-5
Baby's breath	18-20
Balsam	5-8
Candytuft	5-8
Canterbury bells	12-15
Columbine	15-18
Coreopsis	5-8
Cornflower	5-8
Cosmos	5-8
Dahlia	8-10
Dianthus	5-8
Forget-me-not	12-15
Marigold	5-8
Morning glory	8-10
Nasturtium	8-10
Nicotiana	18-20
Pansy	10-12
Petunia	10-18
Phlox (annual)	15-18
Portulaca	15-18
Shasta daisy	18-21
Strawflower	5-8
Zinnia	5-8

MAY

Weather is a literary specialty, and no untrained hand can turn out a good article on it.

—Samuel Langhorne Clemens,
"The American Claimant"

The May sun climbs higher and higher toward the zenith and daytime temperatures rise. But nights are still cool and ice may tinge northern lakes well into the month. Europeans traditionally considered the last appearance of winter to occur on the days of the three Ice Saints of May on the 11th, 12th, and 13th. After that, good growing weather was assured. In southern Wisconsin, the average date of the last killing frost is between May 3 and May 9. But not so in the north, where the median date of the last frost ranges from May 24 to 31, or later. Memorial Day, on the 30th, is the traditional start of the summer season.❁

May Weather History

MADISON

Day	Record High		Record Low		Record Precip.		Average High/Low
1	93	1952	19	1978	1.30	1896	65/39
2	89	1959	23	1978	1.82	1871	65/40
3	87	1949	25	1971	1.50	1873	65/40
4	90	1952	26	1966	0.99	1913	66/40
5	89	1959	29	1958	1.41	1982	66/41
6	92	1934	25	1970	2.55	1960	66/41
7	86	1880	26	1974	1.19	1904	67/41
8	85	1953,79	26	1966	1.61	1927	67/42
9	92	1934	20	1966	1.50	1890	67/42
10	86	1922,79	22	1966	1.26	1905	68/42
11	85	1922	30	1967	1.60	1912	68/43
12	83	1961,77	24	1981	1.84	1970	68/43
13	88	1977	29	1966	2.39	1977	69/43
14	87	1932	32	1964	1.70	1883	69/43
15	86	1977	30	1983	1.39	1933	70/44
16	87	1951,77	29	1979	1.54	1928	70/44
17	86	1971,87	33	1973,82	1.07	1918	70/44
18	91	1934	32	1976	1.45	1898	71/45
19	93	1975	32	1929	2.84	1933	71/45
20	91	1934	32	1967	1.82	1913	71/45
21	89	1972	32	1967	2.07	1974	72/46
22	92	1975	27	1967	1.60	1907	72/46
23	91	1975	28	1958	3.64	1966	72/46
24	90	1977	32	1925	1.07	1914	73/47
25	89	1977	30	1988	1.80	1883	73/47
26	91	1978	30	1983	2.19	1903	73/48
27	92	1978	31	1971	1.38	1943	73/48
28	89	1977	34	1965	1.86	1927	74/48
29	89	1934	30	1965	0.92	1885	74/49
30	92	1953	30	1965	2.15	1958	74/49
31	101	1934	32	1966	1.71	1919	75/49

May Weather History

LA CROSSE

Day	Record High		Record Low		Average High/Low
1	88	1952	27	1966	65/43
2	92	1959	26	1911	65/44
3	91	1918	26	1971	66/44
4	91	1952	27	1907	66/44
5	91	1909	31	1967	66/45
6	98	1934	30	1944	67/45
7	88	1970	29	1890	67/45
8	89	1874	28	1947	67/46
9	93	1934	26	1945	68/46
10	90	1911	27	1966	68/46
11	89	1922	28	1946	69/47
12	90	1940	31	1967	69/47
13	88	1977	30	1953	69/47
14	93	1932	30	1895	70/48
15	89	1977	30	1983	70/48
16	90	1936	31	1921	70/48
17	90	1987	29	1925	71/49
18	92	1934	32	1945	71/49
19	96	1934	32	1929	71/50
20	94	1934	32	1892	72/50
21	92	1970	31	1883	72/50
22	98	1925	33	1967	72/51
23	92	1972	31	1931	73/51
24	93	1928	34	1925	73/51
25	91	1980	34	1979	73/52
26	94	1967	34	1925	74/52
27	96	1874	38	1907	74/52
28	95	1874	32	1947	74/53
29	95	1934	32	1965	74/53
30	93	1934	36	1873	75/53
31	107	1934	35	1897	75/54

The normal average precipitation for La Crosse in May is 3.61 inches. The wettest May was in 1960 when 8.83 inches was recorded; the driest was in 1887 when only 0.50 inches was received.

Excuses for a May Party

17 Syttende Mai

Each year in May, Norwegian communities in Wisconsin celebrate Syttende-Mai—May 17—in observance of the anniversary of the 1814 signing of the Norwegian Constitution, which established Norway's independence from Sweden. The colorful celebration includes parades, displays of Norwegian heritage, street music and dancing, the presentation of the Syttende Mai king and queen, races, concerts, smorgasbords, and drama.

19 Circus Days

On May 19, 1884, the five Ringling Brothers gave their first performance at Baraboo, confidently billing it as the World's Greatest Show. This was only one of a hundred circuses that had their beginnings in Wisconsin. Thousands of items at the Circus World Museum at Baraboo document the colorful history of circuses.

26 Theater Party

For nearly half a century after their marriage on May 26, 1922, the Fabulous Lunts—Alfred Lunt and Lynn Fontanne—starred together on Broadway, returning at the end of each theater season to their summer home in Genesee Depot. Lunt's love of the theater began at age three, when his mother took him to see a musical extravaganza featuring a company of midgets called the Royal Lilliputians, and was nurtured in his boyhood years at such Milwaukee theaters as the Bijou, the Alhambra, and the Davidson.

29 Statehood Day

On May 29, 1848, Wisconsin became the thirtieth state in the Union. The centennial celebration in 1948 included a mammoth parade, which was 12 miles long and lasted for three hours. At least 125,000 people lined State Street and the Capitol Square in Madison to view the parade. Another 10,000 people were in the parade, along with100 marching bands, scores of floats, and airplanes roaring overhead.

Tornado!

A tornado is nature's most awesome spectacle. No windstorm on earth can do what a tornado can do. They cause several hundred deaths and millions of dollars in property damage in the nation each year. The capricious storms have driven straws into trees, lifted autos high into the air and dropped them gently back to earth without injuring the terrified occupants, and stripped chickens of their feathers.

The Palm Sunday Tornado that struck the Green County community of Monroe on April 11, 1965, left a fragile glass vase lying unharmed in the mud as it swept away a rural farm home, while a sofa and chair in the same room as the vase were never found. And the twister put a large kink in the city's railroad tracks that remains unexplained to this day. Thirty-seven tornadoes developed in the Midwest from the Palm Sunday storm system, and 271 people died. At least five of those tornadoes touched down in Wisconsin and three people were killed.

Meteorologists define a tornado as a funnel cloud that touches the ground. Tornadoes' distinguishing features are nearly always the funnel clouds that narrow down from a parent cloud, which is almost always a cumulonimbus type associated with a thunderstorm. The funnel we see is formed by condensation of water vapor around the whirling column, which normally spins counterclockwise. More than one funnel may develop in a mature tornado system.

While much remains to be learned about tornadoes and how they are formed, scientists have gained considerable knowledge about these violent storms in recent years. Surveys have shown that 75 percent of all tornadoes are associated with temperatures that range between 65 and 84 degrees (F).

The regions of most frequent tornado occurrence migrate with the seasons, moving northward in the spring and retreating southward in autumn. In May and June the zone of greatest frequency encompasses the Northern Plains, Upper Midwest and Great Lakes region — including Wisconsin — and remains potentially active until September, when it moves southward.

Tornadoes may occur at any time of the year, and since 1950, have been reported on every day from January 1 to December 31, with the single exception of January 16. The peak tornado month is May, with 1,423 expected tornadoes in the nation. June has only slightly fewer than May.

Nationally, 25 percent of the expected tornadoes for the year will have normally occurred by April 28. Fifty percent will have happened by June 4, and 75 percent will have been reported by July 20. Tornadoes favor the warmer part of the day, when solar heating and thunderstorm development are at a maximum. Nationally, 60 percent of all tornadoes occur between noon and sunset. But the Midwest and Plains states — including Wisconsin — seem to have a preference for late afternoon and early evening tornadoes.

Tornadoes are consistently inconsistent. On March 16, 1942, twisters struck Baldwyn, Mississippi, twice in a 25-minute period. Irving, Kansas, was left a shambles by two tornadoes that occurred 45 minutes apart on May 30, 1879, and Codell, Kansas, was struck by a tornado on May 20 three years in a row —1916, 1917, and 1918.

Ninety-five percent of the tornadoes that strike Wisconsin occur between April and September. No tornadoes have been reported in the state in December, January, or February. The season's earliest recorded tornado was on March 17, the latest on November 15. Although tornadoes are generally distributed throughout the season, the highest probability is from June 20 to 25, between 3 P.M. and 7 P.M.

The tornado that ravaged the Iowa County community of Barneveld on June 7, 1984, didn't follow the "rules." It struck at 1 A.M., killing 9 people and injuring 79. Ninety-three of the town's 225 dwellings were wiped out, and another 57 were damaged.

But it was not Wisconsin's worst tornado —not by far. That dubious honor goes to a killer storm known as the "Circus Day Tornado," which struck New Richmond on June 12, 1899. Arriving the very same day the circus came to town, the twister roared down the community's main street at 6:30 P.M., killing 117 people.

But even that storm pales by comparison with the Mattoon -Charleston (Illinois) Tornado of May 26, 1916. It left the longest track of any tornado in modern times — a total of 293 miles, 188 miles in Illinois and 105 in Indiana—and remained on the ground for seven hours and 20 minutes. Although not the worst tornado, it lasted an exceptionally long time. The average life of a tornado on the ground is less than 15 minutes, and the average tornado track is about 6 miles long. The shortest track in weather bureau records is a 1954 Wyoming tornado that left a track of only 45 feet.

The worst tornado in U.S. history occurred on March 18, 1925, and is known as the Great Tri-State Tornado. It originated in southeast Missouri, swept across southern Illinois, and dissipated in southwestern Indiana. The tornado stayed on the ground for three and one half hours, and covered 219 miles. A total of 695 people were killed in the three states, 2,027 were injured, and property damage in 1925 dollars amounted to $15.5 million.

In Wisconsin, one of the earliest recorded tornadoes occurred in Fond du Lac County at 3 P.M. on August 28, 1844. There were no deaths, and the amount of property damage went unrecorded.

A tornado in Vernon County on June 28, 1865, is one of the earliest recorded tornadoes in Wisconsin in which loss of life was reported. Twenty-four persons died as the twister cut a path from west of Viroqua to Hillsboro. The day was documented by county clerk John M. Bennett, who was an avid weather watcher.

At 3 P.M., Bennett recorded in his diary, the air was so muggy that "we felt as if we were in the very rain clouds." At about 3:45, there appeared "a dark, ragged cloud passing swiftly south, and another going north at the same time... We had never seen a tornado, but we now knew these clouds were moving swiftly in a circle."   Awestruck, Bennett stood in his garden and watched the tornado develop. "The bottom [of the cloud] was on the ground. The motion of this cloud was so rapid that the time of its revolution was but two or three seconds, and its onward rush was nearly a mile a minute." Among the first of Viroqua's buildings destroyed by the tornado was a warehouse whose stock included a large pile of unsacked fleece. As that building was ripped apart, Bennett, along with his wife and daughter, took shelter in the basement of their home.

Bennett's house disintegrated in the tornado, and he was pinned beneath the fallen timbers, his leg broken. His cap and even the women's hairpins were torn away by the screaming winds. The tornado was last seen about 4 P.M., some 30 miles from Viroqua. Falling from it, like June snow, was the fleece from the Viroqua warehouse it had destroyed.❀
—D.D.

Asparagus against Gout

A medical correspondent of an English journal says that the advantages of asparagus are not sufficiently appreciated by those who suffer with rheumatism and gout. Slight cases of rheumatism are cured in a few days by feeding on this delicious esculent; and more chronic cases are much relieved, especially if the patient avoids all acids, whether in food or beverage. The Jerusa-

lem artichoke has also a similar effect in relieving rheumatism. The heads may be eaten in the usual way, but tea made from the leaves of the stalk and taken three or four times a day is a certain remedy, though not equally agreeable.❀
—*The Hearthstone,* 1887

Oak Leaves and Mouse Ears

Phenology is one area in which folklore and science come happily together. Phenology is the science that examines ways in which climate influences the timing of different stages in the development of flora and fauna.

Phenology-wise gardeners know that corn may be safely planted when oak leaves become the size of a mouse's ear, and that peas, beets, and lettuce may be planted when the first leaves appear on the common lilac. And when that lilac begins to bloom, it will be time to plant corn and beans.❀

Years Ago . . .

LA CROSSE—In the factory of Mons Anderson's establishment the motive power is electricity. In several instances the bangs of female employees in the factory have been drawn into the machinery by electrical attraction, causing considerable trouble. Bangs have been prohibited in the workroom.—*Wisconsin State Journal*, April 22, 1889.

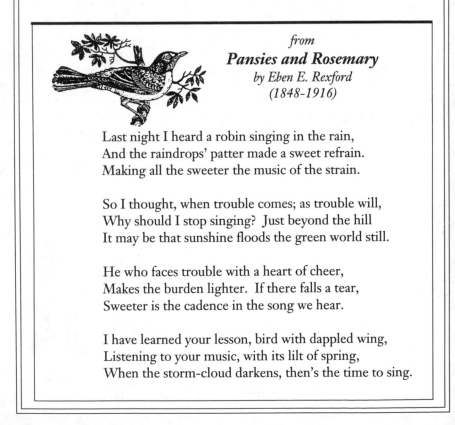

from
Pansies and Rosemary
by Eben E. Rexford
(1848-1916)

Last night I heard a robin singing in the rain,
And the raindrops' patter made a sweet refrain.
Making all the sweeter the music of the strain.

So I thought, when trouble comes; as trouble will,
Why should I stop singing? Just beyond the hill
It may be that sunshine floods the green world still.

He who faces trouble with a heart of cheer,
Makes the burden lighter. If there falls a tear,
Sweeter is the cadence in the song we hear.

I have learned your lesson, bird with dappled wing,
Listening to your music, with its lilt of spring,
When the storm-cloud darkens, then's the time to sing.

Confederate Rest

The weathered stone Civil War markers stand in five neat rows, numbered 1 to 140, each bearing a name, company, and regiment. Some slump like soldiers too weary to come to attention, but the years have not diminished the cold military precision of their formation.

There's nothing unusual about a well-kept Civil War cemetery. Wisconsin, in fact, built one of the first Civil War memorials in the country. But these markers in Madison's Forest Hill Cemetery also bear the inscription "C.S.A."—Confederate States of America.

This burial ground for Southern soldiers is a long way north of the Mason-Dixon Line. While there are individual Confederate burials farther north, officials believe this section of Forest Hill is the northern-most Confederate cemetery in the country.

The men who lie here were prisoners of war — soldiers captured over 125 years ago in a long-forgotten battle for Island No.10 in the Mississippi River. Ironically, the island, once located 15 miles south of New Madrid, Missouri, near the Kentucky-Tennessee border, no longer exists. The Mississippi years ago washed part of it away, cut a new channel, and gave the remains to Missouri.

For reasons lost in time, 1,156 of the 7,000 Confederates who surrendered Island No. 10 on April 2, 1862, were sent to be interred at Madison's Camp Randall, which was then a military camp. They were from regiments located in Alabama, Tennessee, Arkansas, and Louisiana.

Eight hundred eighty-one prisoners arrived in Madison by train from Chicago on April 20, 1862. They were objects of great curiosity, and newspapers of the day carried accounts of good-natured joking between the Southerners and the Madisonians who turned out to greet them.

An additional 275 prisoners arrived four days later, after a long trip by steamboat up the Mississippi to Prairie du Chien and overland by rail. There were no jokes this time. After months of fighting from trenches knee-deep in water, these men were seriously ill with chronic pneumonia and other diseases. Their homespun uniforms were ragged and filthy, and many men lacked shoes.

One prisoner was dead on arrival, and two more died the following day. They were quickly buried in a remote corner of Forest Hill Cemetery, over a mile from the camp.

The arrival of the Confederates created real problems at the onset. Life at Camp Randall — today the University of Wisconsin athletic complex — was no picnic, even for Union troops. The place had been the State Agricultural Fairgrounds barely a year earlier, and had been quickly converted to a rough military camp at the outbreak of the war. Soldiers slept in barracks that had been cowsheds and stables. They itched from the flea-ridden straw, shivered in cold weather and sweltered in hot. The camp hospital, the former Floral Hall building, had no lack of patients, even before the Confederates arrived.

At first there was little real animosity toward the "Secesh" prisoners. Visitors were allowed in the prison compound and many brought food and delicacies to the sick. Printers from a local typographers' union and members of the Masons sought out their fellows among the Southerners. A Union officer provided a barrel of smoking tobacco at his own  expense. Stamps, writing paper, books, and newspapers were made available.

The prisoners quickly settled into a monotonous routine of washing their ragged clothes, playing ball and cards, reading, cooking their meals, and huddling around the campfires. The Wisconsin spring came late in 1862, but while the Confederates complained about the chilly weather, living conditions were far better than they had been at Island No. 10.

By the end of the first week in May, 44 Confederates were dead, and the mood at the camp began to change. There were rumors of gross neglect. Three Confederate surgeons held prisoner at Camp Douglas at Chicago were sent to Madison to help, but the death toll continued to rise. And each day the wagons made the trip up the hill to Forest Hill, sometimes as many as ten times a day.

George Paddock, a Union soldier, wrote in his diary: "The poor Rebels have hard times here. They dye [sic] off like rotten sheep. There was 11 dyed yesterday and today, and there ain't a day but what there is from 2 to 9 or 10 dies."

By the end of May, illness had claimed 114 prisoners and the camp was seething with unrest. Prisoners threw rocks and water at guards. At least one Confederate was shot and killed. Over 500 troops were occupied in guarding 1,000 prisoners. Training programs ground to a halt.

On May 30, all prisoners well enough to travel were sent by train to Chicago. One hundred thirty Confederates remained at Camp Randall. Twenty-six died in the next 30 days. The rest were shipped out in twos and threes as quickly as they could travel. William L. Peacock, Co. D, 1st Alabama Regiment, was the last Confederate taken to Forest Hill. By July 3, the last of the prisoners was gone.

Within a few years, the Southerners who had been at Camp Randall were mostly forgotten. The plot at Forest Hill was nearly lost in a tangle of weeds, and the crude wooden headboards marking the graves were badly decayed.

In 1866, Mrs. Alice Whiting Waterman, a Baton Rouge, Louisiana, woman who had come to Madison after the Civil War, became concerned with the sorry state of the Confederate cemetery. Although she had known none of the men buried there, Mrs. Waterman took it upon herself to care for the graves. She cut the weeds, built a fence around the plot, and replaced decaying markers. Sympathetic Madisonians offered minor assistance, among them Governor Lucius Fairchild, who had lost an arm at Gettysburg.

On Decoration Day of 1872 (now Memorial Day), the Confederates at Forest Hill received an unexpected tribute. Following ceremonies honoring Union soldiers, Governor C.C. Washburn called on those present to join him in honoring the men who had worn Confederate gray. A murmur ran through the surprised crowd, but many who followed the Governor to the Confederate cemetery had worn Union blue.

A reporter covering the ceremonies wrote: "It was an impressive scene, and one not to be forgotten, to see the Governor and old veterans strewing flowers on the graves of their late enemies."

Mrs. Waterman continued to watch over and care for the graves until her death, at age 77, in 1897. At her request, she was buried in the cemetery with the men she fondly called "her boys." Mrs. Waterman's efforts were a labor of love, and in her efforts she unwittingly created a monument to herself. "She found the place a wilderness," read her obituary, "and made it blossom as the rose."

The wooden markers at the Rebels' graves have long ago been replaced with granite stones. On Memorial Day, each grave is decorated with a bronze cross bearing the legend "Confederate Veteran" and a small Confederate flag. And once again, the Stars and Bars flies from the flagstaff at this cemetery so far from Dixie.❀   —D.D.

MAY RECIPE

Door County Cherry Torte

2 cups graham cracker crumbs
    (about 24 squares)
1/2 cup butter, melted
1/3 cup sugar
1/4 teaspoon ground
    cinnamon
1/2 cup sugar
1/4 cup cornstarch
1/4 teaspoon salt

2-1/4 cups milk
2 egg yolks, lightly beaten
1/2 teaspoon vanilla
1 8-ounce package cream
    cheese
1 cup whipping cream
1 21-ounce can cherry pie
    filling

In a medium mixing bowl combine graham cracker crumbs, melted butter, 1/3 cup sugar, and cinnamon. Press mixture into a buttered 12x7-1/2x2-inch baking dish. Bake in a 350° oven for 10 minutes.

In a medium saucepan combine the 1/2 cup sugar, cornstarch, and salt. Add the milk and egg yolks. Cook and stir over medium heat till thickened and bubbly; cook and stir 1 to 2 minutes more. Stir in the vanilla. Cover the surface with clear plastic wrap; let stand to cool about 20 minutes. Spread over the baked crust.

In a small mixer bowl combine cream cheese and whipping cream; beat with an electric mixer on high speed till thickened. Spread atop the custard layer. Spoon the cherry pie filling atop. Chill at least 2 hours before serving. Makes 12 to 15 servings.

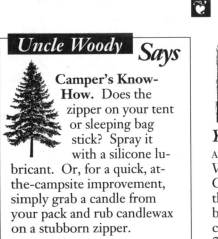

Uncle Woody Says

Camper's Know-How. Does the zipper on your tent or sleeping bag stick? Spray it with a silicone lubricant. Or, for a quick, at-the-campsite improvement, simply grab a candle from your pack and rub candlewax on a stubborn zipper.

Years Ago . . .

ASHLAND—The ladies of the WCTU have requested William Carter to remove certain pictures that adorn both sides of his saloon bar. He has the matter under consideration.—*Wisconsin State Journal*, May 14, 1889.

Wisconsin's Champion Trees

There are no redwoods in Wisconsin. But there are some *very* large trees. The Department of Natural Resources keeps tabs on the champion trees. Foresters and big tree hunters (an excellent sport for those who aren't a good shot) search out state and national champions for most species of trees that grow in Wisconsin.

How can you tell if a tree is a champion? Measure it. The good news is, you can take all the measurements needed without ever leaving the ground. The measurements are added up for a point total based on a system devised by the American Forestry Association (AFA). To measure a big tree:

1. Measure the circumference of the trunk four and a half feet above ground level.

2. Measure the crown spread by setting a stake under the outside edge of the crown farthest from the trunk. Put another stake directly opposite it, again at the outer edge of the crown. Put a third stake under the outside edge of the crown closest to the trunk. Put a fourth stake directly opposite at the outer edge of the crown. Measure both distances (long and short). Add the two measurements, then divide by two to obtain the average crown spread.

3. To measure the tree's height, take along a clear plastic 12-inch ruler. Stand far enough away from the tree that you can sight both the base and the top of the tree between the top and bottom of the ruler. Now, move the ruler (or yourself) forward or backward until the base of the tree lines up with the base of the ruler, and the top of the tree appears across the 10-inch line. Then, sight across the one-inch line and have a companion (you did bring a companion, didn't you?) mark the corresponding point on the tree. Measure the distance from this point to the base of the tree. Multiply by 10 and you have a height estimate.

The circumference, crown and height measurements are used in the AFA point system: circumference in inches plus one quarter of the crown spread in feet plus height in feet equals total points.

Now let's check on Wisconsin's biggest trees:

The state's tallest tree is a 148 foot white pine that has been growing in Forest County for hundreds of years. This monster is 17.5 feet in circumference, weighing in with 372 AFA points, making it the third largest tree in Wisconsin.

Wisconsin's runner-up tree is a 115 foot tall silver maple in Columbia County with a circumference of 24.5 feet, elbowing its way into the record books with 435.5 AFA points. This tree is not only Wisconsin's largest maple, it is the national champion silver maple. That's right, the largest silver maple in the country lives in Columbia County.

And the largest tree in Wisconsin? It's an Eastern Cottonwood in Green Lake County. This 110 foot tall specimen muscles in at 29.5 feet in circumference, and earns 488.8 AFA points.

Some other record holders:

The state's largest paper birch tree is a 242 point giant located in Green Lake County. It is 13 feet in circumference and 77 feet tall.

The largest hemlock is a 96 foot tall monster, with a 13 foot girth and a 261 AFA point total, that lives in Bayfield County.

La Crosse County is home of the state's largest American elm, a 75 foot high, 18-foot-circumference beauty that weighs in with 316 AFA points.

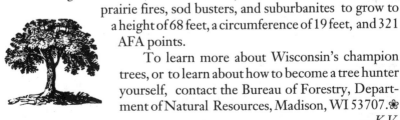

The largest oak is a Waukesha County burr oak that has withstood prairie fires, sod busters, and suburbanites to grow to a height of 68 feet, a circumference of 19 feet, and 321 AFA points.

To learn more about Wisconsin's champion trees, or to learn about how to become a tree hunter yourself, contact the Bureau of Forestry, Department of Natural Resources, Madison, WI 53707. ✾

—*K.V.*

MAY IN THE GARDEN

Highlights:
❈ *Transplant annuals and vegetables*
to outdoor beds
❈ *Sow seeds of most vegetables and annuals*
❈ *Plant new evergreens*
❈ *Stake tall-growing perennials*

May is the busiest month in the Wisconsin garden. Many gardeners of long experience, remembering late frosts of past years, delay in planting the vegetable and annual beds until Memorial Day weekend. But most of us, noting that our growing season is only 177 days long, start in as soon as we have received a decent spell of warm weather and the soil has warmed up tolerably.

You can help the soil to lose its winter chill more quickly if you lay down sheets of black plastic over the vegetable and annual beds. The darkness absorbs the heat of the sun and conducts it to the soil below. Oldtimers used the same principle when they sprinkled coaldust over the receding snows, thus causing them to melt quickly.

Today, coaldust is not so easy to come by—and it wouldn't be recommended, anyway.

The list of May chores is formidable. Early in the month you may divide and thin chrysanthemums and other perennials that bloom in summer and fall, if you have not already done so. Disbud peonies and chrysanthemums to make bushier plants, and set in your dahlia tubers and tuberous begonias. Flowering annuals may be seeded now, and they should germinate quickly and make strong progress through the month. Seedlings of flowering annuals may also be transplanted to the outdoors. Stake delphiniums and peonies before they grow too tall.

Gift Easter lilies may also be set into the garden, but be sure they are hardy for your area or you will be wasting your time.

Evergreens should be planted before they have made vigorous new growth. Growing iris should be given a good dose of bonemeal now, and you may prepare the annual and vegetable beds, if you did not do so in April.

The first asparagus and rhubarb can be harvested early in the month—as a reward for your hard spring work. While harvesting, remove any rhubarb flower stalks.

During the second week, plant bush fruits and grapes. Beginning about the 15th, you may sow seeds of snap and pole beans, sweet corn, melons, squash, cucumbers, and pumpkins. Record the date of strawberry bloom, and note on the calendar that ripe fruit should follow in a month.

Remove faded tulip blossoms, but do not cut away the foliage. Interplant quick-growing annuals around the tulips to hide their browning foliage.

During the last week of May, set out tomato plants—but be prepared to cover them if a late frost threatens. Herb sets may also be transplanted to the outdoors.

The best time to prune lilacs, forsythia, and other early spring-flowering shrubs is immediately after they have bloomed. If you prune in late summer or fall, you will remove next spring's flower buds. ❀ —*J.M.*

The Sturgeon Bay Ship Canal

GEORGE VUKELICH

We spent the weekend at the cabin on the beach just south of the Sturgeon Bay Ship Canal. The foghorn sounded every day and every night we were there and I can still hear it, reverberating through my inner space like some great, nameless animal moaning in a darkened cave.

Two moans within a five-second space, then an uneasy silence for twenty-three seconds, then the pair of moanings again and then the silence, throughout the day, throughout the night. Throughout our fitful dreams. Throughout our fitful lives.

In the darkness, we sat on our piece of secure, rockbound coast and listened to the eternal sound, melancholy, but not frightening, We waited for the foil-wrapped potatoes in the driftwood coals. We waited for the fish to be done. We waited without fear.

Jo and Vince and I sat on the log a pebble throw from the restless alien world and I told them of the dark, stormy nights on the ore carriers, the foghorns washed away on the screaming winds, the seas crashing over the cargo holds, the stern lifted high out of the water, the screw spinning, chattering in mid-air, the ship struggling like a drowning animal, fighting, fighting. In those nights nothing was secure, nothing was rockbound and fear pecked at our spirits the way gulls peck out the eyes of dying fish.

Anyone who has sailed the Great Lakes in the great ships can talk to you of fear. Fear of the November storms on the open lakes. Fear of the holy, mystical powers in these living waters. Fear of the alien world.

A lot of sailors will not put these things into words for you, let alone put the words on paper, but I think they would agree with Mike Link, who did put some of these things on paper in the book *Journeys to Door County*.

"This land," he writes, "should be saved for the sullen, gray foggy days or the blustery, stormy days." He tells of visiting Cave Point with his wife on a thick, foggy day—one that makes you think of London or Maine and foghorns in the gloom.

They were there alone. Billows of damp air rolled in instead of big waves and the water surged, gurgled, and disappeared at the rock's edge. The fog hid the rest of the world and the rocks were wet and seemed to glisten in an otherwise muted scene.

"My thoughts of that day were mixed," Mike Link remembers. "The fog made us seem alone in the world, and the surrealistic setting made my wife's image stand out from a gray background. There was a haunting spell in the air. The fog was not just Lake Michigan water suspended in the sky. There were spirits floating there. Seamen of the fresh water that had tested their mettle in the Great Lakes' storms and had lost. I could feel them."

We stared at the shrouded sea and for a moment, I was back on the fishtug *Ione* out of Two Rivers, watching the LeClair brothers gilling and gutting a ton of laketrout, the waters sparkling and filled with fish and gulls and the laughter of young men who knew damn well they were all going to live forever. ✤

Reprinted from <u>North Country Notebook.</u> Published by North Country Press.

JUNE

What would have become of us had it pleased Providence to make the weather unchangeable?

—*Sydney Smith, "Lady Holland's Memoir"*

"What is so rare as a day in June? Then, if ever, come perfect days," wrote James Russell Lowell. June brings the summer solstice, on or about, the 21st. In Wisconsin, that first day of summer has nearly 15 and 1/2 hours of daylight. While the month produces some of our loveliest weather, tornadoes are most frequent in Wisconsin in June. The highest probability of occurrence is from the 20th to 25th, between 3 P.M. and 7 P.M. Wisconsin's worst tornado struck New Richmond at 6:30 P.M. on June 12, 1899, claiming 117 lives. Since 1950, the Wisconsin counties in which the most tornadoes have occurred are Dodge (40), Chippewa (26), Dane and Fond du Lac (25 each), and Marathon (19). ❀

June Weather History

MADISON

Day	Record High		Record Low		Record Precip.		Average High/Low
1	100	1934	34	1966	1.33	1892	75/50
2	88	1963	35	1956	2.26	1878	75/50
3	91	1972	37	1969	2.40	1883	76/50
4	92	1934	35	1982	2.77	1953	76/51
5	92	1934	35	1982	3.67	1963	76/51
6	94	1952	36	1982	1.10	1917	77/51
7	94	1933	38	1977	1.93	1916	77/52
8	92	1964,85	38	1913	1.40	1874	77/52
9	93	1911	34	1977	2.46	1974	77/52
10	96	1956	31	1972	2.81	1893	78/53
11	94	1956	35	1972	2.41	1876	78/53
12	95	1976	38	1985	1.20	1877	78/53
13	95	1956,76	36	1965	2.31	1947	78/53
14	95	1954,87	39	1965	3.47	1880	79/54
15	92	1954	37	1965	2.59	1981	79/54
16	93	1946	33	1964	3.41	1978	79/54
17	93	1987	36	1972	2.03	1944	79/54
18	93	1954,87	39	1972	1.50	1935	80/55
19	97	1953	38	1982	1.17	1871	80/55
20	101	1988	42	1914	1.50	1877	80/55
21	100	1988	39	1963	3.48	1954	80/55
22	96	1988	42	1963	2.66	1940	80/56
23	94	1923	37	1972	1.53	1894	81/56
24	96	1923	44	1972	1.49	1882	81/56
25	97	1988	36	1979	2.17	1969	81/56
26	96	1931,80	45	1974	2.45	1873	81/56
27	97	1933	45	1970	3.33	1869	81/56
28	97	1931	47	1968	1.87	1988	81/57
29	98	1931	43	1989	1.44	1933	82/57
30	99	1931	43	1988	2.50	1978	82/57

JUNE

June Weather History

Day	Record High		Record Low		Average High/Low
1	96	1934	33	1897	75/54
2	93	1934	39	1985	76/54
3	90	1948	38	1946	76/55
4	94	1934	32	1945	76/55
5	93	1934	35	1945	77/55
6	93	1968	40	1983	77/55
7	97	1987	39	1935	77/56
8	98	1985	37	1978	77/56
9	95	1911	39	1937	78/56
10	95	1973	39	1928	78/57
11	94	1956	43	1972	78/57
12	95	1920	41	1874	78/57
13	97	1988	41	1969	79/57
14	98	1895	42	1933	79/58
15	95	1913	42	1927	79/58
16	93	1913	45	1982	79/58
17	94	1987	42	1950	80/58
18	96	1988	40	1876	80/59
19	98	1953	43	1982	80/59
20	102	1933	44	1969	80/59
21	102	1988	45	1972	81/59
22	97	1911	44	1902	81/59
23	97	1874	42	1972	81/60
24	97	1874	44	1887	81/60
25	97	1983	47	1926	81/60
26	100	1931	46	1911	81/60
27	99	1933	46	1926	82/60
28	100	1931	45	1968	82/61
29	101	1931	45	1950	82/61
30	100	1933	42	1943	82/61

The normal average pre-cipitation for La Crosse in June is 4.15 inches. The wettest June was in 1899 when 11.56 inches was re-corded; the driest was in 1910 when only 0.37 inches was received.

Excuses for a June Party

1 Baby Shower

On June 1, 1981, at the International Crane Foundation at Baraboo, little Gee Whiz pipped out of his shell. Because Tex, the chick's mother, preferred human company to whooping crane company, ICF founder George Archibald himself courted Tex for several years. Flapping his arms to perform the crane mating dance and helping her build a nest, he inspired Tex to lay an egg that was artificially fertilized and vigilantly incubated.

10 Woman Suffrage Day

"Mother mends my socks
   and shirts,
Mother mends my coat
Maybe she could mend some
   laws
If she had the vote."

It took years of such slogans and crusading but finally, on June 10, 1919, Wisconsin became the first state to ratify the Nineteenth Amendment to the United States Constitution. Determined that Wisconsin would be first (Illinois had also voted to ratify), suffragette Ada James pressed Governor Emanuel Philipp to sign the papers immediately, then hustled her father onto the next train to Washington to file the papers.

14 Flag Day

In the mid-1880s, Bernard J. Cigrand, the teacher at a one-room schoolhouse in Fredonia, began to campaign for a national Flag Day. He displayed a little 38-star flag in a bottle on his desk to remind the class that the Continental Congress had adopted the Stars and Stripes on June 14, 1777, and he wrote a lot of letters. Finally, in 1916, President Woodrow Wilson proclaimed June 14 as a day to honor the flag. Later, Mr. Cigrand became a dentist and helped to write the Pledge of Allegiance.

Dairyland Days

Strawberries and cream set the pace for warm weather treats in Dairy  Month. Pet a cow, milk a cow, and sample a 500-foot cheese sandwich at the Cows on the Concourse celebration outside the Capitol in Madison. At the Great Dairy Carton Regatta at Vilas Park, watch extremely healthy sailors compete for prizes in boats they built of cottage cheese and milk containers.

Wisconsin's Agricultural Bounty

Suppose you were forced to eat only Wisconsin products for a week. Not to worry. Wisconsin's 300 billion tons of soil produce an agricultural bounty unmatched in the Midwest. Wisconsin agriculture is a $5.7 billion annual business. You can eat three hearty Wisconsin-grown meals a day and never get bored.

To begin, you would certainly have all the milk, butter, cheese, ice cream, and other dairy products you could handle. Wisconsin is, of course, America's Dairyland. Our 1.8 million cows produce more than 25 billion pounds of milk every year. (Milk production is measured in hundred pound increments. A gallon of milk weighs 8.6 pounds, so a hundred pounds of milk is equivalent to 11.6 gallons. Thus our cows pump out 2.9 billion gallons of milk annually.) That's 17 percent of annual national milk production.

Close to 80 percent of the milk is made into cheese — cheddar, brick, colby, Swiss, bleu, muenster, mozzarella, and many specialty cheeses. (Wisconsin is the only state where limburger cheese — 1.1 million pounds annually — is produced.) Wisconsin cheese factories turn out 1.8 billion pounds of cheese annually. That's 35 percent of total United States cheese production.

Our dairy processing plants also churn out 274 million pounds of butter, 23 percent of the national butter output. Ice cream production stands at 23 million gallons, and if you want health food, try digging into the 27 million pounds of cottage cheese made here. And that's not all. Wisconsin processors make condensed milk, powdered milk, whey products for livestock feed and food additives, and Wisconsin is the sole producer of malted milk.

For those who crave vegetables at every meal, Wisconsin growers produce more than 150 million pounds of carrots, 655,000 tons of sweet corn, 115,000 tons of green peas, and 245,000 tons of snap beans every summer. Wisconsin is the number one state in the nation in production of peas and beans for freezing and canning. Our farmers also grow lettuce (15.7 million

pounds annually), cucumbers for pickling (54,000 tons a year), as well as onions, cabbage, beets and rutabagas (Wisconsin is number one in rutabaga production and in production of beets for canning), and even wild rice.

For the meat and potatoes set, Wisconsin is the seventh ranking potato producer, with a harvest of more than two billion pounds every fall. To go with the potatoes, you have a wide choice of meat: Wisconsin beef and dairy farmers annually send 1.4 million cattle to that big pasture in the sky. In addition, Wisconsin is the nation's number one veal producing state, with nearly 400,000 veal calves produced every year.

If you don't like beef, choose from one of the 2.1 million hogs offered up for pork chops, brats and ham. Wisconsin lamb chops and mutton are available courtesy of the 75,000 woolly creatures who meet their maker every year. (Wisconsin wool producers shear 672,000 pounds off their sheep every year. That's a lot of sweaters.)

Should you prefer poultry, you need look no farther than your own back yard (so to speak). More than six million Wisconsin turkeys give their lives so that we might enjoy Thanksgiving and Christmas every year. For less festive occasions, 4.7 million chickens await your call on farms throughout Wisconsin. While they're waiting, they produce 830 million eggs annually. Should you crave something a little more exotic, Wisconsin farmers also raise ducks, geese, and trout.

Now, what about dessert? If you're looking for something to put on your ice cream, Wisconsin growers can supply you with 1.2 million barrels of cranberries, 6.4 million pounds of strawberries, and 3.7 million pounds of cherries, not to mention the odd raspberry, blackberry or blueberry. For a real sweet treat, try some Wisconsin maple syrup on your ice cream.

If dairy products make you worry about cholesterol, bite into the 56 million pounds of apples produced annually by Wisconsin growers. Or sweeten your tooth with some of the 4.2 million pounds of honey produced by Wisconsin's bees every year. Wisconsin really is the land of milk and honey.

Want an after-dinner mint? Go ahead. Wisconsin's mint growers produce 368,000 pounds of the potent stuff every year. That's enough for millions of mints — or millions of tubes of toothpaste. Or tea. If mint isn't your favorite, you might try sipping a little ginseng tea, courtesy of the hundreds of growers who make Wisconsin the nation's largest ginseng producer.

Looking for something cold to wash everything down? If milk isn't your idea of the perfect drink, you might try cranberry juice, cherry cider, apple cider, cran-raspberry, cranapple, or any of the hundreds of combinations of fruit drinks produced with Wisconsin fruit.

Or, you could sample the products of one of our ten wineries. Like a tangy cranberry wine? How about a sweet cherry? Or perhaps a classic chablis or even a Wisconsin version of a fruity Beaujolais.

You can even enjoy an after dinner cigar courtesy of Wisconsin's tobacco growers, who plant the pungent weed on 6,600 acres.

Breakfast, lunch, and dinner. You can feast on Wisconsin's bounty anytime.

And when you take a walk to help settle your meal, you can wrap yourself in another Wisconsin product — mink. Wisconsin is the nation's largest producer of farm-raised mink, supplying 1.2 million pelts annually to the fur fashion industry. ❀   —K.V.

Years Ago...
Rules for Housekeepers. Count all your clothes pins, spoons, knives and forks, towels, napkins, etc., once a week. — *Oshkosh Journal*, June 11, 1870.

Uncle Woody **Says**

Camp Dishwashing. Rub soap on the outside of your pots and pans before cooking. All the caked-on grease and soot from campfire cooking will come off a lot easier. Keep the soap away from all surfaces that will come in contact with food, of course.

Wisconsin's State Parks

Wyalusing

It's not easy to make a state park. First, take 600 million years of sand and sediment layered gently on the bottom of a shallow primeval ocean. When the ocean recedes, let stand for 400 million years while rivers carve a path through the sediments, creating 500 foot high bluffs.

With only 10,000 years to go, add Indian villages and their mysterious ceremonial mounds built in the shape of deer, snakes, birds, and turtles. Speaking of animals, make the area lush and green and home to great blue herons, wild turkeys, eagles, hawks, deer, raccoon, fox and hundreds of other birds, mammals, fish, and reptiles.

With a few hundred years to go, add European explorers, missionaries and fur traders, followed by soldiers, who subdue the Indians, and settlers, who hew farms and towns out of the wilderness. But not all the wilderness.

Perched on the bluffs overlooking the convergence of the Wisconsin and Mississippi rivers sits Wyalusing State Park. Set aside as a state park in 1917, Wyalusing today preserves the bluffs, bottomlands and sloughs, the forest and prairie, the Indian mounds and even the remnants of settlers' farms created over a billion years.

Visit in April or May to watch Dutchman's breeches, shooting stars,

trillium, and hundreds of other species begin the annual flowering extravaganza. Perch on Point Lookout or hike through the woods and watch the birdwatchers counting their share of the hundreds of species that migrate through or live here year round.

In late May, the frozen waterfalls of Sand Cave and Pictured Rock Cave finally melt, revealing the reds and yellows of the sandstone bluffs.

In summer, canoeists meander through the Wisconsin and Mississippi sloughs, while anglers attempt to lure wily bass and walleye, and hikers atop the bluffs gaze down on eagles and hawks as they soar on warm air updrafts through the river valleys.

Come fall, the park is ablaze with the colors of maple, oak, hickory, and elm, anchored by the deep green of pines and cedars. Astors, blazing stars, and goldenrod spangle the prairies.

Winter opens the park to cross-country skiers, snowshoers, and that most illogical outdoors person, the ice fisher. These strange beings hunker down along the Mississippi shore and wait patiently for pike, bluegills and crappies to jump out through a tiny hole in the ice. And Wyalusing is one of the few parks where outdoor enthusiasts can venture where couch potatoes never go — the winter campsite.

Wyalusing State Park encompasses 2600 acres in Grant County, just across the Wisconsin River from Prairie du Chien. The entance is on county highway C west of U.S. Highway 18. The park offers campgrounds, picnic areas and group camping and shelters as well as hiking and skiing trails, swimming, boat launching and a marked canoe trail.❀—*K.V.*

Years Ago . . .

EAU CLAIRE—On arrival at New Richmond Tuesday afternoon, the Eau Claire expedition disembarked in the midst of a scene of horror and desolation where the evidences of death and destruction were visible on every hand. Mr. Louis Dunbar, who returned to Eau Claire today, said, "I had a talk with Dr. Degnan. Dr. Degnan said that he noticed the storm approaching the city a few minutes after six and called to the janitor of the church to 'ring the mischief' out of the bells. He then went out into the yard and gathered the neighbors and got them into the cellar of his house. He went about a block and secured a family of three and put them in his cellar, and a few minutes afterward their house was completely demolished.

"Scattered about the streets were dead horses, dogs, cows, chickens and pigs. Trees had been uprooted and twisted into wisps. Live chickens with all their feathers gone— they had been picked clean by the storm—were numerous. We saw a dozen or 15 of them in a bunch without a feather on them.

"The iron bridge across the pond had been torn from its foundations and landed on the northeast bank. There is no use in trying to tell how the place looked to us. The fiendish work of the storm demon is indescribable. The strip of 1500 feet wide and about a mile long through town marking the course of the cyclone is strewn with wreckage of every kind from stores and buildings, and beneath the ruins of most buildings we knew were buried perhaps scores of victims, and it is thought that some were blown into the pond and drowned."—*Eau Claire Daily Telegram*, June 14, 1899.

1 *Fabulous* *Firsts*

The first bicycle corps in the United States was organized in 1894 at Northwestern Military Academy in Lake Geneva. It consisted of 16 bicycles, each equipped with special clips for carrying rifles and other gear. One of the feats of the corps was a maneuver in which the cadets put themselves and their bikes, which when fully loaded weighed 54 pounds, over a 16-foot wall in two minutes, 48 seconds. They often made cross-country trips. On a 19-day trip in June of 1897, for example, 11 cadets carried a message from Fort Sheridan, near Chicago, to the secretary of war in Washington.

Homey Honey Hints

Pure Wisconsin honey belongs in every Wisconsin kitchen! Used in place of sugar, it helps to keep cakes and cookies fresh and moist. Honey is also rich in nutrition. It contains all the vitamins it needs for its own perfect digestion, and it is also a source of iron, copper, sodium, potassium, magnesium, manganese, calcium, and phosphorous.

In a cake or cookie recipe that calls for sugar, the general rule is to reduce the amount of liquid one-quarter cup for each cup of honey used. Honey may be substituted for sugar cup for cup. When honey is substituted in baked goods, add one-half teaspoon of baking soda to the recipe for every cup of honey used, and bake at a lower temperature.

Store your honey in a tightly-covered container in a dark and cool place. Cold temperatures will not harm the honey but will hasten granulation. You can get rid of granules, however, by placing the jar of honey in a bowl of warm water (no warmer than the hand can stand) until all crystals are melted and the honey is liquid once again. —*Dodge County Beekeepers Association*

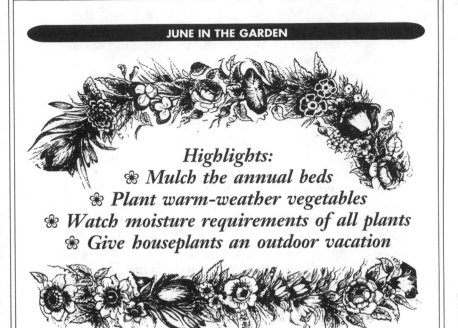

JUNE IN THE GARDEN

Highlights:
❀ *Mulch the annual beds*
❀ *Plant warm-weather vegetables*
❀ *Watch moisture requirements of all plants*
❀ *Give houseplants an outdoor vacation*

June brings the first real summer weather in Wisconsin—and with it, a chance for hard-working gardeners to relax just a little from the frantic pace of May planting. June also brings asparagus, rhubarb, and strawberries!

Still, June is no time for idlers. Perhaps the most important chore is to mulch the vegetable and annual beds. The effort put forth in this endeavor will be repaid many times over as the season progresses. The mulch will keep down weeds, conserve soil moisture, provide a soft and clean bed for ripening fruits, and prevent mud from being tracked into the house. Further, an organic mulch will break down slowly at the soil's surface, thus improving the soil's texture and fertility.

The warm-weather vegetables—eggplant, lima beans, and peppers— may be planted during the first week in the month. It is also not too late to plant other vegetables that you meant to get in earlier but didn't. Late potatoes may also be planted, with an eye toward fall harvest and winter storage. Evergreens may be pruned now, also.

Watch the weather. If we get a dry spell during the month, keep newly planted trees, shrubs, evergreens, perennials, and roses well watered, as well as tender new annuals and vegetables. And always remember that your best ally in a drought is mulch!

The second week of June is the time to stake tomatoes, tall-growing lilies, delphiniums, and other tall-growing perennials. If you have a lot of tomato plants—and a lot of room—you will get a larger harvest per plant by letting the vines sprawl over a thick hay mulch. Tomatoes, after all, are natural creepers, not climbers.

Remove faded peony blossoms, and cut back delphiniums after they have finished blooming. If you're after championship dahlia blossoms, cut back to one shoot per clump, to concentrate the plant's energies.

The third week of June is a good time to try starting some perennials from seed. Choose a protected area and keep it weed-free. Try delphinium, aquilegia, various dianthus, lupin, gaillardia, pyrethrum, viola, and veronica. Be sure to label everything carefully.

Chrysanthemums that will bloom in September should be pinched back for the last time. Thin newly emerging annuals and vegetables that were started from seed.

During the last week in the month, you may take most of your houseplants outdoors for a summer vacation. Choose a spot well protected from strong sun and wind. Keep them in their pots if you sink them into the ground, and keep the lip of the pot above the soil line. Some fit nicely when mixed with flowering annuals in flower boxes, while others look good on patios and porches.

You may plant late crops of rutabaga, cabbage, cauliflower, beets, turnips, and broccoli. Stop harvesting asparagus and rhubarb by the end of the month, and top-dress the beds with compost or well-rotted manure. You can still make weekly plantings of sweetcorn for an extended harvest. Sow seeds of endive and kale now, for crisp greens in the fall.

Trellis and prune red raspberry plants after the first harvest. Remove last year's fruiting canes, if you haven't already done so. And remember to let the lawn grass grow longer during hot and dry spells.❧   —*J.M.*

The Vandergaw Cabbage

The Best Second Early and Summer Cabbage.

Equally as Good for Winter.

COPYRIGHTED 1887.   BY W. ATLEE BURPEE & CO PHILADA

Planting Peas Productively

Plant peas in the early spring, as soon as the ground can be worked. A few light frosts will not hurt them. If you want really quick germination, spread the seeds out in a shallow pan, line the bottom with water so that the peas are just half covered, and place in a dark spot. Just as sprouts begin to show, plant them into the open garden. Treat the seeds with a bacterial inoculant (available at all garden centers) just before planting.

The garden pea is a trailing plant and will appreciate a trellis to climb on. The trellis will afford the plants optimum sun and air and will also make harvesting easier (not necessary with dwarf varieties). Mulch the plants after they have become established, to keep the soil cool. ❧

Uncle Woody *Says*

Outdoor Shirts. For summer, nothing beats the inexpensive, classical blue *cotton* work shirt. It's lightweight, it dries fast, its fabric breathes, and the shirt doesn't show dirt. Make sure that you buy it with long sleeves. Long sleeves can be rolled down, but short sleeves offer no protection for your arms against sunburn.

Years Ago . . .

PORTAGE—The steamer *Boscobel*, with Colonel Fuller of Appleton on board, arrived Saturday. Colonel Fuller, who is the government officer in charge of the Fox River improvements, is on his periodical tour of inspection. He says he intends to have the dredges do some work between that city and Montello soon, and to keep the river navigable.—*Wisconsin State Journal*, June 11, 1889.

JUNE RECIPES

Cherry Cobbler

1/4 cup butter, softened   1-1/2 teaspoons baking
1/2 cup sugar   powder
1/4 cup milk   1 cup flour

Cream butter and sugar. Beat in milk alternately with sifted dry ingredients. Spread into buttered 9x9-inch baking pan. Mix the following ingredients and pour over the dough:

1 1-pound can Wisconsin red tart cherries, drained
1/2 cup cherry juice
1/2 cup sugar
1/4 teaspoon salt

Bake in a moderate oven (350° F.) for 40 minutes. The dough comes to the top and browns beautifully. Serve with whipped cream.
Yield: 8 servings.

Berry Coffee Cake

8 ounces cream cheese,   2 cups flour
    softened   1 teaspoon baking powder
1/2 cup butter, softened   1/2 teaspoon baking soda
3/4 cup sugar   1/4 teaspoon salt
1/4 cup milk   3 cups Wisconsin berries, sliced
2 eggs   1/4 cup brown sugar
1 teaspoon vanilla   1/2 cup chopped nuts

Preheat oven to 350° F. Combine cream cheese, butter and sugar. Beat until light and fluffy. Stir in milk, eggs, and vanilla. Sift together flour, baking powder, baking soda, and salt. Add to cheese mixture; mix until smooth. Spread half the batter in a greased and floured 13x9-inch baking pan. Spread berries evenly over batter. Dot remaining batter over berries. Mix brown sugar and nuts; sprinkle evenly over cake. Bake 40 minutes. Serve warm.
Yield: 15 servings.

JUMBLE PUZZLE

The controversy over whether to permit the sale of colored oleomargarine in Wisconsin was hard fought. One of those who sought to protect the dairy industry by opposing its sale was Senator Gordon Roseleip of Darlington. "If you pass this bill," he warned his colleagues, in a thunderous oration, "you will never be able to look a cow in the face again." Nevertheless, in 1967 it became legal for colored margarine to be sold alongside real butter in Wisconsin grocery stores.

Unscramble the jumbles below, to form ordinary words. Then arrange the circled letters to form the phrase that Wisconsin dairy farmers may well have used to refer to this turn of events. Answers in back of book.

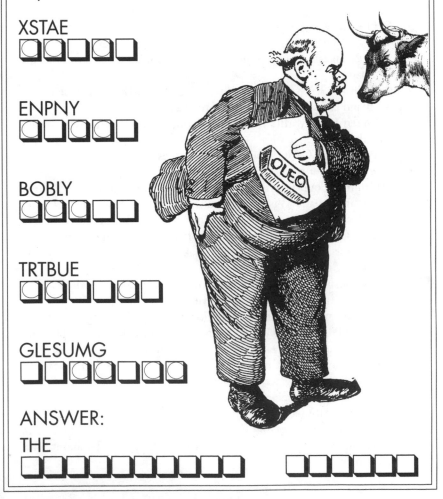

XSTAE
⬜⬜⬜⬜⬜

ENPNY
⬜⬜⬜⬜⬜

BOBLY
⬜⬜⬜⬜⬜

TRTBUE
⬜⬜⬜⬜⬜⬜

GLESUMG
⬜⬜⬜⬜⬜⬜⬜

ANSWER:
THE
⬜⬜⬜⬜⬜⬜⬜⬜⬜⬜   ⬜⬜⬜⬜⬜⬜

Wonderful Wisconsin Water

❀ Wisconsin's average annual snowfall is 45 inches.

❀ Our average annual rainfall is 30.57 inches.

❀ Nearly 1.3 million of Wisconsin's total area of 35.8 million acres is under water. In addition, Wisconsin controls 6.44 million acres of Great Lakes waters and 95,000 acres of Mississippi River waters.

❀ Wisconsin has nearly 15,000 lakes of 50 acres or more.

❀ There are 2444 trout streams in Wisconsin. Put end to end they'd stretch 9560 miles.

❀ Wisconsin has 860 miles of Great Lakes shoreline. Door County has more shoreline —260 miles— than any other county in the United States.

❀ On the west, Wisconsin's Mississippi River shore stretches 190 miles.

❀ Its 28 lakes make the Eagle River chain of lakes the largest in the world.

❀ With a 137,708 acre surface area, Lake Winnebago is Wisconsin's largest inland lake. Its maximum depth is 21 feet.

❀ Green Lake, with a maximum depth of 236 feet, is Wisconsin's deepest lake.

❀ Winnebago County, with 164,224 acres of lakes and streams, has the most water of any county in Wisconsin.

❀ Calumet County, with only 414 acres of lakes and streams, has the least water area of any Wisconsin county. (Though this figure does not include Lake Winnebago, which is considered part of Winnebago County.)

❀ Vilas County has the most lakes of any Wisconsin county.

❀ Crawford County has the fewest lakes — two— of any Wisconsin county.

❀ Wisconsin has 2.5 million acres of wetlands. That's about half the acres that were here when settlers arrived.

❀ Wisconsin has an estimated million-billion gallons of groundwater (that's 1,000,000,000,000,000). We use about 600 million gallons every day in homes, businesses, farming and industry.

❀ Wisconsin was the first state in the nation to set standards for water wells to protect drinking water quality.

❀ There are 174 species of fish in Wisconsin.

❀ We have 50 species of mollusks (mussels and clams).

❀ Our lakes and streams come complete with some 39 species of leeches, though only a few are the bloodsucking types that latch onto fish —or swimmers.

❧ Wisconsin sells more nonresident fishing licenses than any other state.

❧ Wisconsin anglers cumulatively spend nearly 32,000,000 days fishing our waters each year.

❧ It takes an average of 100 hours to catch a 34-inch muskellunge.

❧ The muskellunge is the state fish.

❧ Madison's Lake Mendota is the most studied (by biologists, limnologists, water experts) lake in the world.

❧ Every year the Department of Natural Resources stocks 2.3 million salmon, 140,000 muskellunge, 75 million walleye and 4 million trout in Wisconsin lakes and streams.

❧ To stock those fish, the DNR operates 15 fish hatcheries. —*K.V.*

Uncle Woody *Says*

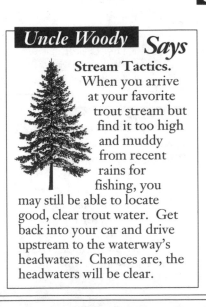

Stream Tactics.
When you arrive at your favorite trout stream but find it too high and muddy from recent rains for fishing, you may still be able to locate good, clear trout water. Get back into your car and drive upstream to the waterway's headwaters. Chances are, the headwaters will be clear.

Years Ago . . .

MADISON—The action of the university faculty respecting the students found to be connected with the red pepper episode at library hall, last Wednesday evening, during the Delta Gamma reception, is as follows: the one who was found in the loft from whence the pepper was thrown has been indefinitely suspended from the university; the other student was suspended for one year.—*Wisconsin State Journal*, June 4, 1889.

CORNUCOPIA OF FRUITS

Region	Usual Date of Full Bloom	USUAL HARVESTING DATES Begins	Most Active	Ends	Principal Producing Counties
APPLES					
East Central	May 25	Sept.15	Oct. 1-Nov. 1	Nov. 10	Door, Kewaunee, Sheboygan
Southeast	May 15	Aug. 5	Sep. 10-Oct.20	Oct. 25	Rock, Ozaukee, Waukesha
Northwest	May 20	Aug. 15	Sep. 10-Oct. 20	Oct. 25	Bayfield, Chippewa
Southwest & South Central	May 15	Aug. 10	Sep. 1-Oct. 10	Oct. 25	Crawford, Richland, Sauk, Dane, Green
TART CHERRIES					
East Central	May 25	July 25	Aug. 1-Aug. 10	Aug. 15	Door, Kewaunee
CRANBERRIES					
Central	July 5	Sept. 20	Oct. 1-Oct. 20	Nov. 1	Wood
West Central					Monroe, Jackson
North Central					Vilas, Oneida
Northwest					Washburn, Sawyer
STRAWBERRIES					
Southeast	N/A	June 10	June 15-July 15	Aug. 1	Washington, Kenosha
South Central					Dane, Columbia
Central					Waushara, Wood
East Central					Outagamie, Winnebago

1 *Fabulous* *Firsts*

The electrobasograph, which records the walking gait in order to distinguish between actual and spurious limps in damage claims for injuries, was first exhibited at a meeting of the American Medical Association in Milwaukee on June 12, 1933.

Site Unseen

MAUREEN MECOZZI

Think of traveling, and you'll likely have an image of going somewhere to see something—the scenery, a museum, a recreation spot. But the greatest pleasure of touring often comes from what cannot be seen, or rather, knowing what was once there that is no more.

County Highway A, a road off State Highway 12 in Sauk County that winds along the western bank of the Wisconsin River about four miles south of Wisconsin Dells, will take you through one of these invisible tourist attractions. There's a story of greed, power, reputations ruined and made, and a whole community literally sold up the river along the shoulders of that highway.

Ready for the tour?

Our story begins in 1850 with an enterprising Ohioan named Joseph Bailey. His eye on the future, young Joe headed west of the new state of Wisconsin and claimed 160 acres along the west bank of the Wisconsin River in the far northwestern corner of Columbia County, just across the river from Dell Creek.

Mr. Bailey had hopes of being hailed as the founding father of a thriving center of commerce and transportation. The site he had chosen was in a direct line between Milwaukee and La Crosse, so Joe had every reason to believe that as the new railroad crossing the state reached northwestern Columbia County, it would span the Wisconsin River at his front door.

Joe had vision, but he lacked cash. To make his dream a reality, in 1851 he sought the friendship and finances of Jonathan Bowman, a lawyer who left behind the relative civility of New York state for wild Wisconsin. The duo bought the land and built a warehouse on the east side of the river. Meanwhile, four other investors recognized the value of the site and bought property on the west bank.

A year later, the Legislature authorized construction of a bridge to link the two sites for commerce and travel. The proprietors of the prospective villages lost no time in contacting one Byron Kilbourn, president of the new La Crosse & Milwaukee Railroad and mayor of Milwaukee, to ensure that the rail line would use the bridge, Kilbourn assured them that it would. The gentlemen also received authorization to build a dam for water power uses on the river in 1853.

The time was right. Bailey and Bowman platted the land on both sides of the river and dubbed the new village "Newport." Lots in the boom town sold for the exorbitant price of $1,000 or more; the population increased rapidly, nearing 2,000 by the summer of 1855. Newportians

could boast of three hotels, 13 stores, a hexagonal house, and the Mary Lyon Female Seminary, a girls' school modeled after Mt. Holyoke College in Massachusetts.

Neither dam nor rail bridge had yet been built, however. As an inducement to secure the railroad crossing at Newport, Bailey and Bowman transferred some of the property they owned near Newport to Byron Kilbourn. The charter to the dam was signed over to the Wisconsin River Hydraulic Company, of which Mr. Kilbourn owned a major share.

When word got out that additional land was being platted for Newport, the real estate market boomed. Lots changed hands at alarming rates; property owners were able to double their profits overnight.

Byron Kilbourn found this amateur wheeling and dealing most amusing. In spite of his promises, he had no intention of laying track through the town or of buying land at inflated prices to build the dam. Kilbourn had secretly purchased land several miles north of Newport on the east bank, where he intended to have the railroad and dam cross the river. He went so far as to have men survey the area at night.

The citizens of Newport panicked when they heard the story of Kilbourn's midnight survey. Anyone who owned land in Newport wanted to sell it, and sell it fast: buyers, unfortunately, were scarce. Property values plummeted, and in the spring of 1857, when the railroad was completed through the new village of Kilbourn City to the north, lots that had once sold in Newport for $1,000 were going for $100 or less.

Within months, many of Newport's buildings were moved to Kilbourn City. The population of the village dwindled. In April 1868, the Newport post office was closed, and lots in the deserted village were dropped from the tax rolls. Newport was no more.

And the fortunes of Kilbourn City? The village named for the mayor of Milwaukee (who later was ruined in a scandal over bribes paid for favorable railroad grants) grew steadily and became an important shipping and supply point for the logging industry. Kilbourn City also had discovered the value of its crowning jewel—the lovely dalles (French for precipices) forming the sides of the Wisconsin River gorge.

The beauty of the site drew summer visitors from far and near, and Kilbourn City soon found that tourism, not logging, held the key to prosperity. In 1931, city administrators hoping to increase the tourist trade decided "Kilbourn City" did not do justice to the spectacular scenery of the area. They changed the town's name to Wisconsin Dells . . . and the rest is history.

As you drive along County Highway A, glance over toward the river and look for Sugar Bowl, Ink Stand and Lone Rock, three outstanding rock formations near the site of Newport. On "A" one mile east of Lake Delton you'll find Dawn Manor, a palatial stone mansion built in 1855 by Captain Abraham Vanderpoel. It's the sole survivor of the boom town.

Ultimately, river rivals Newport and Kilbourn City met the same fate. They were both wiped off the map and swept into the rich history of Wisconsin. ❀

Reprinted from the April 1989 <u>Wisconsin Traveler</u>, <u>Wisconsin Natural Resources</u>- magazine. Courtesy Wisconsin Department of Natural Resources.

Copper Falls

The sound dominating Copper Falls State Park is the roar of waterfalls and rapids created as the Bad River plunges toward Lake Superior. Early French fur traders named it the Mauvais (Bad) because its many rapids and falls made navigation difficult.

The Bad's difficult character didn't just happen. It took millions of years. To make a very long story short, there's been a lot happening around here in the last billion years. The area was once at the bottom of an ancient ocean, into which lava oozed from fissures in the earth's crust. Perhaps 60,000 feet of the stuff covered what is now far northwest Wisconsin. The earth's crust slumped under the weight, the Lake Superior basin was formed, and sediments such as sand and mud began to flow into the basin from higher ground. Naturally, the layers got twisted and angled as the earth's crust shrugged and settled, heaving the compacted lava on top of the sandstone in some areas. To further confuse the topography, a series of glaciers dropped dirt and stone on top of the pile.

Meanwhile, the Bad River was picking out the path of least resistance in its continuing effort to get to Lake Superior. It chewed away the sandstone, but had less luck with the harder lava, so it just jumps off the lava ledges and keeps hammering away at the sandstone. The result is Copper Falls, Brownstone Falls, Red Granite Falls and Tyler Forks Cascades, all now protected in the park.

Copper Falls was indeed a center of copper mining — for the Indians who lived here before white settlers arrived. The settlers tried digging mines, including one located in what is now the park, around the turn of the century, but found little copper. The area was left to farmers and loggers.

Copper Falls State Park was established in 1929, setting aside 2400 acres through which eight and a half miles of river flow over four waterfalls and through narrow, rocky gorges rising 60 to 100 feet above the river. Visitors can meander close to the falls along hiking trails and over three footbridges that provide a bird's-eye view of the cascades.

The park also encompasses two lakes, campgrounds, a picnic area, a swimming beach, and plenty of opportunity to fish for trout, bass, and northerns.

Most visitors stroll the seven miles of trails, listening to the roar of the river, or looking for wildlife. The lucky ones may see a black bear, surprise a deer browsing in the forest, glimpse a coyote, or spy a porcupine lodged overhead in a tree. Early summer visitors will be welcomed by the many banded purple and tiger swallowtail butterflies that visit the park in June and July.

Winter visitors can ski the 14 miles of cross country trails and marvel at the ice formations surrounding the falls.❀   —K.V.

Wisconsin's Big-Water Lakes

Name	Location	Area in Acres
Lake Winnebago	Winnebago County	137,708
Lake Pepin	Mississippi Boundary	27,813
Petenwell Lake	Juneau County	23,040
Lake Chippewa	Sawyer County	15,300
Lake Poygan	Winnebago County	14,102
Castle Rock Lake	Juneau County	13,955
Turtle-Flambeau Flowage	Iron County	13,545
Lake Koshkonong	Jefferson County	10,460
Lake Mendota	Dane County	9,730
Lake Wisconsin	Columbia County	9,000
Lake Butte des Morts	Winnebago County	8,857
Lake Onalaska	La Crosse County	7,688
Big Green Lake*	Green Lake County	7,346
Big Eau Pleine Reservoir	Marathon County	6,830
Lake Du Bay	Marathon County	6,653
Beaver Dam Lake	Dodge County	6,542
Lake Wissota	Chippewa County	6,300
Shawano Lake	Shawano County	6,063
Lake Puckaway	Green Lake County	5,433
Lake Geneva	Walworth County	5,262
Willow Flowage	Oneida County	5,135
Lac Court Oreilles	Sawyer County	5,039
Lake St. Croix	St. Croix County	4,668
Lake Winneconne	Winnebago County	4,507
Trout Lake	Vilas County	3,816
Pelican Lake	Oneida County	3,585
Fence Lake	Vilas County	3,555
Tomahawk Lake	Oneida County	3,392

*Big Green Lake is Wisconsin's deepest lake—maximum 236 feet.
Source: Wisconsin Dept. of Natural Resources

JULY

*When it is evening, you say it will be
fair weather; for the sky is red.*

— *Matthew 16: 2*

July is Wisconsin's warmest month; the all-
time record high of 114 degrees F. was set in
Wisconsin Dells on July 13, 1936. Madison's
all-time record of 107 degrees F. was set the following day. July is much drier than June since
the weather systems are slow-moving without
well-defined storm tracks. As a result, July has
long periods of unchanging weather, with
highly variable rainfall patterns in summer
thunderstorms. July is a busy month for Wisconsin farmers, especially in southern sections
of the state where the corn is coming into tassel.
In most years the southern oat harvest is completed by late in the month.✼

July Weather History

MADISON

Day	Record High		Record Low		Record Precip.		Average High/Low
1	97	1910	40	1965	1.55	1978	82/57
2	96	1911	46	1968	3.04	1960	82/57
3	96	1911	42	1968	3.89	1975	82/57
4	98	1911	44	1972	1.17	1899	82/57
5	98	1911	40	1972	1.56	1871	82/58
6	100	1886	36	1965	2.27	1954	82/58
7	102	1936	46	1984	2.51	1879	83/58
8	100	1936	43	1972	2.46	1949	83/58
9	98	1936	47	1961	2.84	1922	83/58
10	104	1976	44	1968	1.63	1932	83/58
11	100	1936	46	1968,78	3.82	1878	83/58
12	104	1936	45	1975	1.23	1937	83/58
13	106	1936	46	1964	1.40	1912	83/58
14	107	1936	47	1967	1.59	1893	83/58
15	101	1988	41	1967	2.40	1913	83/58
16	97	1931	48	1973	2.35	1950	83/58
17	98	1936	45	1958,76	3.43	1903	83/59
18	95	1894	47	1979	1.43	1977	83/59
19	97	1964	49	1929	3.81	1950	83/59
20	97	1930	45	1970	2.53	1912	83/59
21	104	1901	41	1966	4.32	1881	83/59
22	100	1934	49	1958,77,85	2.21	1885	83/59
23	101	1934	46	1970,85	2.05	1884	83/59
24	101	1901	48	1957	2.35	1929	83/59
25	98	1934	50	1962	2.17	1985	83/59
26	100	1955	46	1977	2.08	1940	83/59
27	100	1955	45	1971	1.62	1877	83/59
28	98	1916	46	1972	1.02	1952	83/59
29	101	1916	43	1965	2.16	1959	83/59
30	97	1916	45	1971	0.70	1872	83/58
31	95	1917,88	43	1971	1.78	1955	83/58

July Weather History

LA CROSSE

Day	Record High		Record Low		Average High/Low
1	100	1931	44	1948	82/61
2	103	1911	47	1924	82/61
3	96	1966	49	1968	82/61
4	100	1911	44	1967	83/61
5	101	1874	47	1972	83/62
6	100	1936	48	1983	83/62
7	104	1980	47	1984	83/62
8	102	1936	47	1891	83/62
9	102	1936	46	1895	83/62
10	100	1980	48	1895	83/62
11	104	1936	48	1895	83/62
12	105	1936	49	1975	83/62
13	106	1936	45	1975	83/62
14	108	1936	48	1926	84/62
15	102	1988	49	1967	84/62
16	101	1931	49	1912	84/63
17	101	1936	45	1911	84/63
18	100	1934	50	1984	84/63
19	97	1974	47	1947	84/63
20	103	1901	49	1970	84/63
21	104	1901	46	1947	84/63
22	102	1934	41	1947	84/63
23	102	1934	48	1948	84/63
24	104	1901	50	1948	84/63
25	98	1874	50	1891	84/63
26	101	1955	48	1911	84/63
27	100	1931	48	1891	84/63
28	98	1955	50	1967	84/63
29	97	1917	50	1968	84/63
30	99	1916	48	1918	84/63

The normal average precipitation for La Crosse in July is 3.83 inches. The wettest July was in 1883 when 11.03 inches was recorded; the driest was in 1967 when only 0.16 inches was received.

Excuses for a July Party

1 Put Out a Spread

On July 1, 1967, the ban on the sale of colored oleomargarine was lifted, ending widespread amateur interstate bootlegging on the part of Wisconsin house-wives. Until then, the only sub-stitute for real butter that could be purchased in Wisconsin was oleomargarine that was "free of coloration or ingredients that cause it to look like butter." Us-ing a yellow pen with yellow ink, Governor Warren Knowles signed the bill while ten women wearing yellow dresses stood by.

4 The Fourth of July

This was the most festive event of the year in the nine-teenth century. Milwaukee commemorated it enthusiastically with parades, music, the firing of cannons, feasting on homemade ice cream and fried chicken, speech making, dancing, and the reading of the Declaration of Independence in English and German. Small towns celebrated too, as an old settler in East Troy recalled: "There were only three of us in the town and one gun, but we fired the gun."

16 Garden Party

Eben E. Rexford (born July 16, 1848) spent most of his life in Shiocton, in Outagamie County, writing numerous books on gar-dening that helped to popularize flower growing in the United States *(Home Floriculture, Grand-mother's Garden, Four Seasons in a Garden)*. An admirer wrote, "To make a flower grow where a rank unsightly weed had been, to make a useful vegetable grow in some neglected, uncared for spot, was, he thought, as religious an act as a man could do." Rexford also wrote sentimental poems and songs, the best known being "Silver Threads Among the Gold."

Surprise Party

The surprise that Mother Nature sprang on Oconto County in July 1952 was an invasion of frogs. In a total

triumph of froggism, the green and bronze army marched out of a marsh between Pensaukee and Peshtigo harbors and in two days was swarming throughout the streets, gardens, and lawns of the town of Oconto. The population figures for Oconto that summer were: humans, 5,030; frogs, 175,000,000 (according to scientists' estimates—frogs are hard to count); mosquitoes, 0.

Why did they call it that, anyway?

Nearby Places with Strange Sounding Names

Ubet. Chequamegon. Hell Hollow. Paradise Valley. Dilly. Butte des Morts. Cornucopia.

Wisconsin place names spring from many roots: melodious Indian names; French names bestowed by fur traders and missionaries; names honoring prominent businessmen, land speculators, politicians, soldiers or a local settler; names to remind of places abandoned to make a new life on the frontier; names evocative of legends and strange happenings; and whimsical, descriptive names based on spur of the moment feelings. Wisconsin has them all.

When the first European explorers arrived, the Indians, of course, had names for most places. The fur traders, missionaries and settlers adopted many of those names, or named their new communities in honor of Indian chiefs, Indian historical events, and Indian legends.

The name Chequamegon comes from the French misspelling (or mispronunciation) of Chippewa words meaning "low land" or perhaps "at the soft beaver dam," referring to land along the shore of Lake Superior.

The city of Oshkosh was named in the early 1840s for Oskosh, the local Menominee chief. The extra "h" crept in in later misspellings.

Similarly, when Tomah was settled in 1855, it was named for Menominee Chief Thomas Carron (Tomah being the French pronunciation of Thomas), who had held a large powwow in the vicinity years earlier.

Lac Court Oreilles (and the community of Couderay, which is the English pronunciation) was named by French explorers who called the resident Chippewa "Court Orielles," which means "short ears" in French. Apparently, the Indians' headgear or haircuts led the French to believe the Indians actually cut off part of their ears.

Butte des Morts means "Hill of the Dead." One version of the origin of the name is simply that the area was an Indian burial ground. Another is that in 1730, the French and the Menominees allied to attack a Fox village on the site, slaughtering all inhabitants. Bodies were buried in a mass grave on the Hill of the Dead.

One of the most melodious of Indian-derived names is Oconomowoc, which was called "Coo-no-mo-wauk" by the Indians at the time the Europeans arrived. The settlers weren't sure how to translate the word, but did agree that the name meant "beautiful water," "river of lakes," "place where the river falls," or a similar term. It probably referred to the Oconomowoc River and the series of lakes between which it flows.

The Dane County community of Waunakee boasts of being "the only Waunakee in the world." The name was chosen in 1870 by local boosters who were developing the area in anticipation of the coming of the railroad. The name was chosen from a list of possibilities compiled by a General Simeon Mills, a Madison resident. It is unclear where the General found the name, but the commonly accepted source of the name is the Chippewa "wanaki," which means "I inhabit a place in peace." It has also been translated "pleasant land" or "pleasant earth."

Some places were named for Indian legends. Maiden Rock, the striking bluff overlooking the Mississippi in Pierce County, is named in honor of a Sioux maiden who, legend has it, was betrothed against her will to a Dakota brave. Her heart belonged to another, however, and immediately after the forced marriage she flung herself from the bluff to die on the rocks below.

As Wisconsin was settled many place names reflected the hope of a better life. Consider the Grant County community called Happy Corners. The Monroe County spot named Paradise Valley. The Jackson County community of Pray. (Of course there's also Hell Hollow in Richland County, and Devil's Corner in Pepin County.)

Some names reflected the settlers' homesickness, or perhaps their belief that their small settlement would one day become a major city. Wisconsin has Paris, Rome, and Vienna. Not to mention Belgium, Denmark, Sweden and Luxembourg. Within our borders are New Amsterdam, New Berlin, New Denmark, New Lisbon, New London, New Rome, and, possibly reflecting tough times on the frontier, New Hope.

It's hard to tell what inspired the names of some communities. The Polk County community of Ubet was supposedly named (in 1860) for a town of the same name in Ohio, which the new settlers had lately vacated to move to Wisconsin.

Luck, another Polk County community, apparently was so named because it was halfway between St. Croix Falls and Clam Falls, and if a traveler got halfway by nightfall, he was "in luck." This explanation ignores the question of why anyone would want to go from St. Croix Falls to Clam Falls.

The origin of the names of the Jackson County community of Disco, of Plugtown in Crawford County, and of Slab City and Slabtown (in Shawano and Jefferson counties, respectively) may be lost in the mists of history. So might the antecedents of Popcorn Corners in Ashland County, Ourtown in Sheboygan County, and Dilly, a Vernon County metropolis.

Certainly, Ino and Ono (located in Bayfield and Pierce counties, respectively) must have long and distinguished histories.

The Waukesha County community of Fussville was named for a Mr. Fuss, the first settler. The twin cities of Krok and East Krok were named for the Czech city of the same name, from which a Judge Stransky emigrated to find himself in Kewaunee County.

Settlers had thousands of lakes, rivers, creeks, hollows, and topographic landmarks to name. They set to it with the best of intentions, but imagination failed them in many cases and they resorted to pure descriptive terms. That's why Wisconsin is blessed with approximately 115 Mud Lakes, and a single Mud Lake Number 2. We are also endowed with dozens of Long, Lost, Deer, Loon, Crystal, Perch, Pine, Round, Silver, and Spring lakes.

Some namers took it on themselves to be a bit more creative, however, and produced monikers such as Big Dummy Lake and the nearby Little Dummy Lake, named, presumably, for either an early Barron County settler or a characteristic trait of an early Barron County settler. There's Left Foot Lake in Marinette County, but no Right Foot Lake to be found. Vilas County boasts Nudist Lake, named perhaps for the activities occurring there, and Crawling Stone Lake, which was named for either an Indian legend or by the local drunk after a night on the town. In deference to the summer bug hatches, Vilas County also contains Noseeum Lake, named, undoubtedly, by an irritated fisherman.

There's Ding Dong Creek in Ashland County, and the ominous Smallpox Creek flows in Oneida County. And apparently an early explorer who spent a lot of time being lost named Million Acre Swamp in the heart of Price County.

Finally, some people know how to name a place to evoke just the right feeling. Wouldn't you love to spend your vacation on the shore of the Lake of Dreams? It's in Florence County. Or if you want to be honest about your leisure time endeavors, a few days on Columbia County's Lazy Lake would be just perfect.❀   —K.V.

Each state can place two statues of deceased citizens—commemorating distinguished civic or military service—in Statuary Hall in the United States Capitol. The two that Wisconsin so honors are Jacques Marquette and Robert M. LaFollette.❀

Soldier in Ouisconsin

In July of 1830, when Wisconsin was still part of Michigan Territory, and the name was spelled Ouisconsin, a young U.S. Army lieutenant led a file of mounted soldiers out of Fort Winnebago, at the Portage between the Fox and Wisconsin rivers. At dusk, they camped beside a lake in the Four Lakes country. Not even he realized it, but the lieutenant was a man of destiny. He would, in the next three decades, marry the daughter of a future President of the United States and serve the nation as congressman, senator, and secretary of war. As President of the Confederacy, he would lead part of this nation in a tragic war against itself. His name was Jefferson Finis Davis, and on that July evening in 1830 he was camped beside Lake Mendota near the future site of Madison.

In 1885, Davis wrote of his visit to the Four Lakes in a letter to Professor J.D. Butler of Madison:

> "While on detached service in the summer of 1829, I think, I encamped one night about the site of Madison. The nearest Indian village was on the opposite shore of the lake. Nothing, I think, was known to the garrison of Fort Winnebago, about the Four Lakes region before I was there. Indeed, sir, it may astonish you to learn, in view of the (now) densely populated condition of that country, that I and the file of soldiers who accompanied me, were the first white men who ever passed over the country between the Portage of the Wisconsin and Fox Rivers, and the then village of Chicago. When sent out on various expeditions, I crossed the Rock River at different points, but saw no sign of settlement above Dixon's Ferry [now Dixon, Illinois]."

Davis wrote of the event 55 years later and had the year wrong. Army records show him on detached service from Fort Winnebago in 1830. A graduate of West Point, he had been assigned to the Wisconsin frontier and arrived at Fort Crawford, in Prairie du Chien, in the spring of 1829. He was soon ordered to the Portage, where one of his duties was to cut lumber to be used in the building of Fort Winnebago.

Two years later, Davis was ordered back to Fort Crawford, and there he began to meet and associate with people with whom he would be involved for much of the rest of his life. There was Lt. Robert Anderson, who would have the misfortune to one day be the commanding officer at Fort Sumter, S.C., where the first shots of the Civil War were fired, and Albert Sidney Johnson, a school chum from Transylvania College in Lexington, Kentucky. Johnson would become one of the Confederacy's ablest generals, only to die in a hail of bullets at Shiloh, in Tennessee. His son William, born at Prairie du Chien, would serve on Davis' staff while he was President of the Confederacy. And when his duties took him into the southwestern corner of the state, Davis would stop at Sinsinawa Mound to visit George Wallace Jones, another friend from Transylvania College. Jones, whose two sons were to serve the cause of the Confederacy, became a Congressman from Michigan Territory and a U.S. Senator from Iowa. Because of his frontier friendship with Davis, Jones was imprisoned at the outbreak of the Civil War.

JEFFERSON DAVIS

In 1832, Colonel Zachary Taylor was named commanding officer at Fort Crawford and Jefferson Davis was named his adjutant. Davis fell in love with Taylor's youngest daughter, Sarah Knox, whom everyone called Knoxie. Eighteen years old (Davis was 23), she was slender and beautiful, with wavy brown hair and gray eyes. They began an ardent, but discreet, courtship, and Davis eventually spoke to Col. Taylor about marriage.

Taylor refused permission, and Davis and Knoxie became secretly engaged. When Colonel Taylor and Davis had a falling out over military matters, Taylor refused to allow Davis to call at his Prairie du Chien home, and forbade Knoxie to see him at all. Aided by mutual friends, the young lovers continued their courtship in secret. In warm weather, Knoxie would often take her younger sister and brother, Dickie, for long walks in the woods, where the trio would "happen across" Lt. Davis, and the children would run ahead and play. Thirty years later, Dickie Taylor, who was then six, became General Richard Taylor, Confederate States of America. His was the last Confederate Army east of the Mississippi to surrender at the conclusion of the Civil War.

Whether or not Colonel Taylor was involved is sheer speculation, but in 1833 Davis was assigned to a new regiment and sent to serve in the Southwest. Davis again requested Knoxie's hand in marriage, and Taylor again refused.

Jefferson Davis left Prairie du Chien at the end of April 1833. Sarah Knox gave him a heartsease, a type of pansy, to carry with him, and Davis often mentioned the flower in long love letters he wrote to Knoxie from the Southwest.

Dissatisfied with military life, Davis resigned from the army in 1835, and Sarah Knox Taylor decided to marry him, with or without her father's permission. Early that summer she took a riverboat to Louisville, Kentucky, and there, on June 17, she and Jefferson Davis were married. Davis took his bride to honeymoon at his sister's home in Louisiana, and tragedy struck. Both he and Knoxie were stricken with malaria and on September 15, less than three months after her marriage, Sarah Knox Taylor died.

Devastated, Davis went into seclusion for over eight years. Eventually he and Zachary Taylor were reconciled — tradition says it was during a chance meeting on a riverboat in 1845. Regardless, Davis led a regiment of Mississippi volunteers in the War with Mexico — under the command of Zachary Taylor.

After that war, Davis was elected to the U.S. Senate, and Taylor was elected President of the United States. Senator Davis was selected to help plan the inaugural ball, and was among the dignitaries who escorted President-elect Taylor to take the oath of office. And Davis was with family members at Taylor's bedside in the White House when he died in 1850.

Jefferson Davis was a senator from Mississippi when the Civil War clouds loomed on the horizon and that state seceded from the Union. Left without office, he returned home, anticipating serving the South in a military capacity. Instead, he was elected President of the Confederacy. On the day of his inauguration, March 5, 1861, Jefferson Davis was escorted from his hotel to the statehouse in Montgomery, Alabama, by members of the 1st Alabama Volunteers.

And therein lies a painful irony. A year later, the regiment surrendered Island No. 10 in the Mississippi River to overwhelming numbers, and over 1,000 Confederate prisoners of war were sent to Madison, Wisconsin. One hundred forty of them died — many from the 1st Alabama —and were buried in Madison's Forest Hill Cemetery. From the entrance to that cemetery, one can look down upon the lake beside which Jefferson Davis camped in 1830.❁   —D.D.

Fishin' Time
By Marian Phelps

Sunbeams playin' hide and seek
With the shadows 'long the creek
   Set a fellow wishin';
Every little breeze that brings
Spicy smells o' woodsy things
   Whispers: "Let's go fishin'."

Wish I was a little lad,
Barefoot, freckled country tad,
   Where the water's gleamin',
Just a wee, contented soul
With a saplin' fishin' pole,
   And a heart for dreamin'.

Bent pin fish-hook on a string
Seemin' quite the proper thing—
   How it sets me wishin'
For the good old dreamin' days
And the simple country ways—
   Say! I'm goin' fishin'!

Outdoor Recreation January 1925

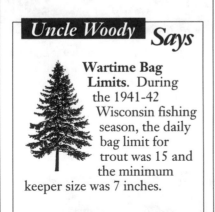

Uncle Woody *Says*

Wartime Bag Limits. During the 1941-42 Wisconsin fishing season, the daily bag limit for trout was 15 and the minimum keeper size was 7 inches.

Invented Right Here!

The Ice Cream Sundae

Ice cream etiquette was much stricter in the 19th century. In those days, a dish of ice cream was a dish of ice cream. Period. One summer day in 1881, George Hallaver strolled into Edward Berner's ice cream parlor in Two Rivers and in an instant changed the course of dairy history as he shattered all the rules of ice cream.

Hallaver asked Berner to put chocolate sauce, normally reserved for ice cream sodas, on top of his dish of ice cream. The stunned Berner complied.

Once a rule is broken, it can never be mended. The five-cent ice cream and chocolate sauce combination was an instant hit. A rival confectioner, alarmed about the low price, convinced Berner to sell the combination only on Sundays. Fortunately, a ten-year-old girl walked in during the week and asked Berner for one of the Sunday confections. Recognizing success when it hit him in the face, Berner began selling the dish every day. The name that has made millions of mouths water was coined by a glassware salesman when he placed an order for "sundae dishes" — the slender canoe-shaped dishes in which the concoction was served.❀   *—K.V.*

This 1895 garden near Phillips shows a wide variety of both vegetables and flowers. Father and son, in the foreground, proudly hold enormous turnips, carrots and a champion-size cabbage. Mother, in background, apparently was in charge of the flower garden.

—*State Historical Society of Wisconsin photo.*

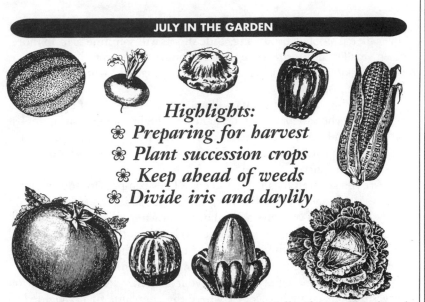

JULY IN THE GARDEN

Highlights:
❀ *Preparing for harvest*
❀ *Plant succession crops*
❀ *Keep ahead of weeds*
❀ *Divide iris and daylily*

The warm and humid weather of July, especially when it is combined with ample rainfall, is a boon to all Wisconsin gardens. Everywhere, cabbages are forming large and solid heads, broccoli is being harvested by the bushel, and bean pods seem to be lengthening on the bush by the hour.

Early tomatoes are now being harvested, and the standard varieties are already growing heavy on the vines. The sweet corn thrives in the heat of July, even if it got off to a slow start in the cool of May, and the squash are fairly bursting from their hills, threatening to overtake everything else in the garden. In July, we wonder why we fretted so much in May.

July is also the time when beginning gardeners learn the error of their spacing ways. Those tiny cabbage seedlings seemed to be so far apart when we set them out according to directions in April. So we moved them closer together, and now—oh my!—they are fighting for space and breathing room. *Follow the spacing directions.*

July is a month of harvest, of canning and preserving, of tending to growing crops— and of planting. All in all, a busy month for all of us. Consider the following:

When you pick that first head of beautiful broccoli, don't think that the plant has stopped producing. Side shoots will continue to form more, albeit smaller, heads for some time to come—right up to heavy frost, if you're lucky. These smaller heads are just as good-tasting as the main head—not just as showy.

All rapidly-growing plants will appreciate a feeding of compost tea right now, when their energy demands are high. Steep some compost or manure in buckets of water for a few days, then pour some of the tea around each plant. Plants—just like teenagers—need extra food during their growth spurts.

Are you keeping ahead of the weeds? They compete for soil nutrients and moisture, and they harbor harmful insects, so it pays to keep on top of the problem. If you have a good mulch down, your weeding time will be close to zero. If not, it's still not too late to gather up some spoiled hay or straw to mulch the vegetable garden. A few hours spent mulching mean very little weeding for the rest of the season!

Are there some empty spots in your garden? Perhaps where you harvested spinach or lettuce, or where the eggplants finally yielded to insect attack? If so, why not take an hour to put in some succession crops this month? You can plant a number of short-season crops now, and harvest them in September. The list of succession crops includes beans, broccoli, carrots, collards, late cabbage, beets, kale, cucumbers, and bunching onions. Chinese cabbage should be planted now, also, so that it can crisp up in the cool of September and October.

During the first week of the month, stop harvesting asparagus and rhubarb to allow plants to gain strength for next year's production. Dust squash vines with rotenone to kill squash borers. Inspect vines at soil level for signs of the borers. During the second week, stop feeding roses and other ornamental plants. Renovate old strawberry beds, and dig manure into the asparagus bed. During the third week, you may divide iris and daylily. Pinch back chrysanthemums to encourage branching. Transplant seedlings of broccoli, brussels sprouts, and cauliflower for the fall harvest.

Are you keeping up your garden diary? Be sure to note the dates on which you harvest each vegetable, when each crop finally petered out, and how satisfied you were with it. Your diary will be an invaluable aid in planning next year's garden. It is best to write in your diary while lying in a hammock under the cool shade of a tree, with a helpful glass of iced tea on a table by your side.❀ —J.M.

1 Fabulous Firsts

On July 29, 1847, the first Norwegian-American newspaper in the United States was published in Muskego. Its name was *Nordlyset* ("The Northern Light"); its editor was James DeNoon Reymert.

JULY RECIPE

Spicy Cranberry and Peach Salad Mold

1 28-ounce can sliced peaches
1/2 cup sugar
1/3 cup vinegar
1 large stick whole cinnamon
6 whole cloves

2 three-ounce packages orange gelatin
1-1/4 cup cold water
1 one-pound can whole berry cranberry sauce

Drain peaches, reserving juice. Measure juice and add water to make 1-1/2 cups liquid in all. Combine with the sugar, vinegar, and spices. Bring to a boil and simmer 5 minutes. Add sliced peaches and simmer 5 minutes longer. Remove peaches and spices from syrup. Measure syrup and add boiling water to make 2-1/2 cups in all. Dissolve the gelatin in this. Add the cold water. Cool. Chill until the consistency of heavy syrup. Break the canned cranberry sauce into small chunks with a fork. Add the peaches and cranberries to the gelatin. Turn into a 10" x 6" cakepan. Chill until firm. Cut into squares and serve on lettuce. Serves 8.

—*Betty Ringelspauch of Tomah.*

Pinch Those Onions!

For better onions from your garden, pinch off the flower buds from the onion plants as soon as you see them. If you can recognize the seed stalk coming from the neck of the onion, in fact, is is better to cut the stalk right then, to prevent the neck from becoming large and stunting the bulb. When the tops begin to wither and fall over, the onions are mature. When most of them have reached

this stage, you can knock down the others. —*Wisconsin Garden Guide*

JULY RECIPE

Fresh Berry Muffins

2 cups sifted flour
2 teaspoons baking powder
1/2 teaspoon salt
2 tablespoons sugar
1 egg, beaten
1 cup milk
2 tablespoons shortening,
    melted

1/2 cup Wisconsin berries, sliced

NOTE: 2 cups sliced, fresh berries equal two 10-ounce packages frozen unsweetened berries. Either strawberries or raspberries may be used.

Sift the dry ingredients, then moisten with the combined egg, milk, and shortening. Stir in berries, stirring only enough to thoroughly blend. Bake in well-greased muffin pans at 350° to 400° F., 20 to 25 minutes. Yield: 12 muffins.

Years Ago . . .

Madisonians may well feel proud of their splendid celebration of the nation's natal day. Flags and buntings floated from nearly all the business houses; private residences were also gaily festooned. The national colors fluttered from every flagstaff and were in the hands of a thousand patriotic persons—men, women, and children. As early as 4 o'clock yesterday morning the rattle and bang of cannons, firecrackers, and muskets awoke the echoes and notified all concerned the natal day had arrived. Through the day, crowds thronged the capitol park and streets or skimmed over the lake in steamers and row boats or visited the summer resorts along the shores. The parade was a grand affair. The floats representing the different lines of business were splendidly gotten up. The chariot containing forty-two young women representing the forty-two states of the union attracted great attention. The most telling design of the whole parade, however, was the large float representing soldier boys in camp while marching through Georgia, with their tents up, guns stacked and campfires burning brightly. In the evening many private displays of firecrackers were made.—*Wisconsin State Journal*, July 5, 1889.

AUGUST

Never return in August to what
you love;
Along the leaves will be rust
And over the hedges dust,
And in the air vague thunder and
silence burning . . .
Choose some happier time for your
returning.

—*Bernice Lesbia Kenyon, "Return"*

The month of summer's "dog days" brings
noticeably shorter days —the amount of
sunshine drops by more than an hour and a
quarter from the 1st to the 31st. August is the
second wettest month of the year —Madison
received a record rainfall for the month of
4.96 inches on August 8, 1906. August 8,
1882, produced a snowstorm on Lake
Michigan that covered the decks of ships
with six inches of snow. Snow showers were
observed at several points on shore that
strange summer day.❀

August Weather History

MADISON

Day	Record High		Record Low		Record Precip.		Average High/Low
1	101	1988	47	1976	2.79	1931	83/58
2	98	1988	44	1965	0.71	1963	83/58
3	96	1958	43	1966	1.68	1924	83/58
4	98	1947	41	1972	2.52	1916	83/58
5	97	1918	46	1957,78	2.01	1977	83/58
6	97	1918	45	1971	3.18	1935	82/58
7	94	1918	42	1976	2.61	1965	82/58
8	96	1941	44	1976	4.96	1906	82/58
9	95	1936	40	1972	1.80	1960	82/58
10	94	1958	44	1982	1.55	1887	82/58
11	98	1941	39	1967	1.42	1887	82/58
12	97	1918	38	1967	1.50	1875	82/58
13	93	1965	43	1967	1.93	1911	81/57
14	95	1988	37	1964	2.09	1981	81/57
15	95	1955,88	37	1979	2.20	1882	81/57
16	102	1988	38	1979	3.25	1886	81/57
17	102	1988	45	1981	0.71	1948	81/56
18	101	1936	41	1977	1.65	1965	81/56
19	97	1983	43	1981	1.33	1904	80/56
20	98	1916	39	1967	1.61	1952	80/56
21	101	1955	43	1970	1.85	1966	80/56
22	101	1947	44	1967	1.40	1892	80/55
23	100	1947	43	1952	3.00	1910	79/55
24	100	1947	41	1977	1.11	1892	79/55
25	94	1953	37	1958	1.74	1972	79/55
26	95	1953	39	1964	2.28	1986	79/54
27	95	1953	35	1968	2.78	1959	78/54
28	95	1955	38	1968,82	3.00	1869	78/54
29	94	1953	35	1965	1.78	1957	78/53
30	97	1953	40	1967	1.50	1956	77/53
31	100	1953	37	1967	1.54	1981	77/53

AUGUST

August Weather History

LA CROSSE

Day	Record High		Record Low		Average High/Low
1	105	1988	49	1976	84/63
2	103	1988	45	1948	84/63
3	101	1988	44	1894	84/63
4	99	1896	45	1912	84/62
5	96	1947	45	1948	84/62
6	98	1968	45	1948	83/62
7	98	1988	49	1976	83/62
8	101	1874	43	1904	83/62
9	98	1936	44	1927	83/62
10	96	1944	45	1982	83/62
11	96	1874	45	1982	83/62
12	98	1936	46	1982	83/61
13	95	1978	47	1946	82/61
14	95	1978	43	1964	82/61
15	100	1936	46	1929	82/61
16	101	1988	44	1976	82/61
17	103	1988	48	1981	82/60
18	98	1947	44	1943	81/60
19	97	1916	43	1950	81/60
20	97	1955	49	1967	81/60
21	103	1955	46	1921	81/60
22	96	1968	43	1923	80/59
23	102	1948	43	1891	80/59
24	104	1948	41	1934	80/59
25	99	1948	43	1958	79/58
26	95	1948	41	1934	79/58
27	95	1973	42	1915	79/58
28	97	1955	39	1891	78/58
29	95	1966	40	1965	78/57
30	95	1966	35	1915	78/57
31	95	1953	42	1967	77/56

The normal average precipitation for La Crosse in August is 3.70 inches. The wettest August was in 1980 when 9.84 inches was recorded; the driest was in 1894 when only 0.35 inches was received.

Excuses for an August Party

12 Betty Picnic

To honor all of Wisconsin's charming, good-natured, hard-working homemakers named Betty, this event recalls Elizabeth Fisher Baird. She was the great-granddaughter of an Indian chief, daughter of a fur trader, wife of a frontier lawyer, and chronicler of the distaff side of pioneer life in Wisconsin. Married at age 14 on August 12, 1824, she overcame the hardships of pioneer life, became an efficient wife and mother and a convivial hostess, and wrote with wit and perception about social life, travel and entertainment, and the customs of early Wisconsin.

15 Ice Water Appreciation Day

Especially the water of Wau-kesha. It was a hot August day in 1868 when Colonel Richard Dunbar happened to stop in Waukesha. Thirstily he drank from a mineral spring in a pasture near the edge of town. When he awoke the next day he was cured of his diabetes, or so he believed. The local paper wrote, "There has gurgled forth a fount of God's elixir of life, and the afflicted of every country shall look here for a revival of lost hopes." Dunbar and others promoted the Waukesha waters and built hotels and boarding houses. In a few years Waukesha was a fashionable and busy summer resort.

20 Family Reunion

Wisconsin is indeed the geographically correct location for a gathering of the clan, being equally convenient from both coasts. Furthermore, the town of Poniatowski, in Marathon County, is at the exact center of the northern half of the western hemisphere (lat. 45° N, long. 90° W), meaning that it is exactly halfway between the north pole and the equator, and is a quarter of the way around the earth from Greenwich, England.

Boating Party

In 1673, Father Jacques Marquette and Louis Jolliet set out on their brave explorations. They traveled the length of the Fox River, portaged to the Wisconsin River, and paddled far enough down the Mississippi River to conclude that it probably emptied into the Gulf of Mexico. They both kept journals of the trip but Jolliet lost his when the canoe overturned.

Invented Right Here!

The Outboard Motor

Ole Evinrude grew up on a farm on the banks of Lake Ripley, near Cambridge. As a boy, he developed a lifelong love of boats and boating by designing and building sailboats. When he left the farm, learned metalworking and engineering, and settled in Milwaukee, his work involved building gasoline engines.

In 1909, Evinrude was picnicking on Okauchee Lake in Waukesha County. He bought some ice cream and rowed out to the picnic site. When he arrived, the ice cream had melted. Irritated by the experience, he went home and, combining his knowledge of boats with his engine-building skills, he designed his "detachable rowboat motor," to get a rowboat to the picnic before the ice cream melted. Evinrude's first outboard motor was a 1.5 horsepower unit weighing in at 62 pounds.

He sold his Evinrude Motor Company in 1913, but went on making outboard motors. In 1929, he merged several companies with his original Evinrude Company to form the Outboard Motor Corporation.❧ —K.V.

Dog Day Fishing

During the hottest part of summer, many gamefish move into colder areas of lakes when the water temperature climbs. Try fishing in areas where cold water streams enter lakes. Also, take advantage of lake maps and find out where underwater springs flow up from the bottom. We've taken large northern pike from such places where the water was from only two to five feet deep.

Much of the best dog day fishing is found in early morning and evenings when large fish move into the shallows to feed. Top-water and shallow-running lures are good. Work them around the edges of shore-lines, stumps, and off the edges of sand and gravel bars.

Dawn, dusk, and night hours are particularly productive on trout streams, too. In fact, many trophy-sized stream trout confine their feeding exclusively to night hours. A large dry fly skittered across your favorite pool at night is capable of producing memorable action.❧

AUGUST IN THE GARDEN

Highlights:
❋ *Sow seeds of perennials*
❋ *Divide established perennials*
❋ *Start new lawns and repair old ones*
❋ *Plant vegetables for fall harvest*

Songs Spring thought perfection
Summer Criticizes:
What in May escaped detection,
August, past surprises,
Notes—and names each blunder.
—Robert Browning

Browning was speaking to the gardener. August is truly the test of our spring garden plan. The mistakes we have made through the first four months of the gardening season now stand out like so many sore thumbs. There's no hiding the fact that we planted the tomatoes and cabbages much more closely than was recommended. That we didn't bother to stagger the plantings of sweetcorn. That we mulched too thinly. And especially that we planted the marigolds behind the delphiniums! Horrors! August, indeed, names each blunder. And now is a good time to note those blunders, ourselves—in a garden diary, so that we don't make the same mistakes next season!

In another sense, however, August forgives all, for this is the month of harvest in Wisconsin, and our dinner plates overflow with succulent sweetcorn, deep green broccoli, tangy red tomatoes, and tender new potatoes. Our salad bowls truly runneth over. And, for the good gardener, there is plenty to can, dry, and freeze for next winter's enjoyment. With all our mistakes, Mother Nature has been kind once again.

The first half of August is a good time to sow perennial seeds outdoors. The list is a long one, and includes achillea, lychnis, arabis (rock cress), foxglove, armeria, carnation, columbine, lantern plant, baby's breath, geum, gaillardia, delphinium, garden pinks, sweet william, hollyhock, hibiscus, shasta daisy, pyrethrum, flax, platycodon (balloon flower), liatris, tritoma, and soapwort. You may also divide established perennials this month, and exchange some with friends to broaden your collection.

Early in the month, make the final plantings of radishes, lettuce, spinach, and beets for fall harvest. You can also start new lawns and repair old ones at this time. Evergreens may be transplanted anytime during the month.

Don't neglect the soil moisture needs of fruiting vegetables, fruits, and blossoming flowers. Give some compost tea to all such active plants, to encourage their good performance.

You may set out nursery-grown chrysanthemum plants now for color in September and October. For growing indoors over the winter, take cuttings of geraniums, coleus, and basil. Dig and pot up some chives and parsley for the winter windowsill garden, also. ❀   —J.M.

Tips on Using Fresh Cherries

When cooking with fresh cherries, it is helpful to chill the cherries in very cold water for 2 to 3 hours (not longer). This allows the fruit to firm, so that it won't fall apart when pitted. If you don't have a cherry pitter, use the classic hairpin or paper clip, kitchen fork or plastic straw punch. Gather the family together and make pitting a family affair. Bleach or lemon juice works well to remove dark stains from hands after pitting. ✿

—*Wisconsin Red Cherry Growers Association*

Keeping Cabbages

Cabbages can be stored for a short time in a cool cellar, by pulling out the head, getting as much of the root as possible, tying a paper bag around the head, and hanging it up by the root. Or, you may store them underground, covering them with layers of soil and straw to protect them against freezing. ✿

Winter Beets

Beets planted in early- to mid-August can be harvested just before the first severe frost of the autumn. Packed in sand and kept barely moist at a temperature of 35 to 40 degrees F., they will last for several months, probably into January. For best results, use a variety especially developed as a winter beet, such as Lutz Green Leaf. ✿

—*Wisconsin Garden Guide*

AUGUST RECIPE

Green Beans and Tomato Vinaigrette

3/4 pound fresh green beans
Salt to taste
2 teaspoons Dijon-style mustard
1/2 teaspoon minced garlic
2 tablespoons red-wine vinegar
4 tablespoons olive or
    vegetable oil
Freshly ground pepper to taste
1/8 teaspoon ground cumin
2 tablespoons chopped fresh
    basil or chives
3 red ripe tomatoes, about one
    pound, sliced 1/4 inch thick
1/4 cup finely chopped red onion.

Trim off the ends of the beans. Drop them into boiling salted water to cover, and cook until crisp-tender, about 5 minutes. Do not overcook. Drain and let cool.

Place the mustard, garlic and vinegar in a salad bowl. Gradually add the oil while stirring with a wire whisk. Add salt, pepper, cumin, and basil or chives. Stir and blend. Add the green beans, tomatoes and red onion. Toss and serve.

Yield: 4 servings.

AUGUST RECIPE

Speedy Swiss-Stuffed Eggplant
(A Microwave Recipe)

2 eggplants (about 1 pound each)
1/2 cup sliced green onions, including green tops
1 large clove garlic, minced
1/3 cup tomato juice or water
2 tablespoons olive oil or vegetable oil
2 cups seasoned croutons
2-1/2 cups (10 ounces) shredded Wisconsin Swiss cheese
1/4 teaspoon thyme
1/8 to 1/4 teaspoon pepper
Paprika

Halve eggplants lengthwise.   Loosen and scoop out pulp leaving shells about 1/3 inch thick; reserve shells. Coarsely chop pulp; combine in 2-quart microwave dish with onions, garlic, tomato juice and oil. Microwave, covered with plastic wrap, on high power 2 minutes. Mix; microwave, covered, 2 minutes longer. Add croutons, 2 cups of the cheese, the thyme and pepper. Toss to mix. Spoon into eggplant shells, dividing equally. Sprinkle tops with the remaining cheese. Dust with paprika. Place on microwave platter, spoke fashion. Microwave at high power 8 minutes, turning a quarter turn every 2 minutes. Let stand 5 minutes.
Makes 4 servings.

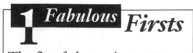
Fabulous Firsts

The first father and son to serve together in the United States Senate were Wisconsin Senator Henry Dodge and Iowa Senator Augustus Caesar Dodge. They sat from December 7, 1848, to February 22, 1855. Previously they had served as delegates to the House of Representatives, from March 4, 1841, to March 3, 1845, before their territories had attained statehood.

The Chinaberry Tree
ANN C. HALLER

To say they don't make women like my grandmother anymore would be absurd. They never did. She was, I think, unique.

When others wax nostalgic about their grandmothers' kitchens I can go along—up to a point. Certainly her kitchen contained all the ingredients for nostalgia. There was the usual massive black iron range from which rose the mouth-watering aromas. There was the coffee grinder for the freshly roasted beans, the egg basket, even the old soapstone sink above which hung the communal dipper. The dipper was germ free, of course. Grandmother did not believe in germs. What she did not believe in did not exist, at least not in her house.

Unfortunately for me, the kitchen also frequently contained my grandmother.

For many years I thought that my grandmother disliked me. Through a rather erratic process of reasoning in my later years I have come to believe that I may have done her an injustice She was very much a person of absolutes: black and white, good and evil, your way and her way. Her first grandchild, my older sister, could in her eyes do no wrong. I was her second. It may have been simply a matter of balance.

Grandmother rarely raised her voice. If something annoyed her it was banished immediately, mentally and/or physically from her presence. And no matter how hard I tried to practice the virtues expected of me, inevitably I erred. Her pale blue gaze would sweep over me, she would point with a full-armed swing to the back door, and she uttered one word, *"Heraus!"* I spent a great deal of time under the old chinaberry tree in the backyard, counting my sins like a doleful rosary.

It was small comfort to realize finally that she applied this tactic impartially. Aunts, uncles, cousins, the iceman, the milkman, my grandfather, even my own mother, at one time or another suffered banishment. No one ever argued. They departed quickly and quietly.

The results were not all bad. I became a very well-behaved and obedient child. Thin and nervous and fast on my feet perhaps, but most certainly obedient. Even today, half a century later, if someone said *"Heraus"* in my ear in the proper tone of voice, I would probably scuttle mindlessly to the nearest exit and the comforting shelter of the chinaberry tree.

Grandmother's use of the word *heraus* stemmed from a firm if mistaken belief that she spoke fluent German. Brought to this country at the age of six months, she developed over the years a language all her own, one understood only by her immediate family. At one gathering a puzzled European asked which German dialect she was speaking. "My own," she answered, and courteously continued a polite social dialogue intelligible only to herself.

As I grew old enough for comparisons I began to admire and envy her superb sense of her own worth. She would not have understood today's women with their liberation movements and fights for equal rights. If she thought about it at all, which I doubt, I am sure she considered herself the equal if not the superior of most of those whom she encountered in her lifetime. Her creed was summed up in the remark with which she ended one minor skirmish with my grandfather. "I am right and I know I am right. Even if I am wrong I am still right," she said. Nobody laughed.

When I was twelve we moved to another city. Returning after an absence of several years, I was shocked when I saw my grandmother. The head of the woman I remembered as ten feet tall came barely above my shoulder, and I am not a tall woman. We chatted pleasantly for a while, my grandmother was quite charming, and I became vaguely uneasy. Either my memory was totally at fault or someone had switched grandmothers on me.

It was, of course, merely a lull. At dinner my grandmother announced that she had decided to attend a movie that evening. A nod in my direction told me who would accompany her. A grandson hurriedly called his girl and told her he would be a little late. I began to feel more at home.

At her appointed time Grandmother was tenderly handed into the car and carefully driven the two full blocks to the neighborhood theater. It was obvious to me that she had been there before. The young woman selling tickets turned pale and gave us an overly cordial greeting. The ticket taker snapped to attention as we entered. The odd behavior of the flashlight in the hand on the usher was explained when I realized he was trembling, although Grandmother spoke kindly to him as we followed him down the aisle.

Where a wide aisle bisected the theater our small cortege halted. Stabbing with her cane in the direction of the two end seats, my grandmother uttered the single word *"Heraus!"* A large bag of popcorn supported by two small boys immediately arose from the seats and vanished into the darkness.

Grandmother's hand on my arm guided me firmly toward the second seat. I had the strangest feeling that if I looked down I would find I was wearing the ruffled organdy, the white silk socks, and the gleaming patent leather slippers of my long-vanished childhood. Whoever said you can't go home again had obviously never known my grandmother.

The people who ran the movie theater just as obviously did. Settled comfortably in her chosen seat, Grandmother waved away the hovering usher and glanced back over her shoulder. The house lights promptly dimmed. Nodding regally in the direction of the screen, Grandmother allowed the movie to begin. ❧

From: <u>We Were Children Then, Volume II</u>, published by NorthWord Press, Inc., Minocqua, WI.

Years Ago . . .

LAKE GENEVA—Lake Geneva is becoming a very popular resort. Thousands are now camping on its shores in the various camps and parks surrounding the lake. It is worthy of note that, while some of the wealthy are enjoying rest and recreation themselves, they have not forgotten the poor and have put their hearts to noble deeds of charity by establishing a Fresh Air camp for the poor children of Chicago.— *Wisconsin State Journal*, August 10, 1889.

AUGUST RECIPE

Eggplant and Zucchini Casserole

2 small eggplants, about 3/4 pound
2 small zucchini, about 3/4 pound
4 tablespoons olive oil
1 tablespoon finely chopped garlic
1 cup coarsely chopped onions
1 bunch scallions, cut into 1-inch lengths
4 ripe plum tomatoes, about 3/4 pound, cut
    into 1/4-inch cubes
4 sprigs thyme or 1 teaspoon dried
1 bay leaf
2 sprigs fresh rosemary or 1 teaspoon dried
2 teaspoons grated orange rind
1/2 cup coarsely chopped fresh basil or parsley

1. Trim ends of eggplants; do not peel them. Cut into 3/8-inch cubes. There should be about 4 cups.

2. Trim ends of zucchini; do not peel. Cut into 3/8-inch cubes. There should be about 4 cups.

3. In a heavy casserole, heat oil. When it is very hot, add eggplant and zucchini. Cook, stirring, for about 4 minutes. Add garlic, onions and scallions. Cook, stirring, about 5 minutes.

4. Add tomatoes, thyme, bay leaf, rosemary, and orange rind. Stir well and cook over medium heat for 10 minutes. Stir often.

5. Remove bay leaf and add basil. Check seasoning. Serve immediately.

Yield: 4 servings.

Wisconsin Cheddar

Cheddar is America's favorite cheese! Americans eat an average of 10 pounds per person each year. Wisconsin is the leader in Cheddar making ... 850 million pounds each year or 37 percent of the nation's total production. Cheddar is just one of Wisconsin's 200 varieties, styles, and types of cheese. Wisconsin cheesemakers consistently win the National and World Championships for Cheddar, making "Wisconsin Cheese the taste worth looking for." Wisconsin Cheddar is so versatile ... use it on cheese trays, as a snack, or for cooking. It's perfect!

How is Cheddar made?

"Cheddar" refers to the traditional method used to make this popular variety. A cheese that is "Cheddared" has its compacted curd cut into slabs which are turned and stacked at intervals of 10-15 minutes for about 1-1/2 hours. This procedure presses out the excess moisture and forms tightly knit, uniformly textured cheese. The compacted curds are then broken into small pieces (milled), packed into molds, and pressed before being stored for aging.

What is the difference between Golden and White Cheddar?

White and Golden Cheddar are the same. It is a matter of personal and regional preference. The rich yellow-orange color comes from the addition of a natural vegetable dye called "annatto."

What does "mild," "medium," "sharp," or "extra sharp" Cheddar mean?

As Cheddar ages, the moisture content decreases and it becomes more crumbly in texture and sharper and more tangy in flavor. The more aged the Cheddar, the easier it melts and blends into sauces. The younger the Cheddar, the stretchier it is when melted.

"**MILD**" Aged up to 3 months. Mellow subtle flavor, slightly stretchy texture makes it best for snacks and casseroles.

"**MEDIUM**" Aged from 3 to 6 months. Rich full-bodied flavor, melts evenly in sauces, great for snacks and for cooking.

"**SHARP**" Aged from 6 to 12 months. Strong savory flavor, melts evenly in sauces and adds more flavor to recipes and snack trays.

"**EXTRA SHARP**" Aged from 12 to 24 months. Tangy assertive flavor, crumbly; excellent for full Cheddar flavor in sauces, cooked dishes, and snack trays.

By federal regulations, raw milk Cheddar (made from unpasteurized milk) must be aged a minimum of 60 days.

How to care for Cheddar

Keep all cheeses clean, cold, and covered. Plan to use within a month or two.

Cheddar may be frozen in one-pound pieces or less for up to 3 months. Freeze quickly . . . thaw slowly. Cheese that has been frozen may have a crumbly texture. It is best to use for cooking. ✿

Years Ago . . .

MADISON—A local sportsman fishing off Picnic Point was surprised by a fearful splash and a rush through the water nearby the boat and saw some great monster going by at a fearful rate. "What it was I do not know, but I am certain it was at least five to ten feet long and of a peculiar shape. Its violent plunge through the water rocked the boat so much that I was nearly pitched out. I got out of that locality and rowed for home as lively as I could make the boat fly through the water and I have never been over to that part of the lake alone since. I believe the boys who saw a serpent ten feet long on the banks of the Catfish in the town of Westport may have seen that very same animal that struck terror in my mind. I would not go bathing in Lake Mendota for $50, no sir."— *Wisconsin State Journal,* August 17, 1889.

SEPTEMBER

By all these lovely tokens
September days are here,
With the summer's best of weather
And autumn's best of cheer.

—Helen Hunt Jackson, "September"

September's weather swings back and forth from summer to autumn and autumn to summer. It is a time for gathering the harvest, of reaping nature's bounty. The full moon nearest the first day of autumn is called the Harvest Moon. Fall begins with the autumnal equinox, on or about the 21st. On that day the sun rises in the true east and sets in the true west; day and night are of equal length everywhere on the earth. As temperatures cool, Wisconsin's leaves put on a magnificent display of color, moving from north to south as the month progresses. On September 1-3, 1905, known as "Black September" on Lake Superior, an early season storm wrecked four ships with the loss of 39 lives.❧

September Weather History

MADISON

Day	Record High		Record Low		Record Precip.		Average High/Low
1	99	1953	36	1967	3.04	1937	77/52
2	98	1953	37	1976	1.43	1887	77/52
3	92	1960	38	1974	1.03	1953	77/52
4	94	1925	35	1974	2.10	1947	76/51
5	93	1954	36	1962	1.46	1946	76/51
6	97	1922	34	1962	2.28	1938	75/51
7	97	1939	36	1986	3.33	1942	75/51
8	97	1978	37	1986	2.79	1941	75/50
9	97	1955	36	1975	1.92	1965	74/50
10	95	1931	33	1967	2.00	1876	74/50
11	93	1931	34	1955	1.57	1879	74/49
12	91	1927	31	1955	3.21	1915	73/49
13	93	1939	31	1964	2.34	1961	73/49
14	96	1939	32	1963	2.63	1914	73/48
15	96	1939	33	1966	1.60	1931	72/48
16	91	1931	33	1966	1.74	1915	72/48
17	90	1955	36	1980	2.64	1907	72/47
18	92	1955	33	1959	3.40	1874	71/47
19	89	1948	32	1956	1.88	1931	71/47
20	89	1908	28	1956	3.34	1878	71/46
21	90	1908	33	1974,82	1.42	1950	71/46
22	89	1937	25	1974	1.37	1988	70/46
23	90	1937	26	1974	2.55	1970	70/45
24	88	1935	26	1976	2.07	1899	70/45
25	89	1920	30	1942	1.74	1931	69/45
26	87	1974	27	1966	1.27	1880	69/44
27	87	1954	29	1964	1.57	1902	69/44
28	89	1971	27	1964	1.21	1904	68/44
29	90	1953	28	1967	1.52	1986	68/44
30	88	1971	30	1967	1.72	1881	68/43

SEPTEMBER

September Weather History

LA CROSSE

Day	Record High		Record Low		Average High/Low
1	98	1913	36	1949	77/56
2	98	1937	40	1946	77/56
3	95	1925	38	1974	76/55
4	95	1925	37	1891	76/55
5	95	1922	40	1918	76/55
6	101	1922	41	1988	75/54
7	100	1978	40	1986	75/54
8	99	1978	35	1883	74/54
9	100	1955	38	1924	74/53
10	99	1931	34	1917	74/53
11	97	1895	34	1943	73/53
12	92	1931	35	1955	73/52
13	94	1939	32	1902	73/52
14	96	1939	31	1923	72/52
15	96	1939	34	1916	72/51
16	94	1931	34	1916	72/51
17	93	1988	31	1943	71/51
18	95	1955	32	1929	71/50
19	94	1895	34	1929	71/50
20	93	1908	33	1897	70/50
21	93	1891	32	1918	70/49
22	94	1895	33	1913	70/49
23	91	1891	32	1983	70/49
24	92	1891	29	1950	69/48
25	89	1920	28	1947	69/48
26	88	1986	29	1984	69/48
27	86	1987	30	1889	68/47
28	89	1904	27	1942	68/47
29	87	1898	23	1949	68/47
30	86	1971	24	1899	67/47

The normal average precipitation for La Crosse in September is 3.47 inches. The wettest September was in 1881 when 10.87 inches was recorded; the driest was in 1940 when only 0.29 inches was received.

Excuses for a September Party

Labor Day (first Monday)

In 1886 thousands of Milwaukee workers went on strike to demand an eight-hour day. Governor Jeremiah Rusk suppressed riots by calling up the militia, but lives were lost. Defending his action, he declared, "I seen my duty and I done it." Wisconsin was the first state to provide jobless benefits. In 1936 a check for $15 to a Madison man was the first unemployment check issued in this country from a state unemployment fund.

4 I-90/94 Appreciation Day

Seven miles of I-94 in Waukesha County was the first stretch of Interstate Highway in Wisconsin. Miss Concrete, Miss Black Top, and state and county officials gathered for the dedication ceremony on September 4, 1958, when Governor Vernon W. Thomson cut the ribbon that officially opened the highway. Today approximately 400 miles of Wisconsin's 108,000 highway miles are part of the Interstate system.

7 Shirley Abrahamson Day

On September 7, 1976, Shirley S. Abrahamson was sworn in as the first woman justice on the Wisconsin Supreme Court. Twenty years earlier, although she ranked first in her class in law school, the dean advised her that she could not expect to find employment as a lawyer since so few firms would be willing to hire a woman. She did become a lawyer, however, as well as a professor, legal scholar, and lecturer at home and abroad. She frequently travels around the state to speak in schools and before civic groups about the court system.

Back to School

In Watertown in 1856 Margarethe Meyer Schurz formed the first kindergarten in America, consisting of six children, two of them her own. From her native Germany she brought the concept and skills for its organization and teaching, as well as the German word *kindergarten*.

The Last Covered Bridge in Wisconsin

Weathered to a silver gray, Cedar Creek Bridge stands majestically beside a small roadside park in Ozaukee County —three miles north of Cedarburg and five miles from the shores of Lake Michigan. Built to span Cedar Creek in 1876, the bridge served faithfully until it was retired in 1962—the last covered bridge in Wisconsin.

Few things in today's world evoke more images of a bygone era or the romance of rural America than does a covered bridge. Happening across one of the narrow, one-lane roofed structures quickly takes you back to the nineteenth century. Look inside, and you'll quite likely find century-old dates and initials carved into the massive beams. It takes but little imagination to hear the creak of a buggy and the clip-clop of horses' hoofs, or to picture grandpa giving grandma a peck on the cheek in such a place. In fact, in the last century, covered bridges were often called Kissing Bridges or Tunnels of Love.

While Wisconsin was on the northernmost edges of the covered bridge belt in the Midwest, there were still about 60 covered bridges constructed in the state.

As settlements, mines and mills sprang up, and trails were cut into the interior, stage lines first made their appearance in Wisconsin (then part of Michigan territory) in the 1830s. Fording places on many streams were frequently flooded and an early need arose for bridges at key points. Covered bridge building reached its peak in Wisconsin between 1870 and 1880, with most of the structures built within the Wisconsin River watershed and the upper Rock River.

The biggest concentration of covered bridges in Wisconsin was on the Baraboo River, with seven in Sauk County, six of which crossed the Baraboo River. Three of these were located in the city of Baraboo and remained in service until the 1920s, when they were razed.

Dozens of romantic theories have been offered as to why bridges were covered, but the roof and weatherboard siding were not for the protection of travelers, or horses, or loads of hay, or to keep snow off the bridge floor. The real reason was unromantically practical—the roofs and sides were added to protect the main structural trusses from weather in a time long before the development of wood preservatives.

Most people think of covered bridges as a trend that began in Colonial America, but the idea of roofing a bridge came from Europe. There are covered bridges standing in Switzerland that date back to medieval times.

The covered bridge-building era in the U.S. began at Philadelphia in 1805 and lasted for most of the nineteenth century. Between 15,000 and 20,000 covered bridges were built. Most were constructed without nails— fitted together and held in place with "tree nails"—wooden pegs which were hammered into position. The twentieth century has been hard on the old roofed structures. By the 1930s, 75 percent of those built were gone—lost to neglect, old age, vandalism, fire, food, and "progress." Today only about 950 historic covered bridges are left in America.

When old timers in Wisconsin talk about covered bridges, four famous bridges come to light —the span across the Wisconsin River at Bridgeport, near Prairie du Chien; the Boscobel Bridge; the Portage span across the Wisconsin River; and the Clarence Bridge across the Sugar River near Brodhead.

The 630-foot **Portage Bridge**—a massive three-section span across the Wisconsin River—was built in 1857 at a cost of $41,146, and was one of the first covered bridges in the state. It carried traffic into the twentieth century, only to be demolished by a cyclone on August 8, 1905.

The **Bridgeport Bridge**, a 650-foot span across the Wisconsin River about six miles south of Prairie du Chien, was on the old Military Road. Erected in 1857, and rebuilt in 1892, it was close to the water, with an iron drawbridge for river navigation on the Bridgeport side, plus a lengthy trestle stretching to the south shore. It was privately owned and operated, and was a toll bridge from 1870 until 1930, when the state bought it. The old bridge was dismantled and replaced by a modern steel structure in 1934.

The granddaddy of all Wisconsin covered bridges was the **Boscobel Bridge**, which spanned the Wisconsin River between Grant and Iowa counties. It was an odd 655-foot combination of iron from Pittsburgh and wood from Green Bay. From the north bank, where the village of Manhattan once stood, a single covered span connected with a 150-foot iron draw bridge (the Wisconsin River was still navigable at the time). Next came two more covered spans, then a fixed iron truss that carried on to the Boscobel side.

No less a personality than famed Wisconsin historian Ruben Gold Thwaites, who admittedly disliked covered bridges, described the Boscobel Bridge as "an ugly, clumsy structure, housed in like a tunnel and dark as a pocket." Perhaps the famed historian was afraid of the dark. Regardless, the Boscobel toll bridge kept going for 60 years until the city sold it to the state in 1935 for $22,778. The bridge was demolished and replaced with the current open iron structure in 1937.

The **Clarence Bridge**, which spanned the Sugar River three miles southwest of Brodhead, in southern Wisconsin, has achieved more fame

Cedar Creek Bridge.

in passing than while it was still in existence. Built in 1864, it stood until 1934. Its fame came via Brodhead barn painter Frank Engebretson, whose huge barn murals of Wisconsin scenes gained national attention. When photos of Engebretson's mural of the Clarence Bridge, painted on a small barn in Brodhead, appeared in *Life* magazine, the bridge's fame was assured.

When the plans were drawn for a bridge near Cedarburg, in Ozaukee County, in 1876, it was decided to build it with white pine from the Baraboo Bluffs. All the timbers and planks were cut and squared at a mill near Baraboo, then hauled some 75 miles to the bridge site. The bridge was built on the Town lattice design. The design, patented by Ithiel Town in 1820, uses a criss-cross arrangement for the interior framing, much like that of a rose trellis in a flower garden. The single 120-foot span, erected over Cedar Creek on a town road, was given a board-and-batten finish, and has openings near the roof line to admit light.

Through the years the suburbs of Milwaukee stretched northward, and what was once a rural road past Cedarburg to the covered bridge became a busy highway. A strengthening center pier was placed beneath the bridge in 1927, and as early as 1940, the bridge was marked for permanent preservation as a historic monument by a far-sighted Ozaukee County Highway Commission. After years of discussion, during which traffic on the old bridge became heavier and heavier, the bridge was retired in 1962. Still standing on its original location, the bridge remains open to foot traffic, serving as a tribute to a time long past.✵   —*D.D.*

Celsius vs Fahrenheit

While it has not gained acceptance in the United States, the Celsius temperature scale is used virtually everywhere else in the world. Celsius measures the freezing point of water as 0 degrees C and the boiling point as 100 degrees C at sea level. The scale was devised in 1742 by the Swedish astronomer Anders Celsius (1701-1744) and was originally called centigrade. While the designation Celsius has been official since 1948, centigrade remains in common use.

One degree Celsius is 1.8 times bigger than a degree Fahrenheit, the temperature scale commonly used in the United States. However, -40 degrees is the same on both scales.

To convert degrees Celsius to Fahrenheit, use the formula T (degrees C) = 5/9 T(degrees F) - 32. ❀   —*D.D.*

SEPTEMBER RECIPE

Cream of Potato-Broccoli-Cheese Soup

3 cups chicken broth	4 tablespoons butter
1 cup chopped onion	4 tablespoons flour
2 cups diced potatoes	1 teaspoon salt
1 cup cut broccoli	2 cups milk
8 ounces shredded	dash white pepper
Swiss cheese	dash dill weed

In large saucepan combine chicken broth, chopped onion, diced potatoes, and cut broccoli. Bring mixture to boiling. Reduce heat; cover and simmer until vegetables are tender. Place half the vegetables in blender. Blend 30 to 60 seconds, or until smooth. Pour blended vegetables back into unblended vegetables. In another saucepan melt butter. Blend in flour and salt. Add the milk all at once. Cook and stir until mixture is thickened and bubbly. Stir in shredded cheese; stir until melted. Pour into vegetable mixture. Heat through; add pepper and dill weed to taste. Serves 6-8.

—*Shirley Silberhorn, Fort Atkinson*

Wisconsin's Orient Express

If you were visiting friends in China or Korea, what gift from Wisconsin would they most like you to bring along? Chances are, they'd be very pleased with a gift of ginseng root.

Ginseng? Wisconsin growers have been cultivating this most Oriental herb since the 1890s. Today, more than 1200 growers, the majority in Marathon County, are the source of 90 percent of the ginseng grown in the U.S. And 95 percent of American-grown ginseng is exported to the Orient.

Ginseng is one of the most important ingredients in Oriental herbal medicines. It is a cure-all, recognized as a tonic and a sedative. It strengthens the heart, promotes body secretions, and strengthens the body's resistance to physical and mental stress. It is alleged to cure asthma, amnesia, dizziness, headaches, nausea, and fever. And, according to rumor, it's an aphrodisiac.

The herb is taken as a powder in a capsule, in a liquid extract, or a piece of the root is chewed. The powdered root or leaves can be made into tea.

Oriental ginseng, a different species from the North American species grown in Wisconsin, has been part of Oriental medicine for more than two thousand years. American ginseng was used by the Indians. A Jesuit missionary in sixteenth century China became familiar with ginseng and theorized that ginseng might also grow in Canada, with its similar climate. In 1716, a Jesuit in Canada read the theory, and did indeed find wild ginseng. Within a few years, French fur traders and their Indian helpers were gathering American ginseng for shipment to China.

American pioneers, including Daniel Boone, supplemented their income by gathering wild ginseng for export to China. Thus, Americans have been exporting ginseng to the Orient for more than 200 years. Surely ginseng is one of the earliest American exports to the Far East. And today, Wisconsin leads that Orient Express.

Wisconsin's ginseng growers plant seeds or seedlings in spring. Because the plants are native to the forest, they need lots of shade. They are grown in raised beds under lath-roofed or net-covered open-sided sheds. In four to six years the roots are ready for harvest. In mid-October, the grower carefully digs the mature roots, being careful to avoid damage. Only intact roots bring a good price. The roots are then dried. In a good year, ginseng roots bring $40 to $60 per pound, making ginseng production a $40 million business. ❧   —*K.V.*

Working Girls on the Farm
It's a Cow's Life

Cows have long been an integral part of Wisconsin. After the Civil War, wheat and hops, the previous agricultural mainstays, were slowly replaced by dairy farms as immigrants from Switzerland, Germany, and Scandinavia brought their dairying skills to Wisconsin.

Of course, the development of an industry is never smooth, and the first Wisconsin-produced butter did nothing to make our reputation as the dairy state. The butter was so bad that buyers used it to lubricate wagons and equipment. No one, apparently, actually ate it.

But Wisconsin's dairymen persisted. The butter got better. And the first commercial cheese factory opened in Fond du Lac in 1864. Wisconsin's 200,000 cows had hit their stride. Soon hundreds of cheese factories were producing. Wisconsin cheese-makers developed Colby and brick cheese, both of which were well received throughout the United States. In 1872 Wisconsin cheese was exported to England, the beginning of a world-wide reputation.

And just who is responsible for Wisconsin's place at the top of the dairy heap? Our Holsteins, Guernseys, Brown Swiss, Ayrshire, Milking Shorthorns, and our beautiful doe-eyed Jerseys. Wisconsin is the home of 1.8 million of these bovine beauties.

Their tasks in life are uncomplicated: eat, produce milk and calves, and, at the end of long and dedicated service, to become the main ingredient in a fast-food hamburger.

In spite of their current trendiness in such cosmopolitan centers as New York, a cow's lifestyle is anything but fast paced or stressful.

Let's start with cow basics. The average cow weighs between about 900 and 1600 pounds, depending on the breed. Wisconsin cows produce, on the average, 13,500 pounds of milk annually. (That's nearly 1600 gallons a year, or about 4.3 gallons every day, 365 days a year.) To produce the milk, she'll drink some ten to thirty gallons of water every day, and chow down in the neighborhood of 5000 pounds of grain and feed concentrates annually — not to mention plenty of grass and hay.

While life is simple for a cow, it is more complicated in this age of high-tech than it was for her great-grandsires and great-granddams. These days, milking is done by machine. Feed can be dispensed by computer-controlled machines. And her sex life is usually limited to an annual visit by the artificial insemination technician, with his long rubber glove and syringe. These days, close to 75 percent of Wisconsin's dairy farmers have their cows bred by artificial insemination.

How a cow spends her day varies with the time of year and whether or not she's giving milk. During the warm months, cows spend most of their time outdoors, hanging around the barnyard or pasture, grazing or chewing their cuds. (Cows gulp down their food without chewing. Later, they regurgitate the "cud" and chew it leisurely.) Cows spend about six hours a day eating, and another eight chewing their cuds. Mix in two milkings — one early in the morning, and one late afternoon — sleeping, and just standing around swatting flies, and you've got a pretty full cow day.

In the winter, cows stay inside the barn virtually all the time. Since cows are not physical fitness fanatics, they don't seem to mind eating, chewing cuds, and getting milked without having to move.

Because of their placid nature, cows like routine. Herd dynamics are important to a cow's well-being. In every herd, each cow has her place. The dominant cows get the best shade in the pasture. They choose the order in which the cows enter the barn to be milked. And they get whatever other little courtesies cows make to each other. Dominance is established by the rather unladylike method of pushing and shoving. The most aggressive cows become the head cows. Perhaps cows are more like humans than we give them credit for.

A cow's year is centered around the birth of her calf. After a heifer (young cow that has never had a calf) reaches maturity, usually at about one and a half years of age, her owner calls in the artificial insemination technician and has her bred. Her pregnancy lasts almost nine and a half months. She starts giving milk when the calf is born. The farmer, however, takes away the calf after a day or two, leaving both cow and calf brokenhearted. The farmer then milks the cow for about 10 months. About two months after her calf is born, a cow comes in heat again, and the artificial insemination technician pays another visit. A couple of months before the next calf is due, the farmer quits milking her. During this period, the cow just hangs around being pregnant. As one farmer says, "My cows work ten months, then get a two-month vacation." And those are the basics of a cow's lifestyle. Not flashy. Just slow, steady, and maternal. And after ten or twelve years of faithful service, the farmer takes her off to the local slaughterhouse, where she is made into hamburger. ❧

—K.V.

Famous Cows

While cows are not as flashy as, say, horses — there's no cow equivalent of Man O'War — a few do stand out in both bovine and human history.

Take **Mrs. O'Leary's cow**. On the evening of October 8, 1871, the Great Chicago Fire started when one of the cows who lived in the barn behind Mrs. O'Leary's home kicked over a lantern. The resulting fire destroyed more than 17,500 buildings, essentially razing the city of Chicago. No one has ever documented which of Mrs. O'Leary's cows actually kicked over the lantern.

Elsie the Borden cow. Probably one of the most famous advertising symbols in history, Elsie, unlike Betty Crocker, her human counterpart, was real. Actually, she was a series of Jerseys used by the Borden Company beginning in the 1930s. She was so successful with her appearances around the country, including a movie and television guest appearances, that the company created a calf, Beauregard, to join her as company mascot.

Easter, the Wisconsin tourism cow. In 1985, the state Division of Tourism used Easter, a Walworth County Holstein, as the centerpiece of its "Escape to Wisconsin" advertising campaign. Easter was pictured standing on a pier wearing large pink-rimmed sunglasses, holding an "Escape to Wisconsin" booklet in her mouth. She must have had some indefinable star quality, because requests for information about escaping to Wisconsin nearly doubled.

G. Metcalf Valiant Mist E.T., the most expensive cow in history. In 1985, Mist, as her friends call her, a four-year-old Holstein who was a champion milk producer, was sold for $1.3 million. (An average four-year old dairy cow might sell for $1000.) She lives in luxury on a farm in Montpelier, Vermont. Mist is incredibly valuable because embryo transplant technology will allow her to produce as many as 100 high-priced offspring during her life, rather than the 10 or so calves that cows produce normally. Mist's embryos are transplanted into other cows, though she still does produce an occasional calf the old-fashioned way.❀ —*K.V.*

Weather, Whether or Not

"Some people are weatherwise but most people are otherwise."
Benjamin Franklin

Ben was right about many things, but he may have missed the mark here. Weather affects every single living thing — we have to live with what Mother Nature doles out at the very least—and everyone is conscious of the weather, even if only to complain about it.

Down through the ages, people have always tried to predict the weather, especially folks like farmers and sailors, whose livelihoods, and lives, depend on it. And some of the old weather proverbs have a definite ring of truth about them. Remember this one?

Red sky in morning, sailor's warning;
red sky at night, sailor's delight.

Nearly everyone learned some version of this as a child. It's one of the oldest weather proverbs and has its roots in the Bible (Matthew 16: 2-3). Like many, it has some basis in fact. Most weather patterns move from west to east, so if "tomorrow's air" and weather lie to westward as a mass of wet stuff, the sun shining through it appears to be a gray or watery yellow disk. But if the air to westward is dry, the sun appears at its reddest.

"The cricket too, how sharp he sings..." is a line from an old weather rhyme that indicates how strongly weather affects insects and animals. Try this some warm summer evening. Count the number of chirps a black cricket makes in 14 seconds and then add 40. This gives you the air temperature in degrees Fahrenheit— at least where the cricket is.

There is a weather adage in the Lake Superior region that goes:

"When pewter sky meets black water and camp smoke rises straight, Gitche Gumme is getting ready to make weather."

This is a good description of the approach of a Lake Superior storm. The clouds are silver-black and dark because they hold more precipitation, and the black water reflects the ominous darkness of the clouds. Camp smoke rises straight because the air is still and heavy in the lowered air pressure as the storm draws near. A Lake Superior storm is an exciting and awesome spectacle, as anyone who has witnessed one from shore can tell you. Sailors will tell you it's an even more awesome spectacle when witnessed at sea, although some may become a bit too exciting.

"A ring around the moon means rain." This is often true, especially in summer. It means a mass of rain-bringing warm air has flowed in overhead, causing ice-crystal cloudforms (the very highest clouds). When the moon shines through these clouds, a halo results. In summer this often means a lasting rain will arrive in about ten hours.

"When the leaves turn their backs, rain is on the way," is another rainy homily that often holds true. Leaves grow in a pattern according to the prevailing winds (generally good weather winds). A non-prevailing or stormy wind turns them over.

Lightning is one of Mother Nature's most brilliant and frightening displays, and has come in for its share of sayings and warnings. Said an old English rhyme:

> *Beware of an oak:*
> *It draws the stroke;*
> *Avoid an ash:*
> *It counts the flash.*

Of course, we know today that all trees are to be avoided during a lightning storm.

In some places in England, pieces of hawthorne cut on Holy Thursday were presumed to guard any house against lightning because Christ had been born beneath a thorn tree. And at Christmastime in many places, a piece of yule log was pulled from the fire as soon as it had been scorched. It was stored away and later thrown on the fire when a thunderstorm began, the theory being that no thunderbolt would strike a house in which the yule log smoldered.

Today we know better, although we still get various opinions on lightning. It is the devil, coming for a man's soul. It curdles milk. It strikes in the North to portend rain, or in the West or South for dry weather.

To escape it you need only jump into water, and hold up a raccoon skin. Or hide the scissors. Or stay away from wet animals. Not so! These are old wives' tales, not to be taken seriously.

Lightning is serious stuff and causes more direct deaths in the United States than any other stormy weather phenomenon. Between January 1940 and December 1976, lightning was reported to have killed more than 7500 Americans and injured 20,000 others.

And it does strike twice in the same place. Tall buildings often receive multiple strikes during a thunderstorm. Ask Virginia Park Ranger Roy C. Sullivan, who on June 26, 1977, was struck by lightning for the seventh time (1942, 1969, 1970, 1972, 1973, 1976 and 1977). Mr. Sullivan would seem to be a person to stay away from on cloudy days.

Rainbows are among the prettiest weather phenomenons, and there is a saying:

Rainbow to windward, foul fall the day;
Rainbow to leeward, damp runs away.

The reasoning is, if the rainbow is to the windward of a sailor, a shower is approaching. But if it appears to leeward, no rain can come from weather that is moving away.

Winter comes in for its share of weather sayings too, especially here in the Midwest, where it seems the longest season. "As the days lengthen, the cold strengthens," goes the old winter post-solstice proverb. January is indeed the cold month. Although the days are getting longer as the sun begins its northward journey after the Winter Solstice (December 21), the days get colder. This is because the incoming solar radiation and the heat loss into space at night do not come into balance until about six weeks after the Solstice — around February 1. So while the days get longer, they also get colder.

The winter warm spell known as the "January thaw" is a reality, especially in the Midwest and the Northeast. It most often occurs between January 20 and 26, although the phenomenon does not necessarily take place every year. Scientists know why the January thaw occurs — the weather patterns line up so there is a strong southerly flow of warm air into the Midwest and Northeast, but why the patterns set up at this particular time is not known.

Predicting winter's length and severity becomes a popular pastime in Wisconsin as the season draws near. There's the formula using the age of the moon at the time of the first snowfall deep enough to track a cat (or anything that leaves a footprint) to determine how many snowfalls winter will bring. On Groundhog Day (February 2) Jimmy, the Sun Prairie groundhog, looks for his shadow to tell us if winter will end early or late.

And then there's the woolly caterpillar. If in autumn you find one with a wide brown middle and a small amount of black at the ends, look for a mild winter. But if it shows lots of black and little brown, look for a rough one. Trust me.❀   —*D.D.*

SEPTEMBER IN THE GARDEN

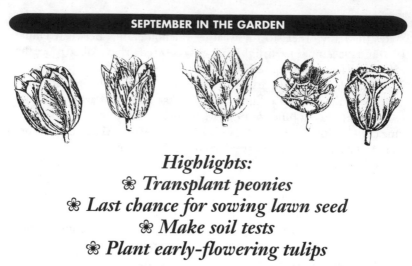

Highlights:
❀ *Transplant peonies*
❀ *Last chance for sowing lawn seed*
❀ *Make soil tests*
❀ *Plant early-flowering tulips*

September is a transition month in the Wisconsin garden. Early on, summer reigns, the bounty of August spilling over into the current month, and the focus is on preserving the harvest for the fall and winter. By the end of the month, though, the first cool winds of autumn have arrived, and frost has come at least to the northern reaches of the state. Our thoughts turn in different directions, as we wonder how summer slipped by so quickly once again.

The list of garden chores also shows a transitional nature, as we deal with summer while preparing for winter. Early in the month, you can bring all your houseplants indoors from their summer vacations, if you did not do it previously. Isolate each plant until you are sure it is not carrying mealy bugs, spider mites, or other insects.

Divide and transplant spring and early summer flowering perennials, including peonies and bleeding heart, during the first half of the month.

Lawn seed may be sown up until the 15th, and the new grass plants will make good progress from now until frost, with moderate temperatures, ample moisture, and little competition from weeds. The 15th is also the last date to transplant evergreens. Do it any later and they won't have a chance to become established before winter.

If early frost threatens, be prepared to cover tomatoes. Get them through the first freeze, and you may enjoy an extended harvest season through Indian summer.

Move amaryllis to a cool basement for its three-month rest period.

September is a big month for apple harvest. Store them at just above 32°.

The latter half of the month is a good time to make soil tests in various garden locations. Do it now, and you won't have to do it when you're so very busy next spring. Make separate tests for the vegetable garden, annual and perennial beds, and the lawn.

Dig up gladiolus corms when the plants' leaves have turned yellow. Cure them for a few days on the ground, in the sun, but bring them inside if rain threatens They are stored much like onions, and can be brought back next spring to serve again.

Harvest gourds before they are touched by frost, if you want to dry and use them for decorative purposes.

To add organic matter to the vegetable garden, sow a cover crop of rye early in the month. It will grow to six inches in height before winter sets in, then can easily be tilled into the soil in spring. Do this every year for problem clay or sand soils.

You can still make cuttings of geraniums and coleus before killing frost.

Plant bulbs of early-flowering tulips during the last week of the month. Bulbs for winter forcing should be brought indoors to the refrigerator now, for the required period of cold storage. If you will be using bulbs from your own garden, choose only the biggest and best.

Pray for the Packers.❀

—*J.M.*

Canvas-Back Ducks in Wisconsin

Janesville, Wisconsin, September 22nd, 1873

Editor of *Forest and Stream:*

Our shooting hereabouts is principally confined to ducks, and we claim to have the best duck-ing grounds in the Northwest, and the only grounds where the famous canvas-back is found in any great number. This ground  is at Lake Koshkonong, Wisconsin, a body of water about nine miles long, from two to four miles wide, quite shallow and filled with wild celery. The shores are indented by numerous bogs and sloughs, and lined with a heavy growth of wild rice, and here in the spring and fall are found nearly every variety of water fowl by the million. It has been disputed by Eastern sportsmen that our canvas-backs are the same as are found in the Chesapeake; but that they are the same is true beyond a doubt, and can be proven to the entire satisfaction of all who will come and see. Teal and mallard shooting begin about September first and last until about Octo-ber. Then comes the canvas-back. Black head, red head, and other northern varieties of ducks, which remain until the lake is closed by ice, and are slaughtered by thousands. Sportsmen in search of ducking grounds would do well to visit Koshkonong, any time from October 10th to November 15th. The best route is via C. and N.W. Railway, Wiscon-sin Division, from Chicago to Fort Atkinson, 111 miles; thence by team three miles south to Mr. H. L. Beemer's, where good accommodations will be found, and necessary information given. Mr. Beemer lives nearest the best shooting grounds on the lake, and all who stop with him will be well taken care of. The fishing is also very fine, and black bass are taken in great numbers. General Phil. Sheridan took in one day last season all his boat could carry, averaging two pounds apiece.

Yours truly,

Valentine

From Forest and Stream, October 16, 1873
From Stephen Miller's Early American Waterfowling, published by Winchester Press,
220 Old New Brunswick Rd., Piscataway NJ 08854.

Training Your Retriever

When training a young dog, make a pup-sized retrieving dummy by cutting up a length of burlap sack. Fold an 8 x 16-inch strip into the size of a woodcock, quail, teal, or other small bird which suits a pup's small mouth. Tie the bundle together with strong twine, so that there are no loose ends. To add spice to your retrieving lessons, sprinkle the burlap dummy with a drop or two of pheasant scent or duck scent. It's available from most outdoor stores.

Do a few retrieves each day. Be sure to end your sessions while your pup is still eager to return the dummy to you. Regular practice, done in the spirit of play, will help create a spirited and competent retriever for your autumn hunting trips. ❧

Apple Tips

❧ Six to eight medium apples will fill a nine-inch pie. (Three medium apples weigh about one pound.

❧ One bushel (96-144 apples) makes 16-20 quarts of applesauce.

❧ Apples should be refrigerated or stored in the coolest place possible without freezing (ideal temperature between 32 and 40 degrees F.). Store in plastic bag.

❧ For a list of pick-your-own apple orchards, contact DATCP, Marketing Div., P.O. Box 8911, Madison, WI 53708. Call 608-266-1531.

—*Wisconsin Apple Growers Association*

Years Ago . . .

MILWAUKEE—Twenty-five ladies and gentlemen from Milwaukee and many from Racine, Chicago and other cities will take part in the great fox hunt at Cold Spring Park. The prizes awarded will be a silver cup to the dog that keeps the best trail, and another to the dog that is in first at the death. A brush mounted over a silver horn will be given to the rider in first to the death of the fox, and a gold-mounted whip, diamond studded, to the rider second on the scene. Besides the fox hunt there will be a greyhound race, a horse race, and a watermelon race.—*Wisconsin State Journal*, September 7, 1889.

Russian Cream Parfaits

1/2 cup sugar
1 envelope unflavored gelatin
1-3/4 cups milk
1 pint dairy sour cream
1 teaspoon vanilla
2 cups fresh or frozen blueberries or raspberries, thawed.

In a medium saucepan combine the sugar and gelatin. Stir in the milk. Cook and stir over medium heat till gelatin is dissolved. Remove from heat; stir in the sour cream and vanilla. Cover; chill about 2 hours or till mixture mounds. Spoon into 8 dessert glasses. Top each with 1/4 cup of the berries. Makes 8 servings.

Preparation time: 30 minutes plus chilling

Years Ago . . .

MILWAUKEE—The steamer *Lady Elgin*, of the Lake Superior line, which left Milwaukee on Thursday evening with between four and five hundred excursionists, when on her return trip was run into by the schooner *Augusta* off Point Winnetka, about ten miles north of Chicago.

Among the excursionists were the Union Guards, Captain Barry, the Black Yagers, and a number of the company known as the Green Yagers, besides a number of the firemen of our city, and many prominent citizens.

The excursionists left Milwaukee on the night of the 6th inst., with every prospect of a happy time and a safe return.

Yesterday morning the first premonitions of the horrible news were whispered about the streets. Cheeks were blanched and hearts were hushed at the tidings that the steamer had gone down with all on board. The rumor grew into a dread certainty as the despatches began to arrive. The dreadful intelligence spread like wildfire and soon the city was agitated by feelings of suspense and apprehension. Then came the confirmation: only thirteen saved out of the four hundred happy pleasure seekers.—*Milwaukee Sentinel*, September 10, 1860.

Uncle Woody *Says*

Rainy Day Whitetails. A day of drizzling rain sends many deer hunters back to their cabins. But to experienced outdoor people, rain signals the best possible hunting conditions. Leaves underfoot are soggy and quiet. Rain dripping off tree branches camouflages sounds made by the hunter. In general, mist and gray weather mean that whitetails can be approached more closely and successfully.

The Hardest Working River in the World

Through the years, glaciers, then man, have twisted, reshaped and dammed the Wisconsin River. Since the glaciers receded 15,000 years ago, the river has provided transportation to Indians, fur traders, settlers, lumberjacks, and, more recently, recreational boaters. It supplies power for the turbines of industry. It offers shelter to wildlife, and to humans seeking solitude. Unfortunately, it was also at one time a convenient place to dump the wastes of town and industry.

The Wisconsin begins in Lac Vieux Desert, a 6400-acre lake that is largely in Michigan. The rivulet that will become the river flows south, exiting the lake on the Wisconsin shore. Gaining size, it flows through Rhinelander, Wausau, Stevens Point, Wisconsin Rapids, Wisconsin Dells, then makes a sharp turn to the west, flowing past Sauk Prairie and other communities until, 430 miles after it began, it joins the Mississippi. Along the way, it has dropped 1000 feet in elevation. The river drains an area of 12,000 square miles, nearly 25 percent of the state.

The Wisconsin was known to early fur traders, who explored the area between Green Bay and Lake Superior in the late seventeenth century. The first map that shows Lac Vieux Desert (colloquial French for "old planting ground") was published in 1718.

The name Wisconsin derives from Indian names of uncertain translation. Two likely candidates are words meaning "a gathering of the waters" or "the stream of the thousand isles." Spellings of the Indian words included Meskousing, Ouisconsin, and Wiskonsan. In 1836, the territorial legislature officially proclaimed "Wisconsin" the correct spelling of both the river and the then-territory.

In addition to giving its name to the new territory, the Wisconsin was a major highway for exploration and settlement of the new land. In 1673, the French explorers Marquette and Joliet paddled the Fox River from Green Bay, then carried their canoes to the Wisconsin at the spot that is now the city of Portage. The two rivers, which flow in different directions, are only about a mile apart at this point. The route became so important that British, then American, military authorities established forts at Green Bay, Portage, and Prairie du Chien to protect it.

As Wisconsin was settled, the river became a major artery for logging operations. Pine cut in the north was rafted down the river to sawmills. Because some rapids were treacherous for loggers, who rode the rafts down the river, the first dams were built on the river north of Wausau. Unfortunately, going over the dams with the log rafts was perhaps nore history.

The logging industry declined and the pulp and paper industry took its place—and demanded a steady source of electricity.

The discovery of electricity opened the next chapter in the river's long history. The logging industry declined and the pulp and paper industry took its place—and demanded a steady source of electricity.

From 1905 to 1907, a group of industrialists persuaded the Legislature to charter the Wisconsin Valley Improvement Company, whose task was to reduce flooding problems and stabilize the river's flow. The first power dams were built at Wisconsin Dells and Prairie du Sac.

Electric utilities, paper companies, and river communities took advantage of the more consistent flow and industrial use intensified.

Today, there are 21 flood control dams and 26 hydroelectric dams on the river (yet the last 92 miles from Prairie du Sac to Prairie du Chien is undammed, the longest stretch of free-flowing river left in the Midwest). Thirteen major paper mills, dozens of river communities and hundreds of smaller industries take advantage of the Wisconsin's water for power, industrial process water, and waste disposal. (For many years the river had few fish and little recreational use because of pollution. In the last decade, $350 million has been spent by government and business to control water pollution. And waste discharges have dropped more than 90 percent.)

The hardest working river in the world will continue to be an important industrial river. But it is also emerging as a major recreational area, with trophy fishing, canoeing, and other water sports attracting visitors from throughout the midwest. And Marquette and Joliet would still recognize much of the river they canoed 317 years ago.✿   —*K.V.*

Rattlesnake Tom

LLOYD M. HOLLIDAY

The Kickapoo area has always been the home of the rattlesnake, and there's almost as many at home now in the hills as there were in the heyday of the snake hunters who took them for bounty.

This is a story about one of those hunters.

Rattlesnake Tom was a long, lean man. His unsmiling face was creased by his ugly disposition. Pale blue eyes stared from under bushy eyebrows. His lumpy Adam's apple had plenty of room to bob up and down in his long scrawny neck, and he had the strength of seasoned hickory. I was told that his crooked nose had gotten its ugly hump from being shoved into other people's business.

If you had had the impertinence to ask Tom in his later years—he lived past ninety—what he'd accomplished in his long life, I'm sure his answer would have been either "None of your damned business" or "I was the champion liar, thief, fighter, boozer, dynamiter, troublemaker, and rattlesnake hunter of my time, and if anyone else has outchampioned me it's because I can't get around anymore."

He wasn't even honest in his bounty hunting! He'd carefully cut off the rattles short of the body and turn the snake loose to live and raise more snakes. "I don't want to destroy the main source of my income," he'd say.

Without his rattles a snake was a deadly menace. Many of these derattled snakes were taken by other hunters who let it be known that another one of Tom's pets had been killed.

Tom's moniker, "Rattlesnake," came from an incident that only he could have hatched.

The local saloon was Tom's first home. There he was himself. A few drinks would add more big devils to his already devil-saturated character. One day the bartender remarked that he'd rather have Tom's rattlesnakes turned loose in his place than the man himself—at least they didn't lie.

Some old crony carried the words to old Tom.

He just grinned and said, "The hell, ya say. I'll oblige."

Late that afternoon when the saloon was full up, he walked in and dropped a live gunny sack on the bar, gave a few jerks at the bottom of the bag, and out rolled a slithering mass of rattlesnakes.

"Barkeep," he said, "here's your rattlesnakes."

But the barkeeper had joined the mob trying to escape through the one lone door.

Tom had the place to himself and proceeded to get drunk—one of his singing, shouting, cursing, fighting drunks. He could be heard all over town. He yelled, "Come back in here, you lousy good-for-nothings. That was just a bag of happy rattlesnakes. Can't ya hear 'em singing?"

"You're sure missing lots of good liquor—there's no one in here to take your money."

"Hey, barkeep, your rattlers are all over the place. I just saw one go through a knothole; some of 'em are trying to crawl up the wall. You might as well crawl around on your belly in here as out there, you varmit."

But no one went in. Most of them were more afraid of the snakes than of him. Everything had been pretty quiet for maybe twenty minutes when Tom staggered out the door, the bag of snakes in one hand and a bottle of whiskey in the other.

"I'm going home, barkeep, and finish off this bottle. I've got all the snakes but one. You can have him for a pet."

The barkeeper and a few friends carefully turned the place upside down, looking for one lone rattlesnake. It couldn't be found.

Tom came in the next morning and offered to find the snake—for a pint of whiskey. He got the whiskey and proceeded to sit down and enjoy it.

"You've got your whiskey. Why don't you start looking?"

"Because I'm a liar," said Tom. "You said so yourself. What did I say when I left here?"

"You said you had them all but one."

"That's right." He got up and left.

"Tom, come back and find that snake."

"What snake?" Tom asked, and kept on going.

The barkeep got the message—all for nothing. He'd get a lot of ribbing over it.

He went to the door and yelled out, "Tom, you're nothing but a stinking, dirty rattlesnake."

Word got around. That night in the saloon everybody wanted to know where the pet snake was. What do you feed him? Goin' to cut his tail off short? Want any more pets? When Tom walked in, someone shouted, "What do you know, fellows, here comes 'Rattlesnake Tom'!"

Tom was grinning, his revenge was sweet, and to him, the moniker was a gleaming halo.

People in the valley miss the old rascal.

From: We Were Children Then, Volume II, published by NorthWord Press, Inc., Minocqua, WI.

Cover Crops for Gardeners

Plant rye in your vegetable garden? It's a good idea, in order to increase soil organic matter, yet not many gardeners pick up on the idea of cover-cropping. Sow the rye, according to package directions, in the fall, at least three weeks before frost. Sow the seed in every part of the vegetable garden that now lies fallow. The new rye will die after the first hard frosts, and can then be turned into the soil in the spring. It will not reseed, but will add considerable amounts of organic material to your soil, at very little cost. Buckwheat is another good cover crop for Wisconsin gardens.❀

Is This Melon Ripe?

How can you tell when a melon is ripe? Thumping is the traditional method, but it is unreliable. A better way is to apply gentle pressure with the thumb between the fruit and the base of the stem. If the fruit separates easily from the stem, the fruit is ripe. Chill the melons and eat them the same day they are picked.❀

Years Ago . . .

ALBANY—The pearl excitement on the Sugar River is now at its height. Although clams are getting scarce and the divers have to dig in the mud on the bottom of the river, the finds are more numerous and valuable than ever. The largest and by far the most valuable pearl in Wisconsin was found yesterday by W. J. Hahn. The weight of the pearl is 252 grams. A New York buyer offered $3500 for it but his figure was considered too low. Hundreds of small pearls are found and sold daily. The purchasers are agents of New York, Chicago, and Paris houses. Visitors and clam hunters are pouring into the village, and the banks of the river for miles are dotted with tents.—*Wisconsin State Journal*, September 6, 1889.

Uncle Woody Says

Storing Your Canoe. Many a garage can be modified into a canoe storage area. If the ceiling is high enough, you can store your canoe near your car parking space, making loading and unloading an easier chore. Secure two small pulleys to an overhead beam. Place them as far apart from each other as the length of your canoe. Then, raise and lower your craft with ropes.

OCTOBER

Oh suns and skies and clouds of June,
And flowers of June together,
Ye cannot rival for one hour
October's bright blue weather

—Helen Hunt Jackson,
"October's Bright Blue Weather"

October begins with red and green and gold, and ends in wintery gray. The month of ghosts, goblins, and jack-o'- lanterns, October often brings "Indian Summer," a period of warm temperatures, light winds, and hazy sunshine. The warm spell often comes after the first frost of autumn or a period of freezing weather known as "Squaw Winter." Indian Summer moves around on nature's calendar, coming any time in October or early November, and may recur two or three times in the same autumn. On October 8, 1871, more than 1,000 perished in Wisconsin's Peshtigo Forest Fire; the Great Chicago Fire occurred that very same night.❀

October Weather History

MADISON

Day	Record High		Record Low		Record Precip.		Average High/Low
1	90	1976	27	1974	1.53	1926	67/43
2	87	1953	22	1974	1.67	1879	67/43
3	85	1976	25	1974	1.16	1917	67/42
4	85	1967	27	1980	1.42	1919	67/42
5	86	1922	23	1980	0.97	1959	66/42
6	90	1963	22	1952	1.26	1949	66/41
7	84	1947	26	1976,87	1.56	1882	65/41
8	83	1949	22	1987	2.05	1881	65/41
9	82	1879	20	1964	1.10	1932	65/40
10	84	1928	17	1964	1.75	1954	64/40
11	84	1928	23	1967,87	0.96	1983	64/40
12	81	1892	21	1988	0.98	1890	63/39
13	90	1975	20	1988	1.45	1883	63/39
14	82	1947	22	1979	1.16	1966	62/39
15	84	1968	23	1885	1.31	1880	62/38
16	81	1938	19	1891	0.99	1914	62/38
17	82	1947	20	1976	1.99	1881	61/38
18	82	1950	18	1976	2.78	1984	61/37
19	80	1953	15	1972	2.27	1937	60/37
20	82	1953	20	1952	1.65	1934	60/36
21	82	1947	20	1960	1.04	1951	59/36
22	82	1947	17	1982	1.54	1979	58/36
23	81	1963	15	1959	1.59	1959	58/35
24	79	1963	18	1981	1.61	1967	57/35
25	74	1964	12	1887	0.86	1932	57/35
26	80	1927	16	1962	1.08	1917	56/34
27	79	1927	15	1976	1.93	1918	56/34
28	72	1974	16	1969	1.06	1874	55/33
29	82	1937	13	1925	1.23	1896	54/33
30	78	1971	13	1988	1.43	1919	54/33
31	78	1950	16	1925	1.21	1960	53/32

OCTOBER

October Weather History

LA CROSSE

Day	Record High		Record Low		Average High/Low
1	92	1976	28	1974	67/46
2	86	1953	20	1974	67/46
3	86	1900	26	1888	67/46
4	87	1922	28	1935	66/45
5	86	1922	27	1935	66/45
6	93	1963	22	1935	65/45
7	86	1916	26	1889	65/45
8	82	1966	26	1976	65/44
9	84	1879	24	1895	64/44
10	86	1928	23	1964	64/43
11	86	1928	22	1987	64/43
12	86	1918	24	1988	63/43
13	86	1975	19	1917	63/42
14	88	1897	24	1937	62/42
15	85	1958	24	1937	62/42
16	85	1910	24	1937	61/41
17	84	1910	20	1948	61/41
18	83	1950	18	1972	60/40
19	79	1953	15	1972	60/40
20	84	1872	19	1952	59/40
21	83	1947	20	1896	59/39
22	83	1947	19	1930	58/39
23	84	1899	17	1895	58/38
24	79	1963	17	1887	57/38
25	77	1897	6	1887	56/38
26	85	1927	18	1962	56/37
27	84	1927	17	1976	55/37
28	73	1912	18	1909	55/36
29	81	1937	12	1925	54/36
30	80	1924	7	1925	53/35
31	79	1933	18	1917	53/35

The normal average precipitation for La Crosse in October is 2.08 inches. The wettest October was in 1900 when 12.09 inches was recorded; the driest was in 1952 when only 0.02 inches was received.

Excuses for an October Party

Oktoberfest

The German tradition of Oktoberfest—a kind of beer-flavored country fair—is celebrated with polka parties, beer tents, and bratwurst. From the early days of Wisconsin history, breweries began to spring up all over the state, but eventually the ones in Milwaukee dominated the industry. By the mid-nineteenth century such Bavarian immigrants and entrebrewneurs as Valentin Blatz, John Braun, Jacob and Philip Best, August Krug, Joseph Schlitz, Adam Gettelman, and Frederick Miller were producing more beer than the state could consume. As an export, the product did indeed make Milwaukee famous.

10 World Series Celebration

In 1957, Milwaukee won its only world championship when the Braves beat the New York Yankees 5-0 in game seven of the World Series. Braves winning pitcher Lew Burdette had been an accomplished stone-thrower at a quarry outside his hometown of Nitro, West Virginia, but he was cut from his high school baseball team.

17 Antigo Silt Loam Awareness Day

Harvest time is a good time to reflect on our soil stewardship responsibilities. Professor Francis Hole, who championed the cause of soil conservation and antigo silt loam in particular as Wisconsin's state soil, has said, "The soil is the realm of lively darkness beneath our feet, where there is life on such a huge scale we can't imagine it." Antigo silt loam was a fitting choice for Wisconsin's official soil because, of the 500 soil types here, it is the only one that supports dairying, potato growing, and timber.

31 Halloween

Kenosha-born actor Orson Welles caused national panic when he broadcast "The War of the Worlds" in 1938 as a Halloween spoof on Mercury Radio Theater. Using a documentary

style of story-telling, he "interrupted the broadcast" to report that extra-terrestrial beings were invading New Jersey. The production was so convincing that many listeners thought that the martians really had landed.

Wisconsin's Ghost Towns

When people think of ghost towns, they usually think of abandoned mining towns in the Rocky Mountains, or withered desert settlements. But Wisconsin has its share of towns that once were, and in some of these long-gone places important things took place.

Old Belmont, Lafayette County. When Wisconsin became a territory in 1836, President Andrew Jackson appointed Henry Dodge as Territorial Governor. Most thought Dodge would pick the booming lead mining town of Mineral Point as the Territorial Capital, but Dodge instead chose Belmont, a new village 12 miles to the southwest. The new legislature was ordered to meet there on October 25.

Platted only two months earlier, Belmont existed mostly on paper. It was promoted by John Atchinson, of Galena, Illinois, who offered the government four buildings, free of charge, expecting to make a handsome profit from nearby lands. The buildings were pre-cut in Pittsburgh, and shipped by steamboat along the Ohio, Mississippi and Fever rivers to Galena, and hauled by wagon to Belmont.

There was a capitol building, home for the governor, and a rough lodging house. The Supreme Court building was not finished when the legislators gathered.

The territorial session lasted for 46 days, during which Belmont was the capital of an area that included present day Wisconsin, Iowa, Minnesota, and North and South Dakota as far west as the Missouri River. During the stormy session, Madison was chosen as the permanent capital, and the legislators agreed to meet at Burlington, Iowa, for the 1837 session. Within two weeks of their adjournment, the territorial furniture and surplus supplies were sold, and Belmont began to die.

Chief Justice Charles Dunn purchased the unused Supreme Court building, moved it across the road, and used it as a residence until his death in 1872. The building then became a barn. The Council House was used as a residence for a time, then moved from the site and converted to a barn.

What remained of Belmont died officially in the 1860s, when the railroad passed three miles to the south and a new Belmont was established on the railroad line. A rail spur ran to the site of the old village, and the depot was named Leslie. The name still appears on Wisconsin road maps.

The Wisconsin Federation of Women's Clubs bought the land in 1910, and in 1919 the Council House was returned and restoration work began. The Supreme Court building was returned to its original site in 1956 and restored.

Old Belmont today is First Capitol State Park and is open to visitors during the summer months. There is a small museum in the Supreme Court Building, and the Council House has been furnished as it was in 1836.

Voree, Racine County. Here lived a man who would be king. In 1843, James Jesse Stang, of New York, arrived in Burlington, Wisconsin, which had been co-founded by Moses Smith. Smith was Stang's brother-in-law, and also one of the founders of the Mormon Church.

Not long after his arrival in Wisconsin, Stang journeyed to Nauvoo, Illinois, then the home of the Mormon religion. There he met Joseph Smith, the Mormon Prophet, and was baptized into the faith, named an elder in the church, and given authority to build a Mormon settlement in Wisconsin.

Stang returned to Wisconsin and chose a spot two miles west of Burlington on the White River. Homes and roads were constructed and the village prospered. Stang named it Voree, which, he told the faithful, meant "Garden of Peace." In June of 1844, Joseph Smith was murdered. Stang hurried to Nauvoo, where he attempted to convince the Mormon Council of Elders that he should succeed Smith as leader of the Mormon Church. He lost his bid to Brigham Young, but when Stang returned to Voree, a number of Nauvoo Mormons accompanied him.

The Wisconsin colony continued to grow, even publishing a newspaper, the Voree *Herald*, with Stang as editor. Plans were made to build a huge temple, but before construction began, Stang had a vision which told him he and his nearly 2,000 followers should leave Voree. In 1849, most of the Voree Mormons followed Stang to Beaver Island, in northern Lake Michigan. There, Stang had himself crowned king — King James — and he began to advocate the practice of polygamy. Stang's reign lasted for six stormy years, until 1856, when he was shot by two of his subjects from ambush.

Mortally wounded, Stang asked to be taken to Voree to die, and two of his four young wives accompanied him back to Wisconsin. Stang died there on July 9, 1856.

Voree no longer exists, although there is a marker designating the spot on Wisconsin Highway 11 where it crosses the White River. The stone house where the Voree *Herald* was published and where Stang died stands nearby.

Stang was buried in the Burlington cemetery, his grave marker bearing only his name and the dates of his birth and death. It is a simple epitaph for a man who was king.

Ulao, Ozaukee County. Only a road sign and a former stretch of turnpike remain of this one-time Lake Michigan port community.

Ulao was founded in 1847 by James T. Gifford, of Illinois, who bought cordwood from area farmers and sold it to passing Great Lakes steamers. The village had a thousand-foot pier stretching out into the lake, a warehouse, sawmill, school, homes, and several other businesses.

Gifford also received a charter from the Territorial Legislature for a plank road starting at Ulao and proceeding westward to the Wisconsin River. Three miles of road were actually built, and have become part of Ozaukee County Highway Q, which is named Ulao Road.

One of Ulao's early residents was Charles Guiteau, who in 1880 shot and killed President James Garfield. Ulao had a fairly short life, fading away after the Civil War. Some of the community's last residents were Mormons who have been driven from their homes on Beaver Island, in northern Lake Michigan.

Gratiot's Grove, Lafayette County. Located a mile south of Shullsburg, the village began life as a lead smelter in 1826, and became an important settlement in Wisconsin's lead mining region. Among its citizens were people educated in the capitals of Europe. By 1838, it boasted a school, several stores, two good hotels, lead furnaces, shops and comfortable residences. The previous year, 81-year-old Mrs. Alexander Hamilton, wife of the famed federalist statesman, who had come to Wisconsin to visit her son William, spent most of the summer there.

The community faded as the lead ore played out, and little remains. But the Gratiot House, a large limestone home built in 1835, and one of the oldest houses existing in Wisconsin, still stands and is in use as a private home.

There were other ghost towns in Wisconsin, places like Oil City, Pleasant Ridge, Helena, Pokerville, La Rue, and Sinipee. Most lived only a short time, but all were important in their day. ❧   —*D.D.*

Years Ago . . .

MILWAUKEE—The annual meeting of the Wisconsin Woman Suffrage Association will be held at the WMCA building tomorrow and continue three days. Lectures will be delivered by Susan B. Anthony and Mrs. S.M.C. Perkins, of Ohio, and it is expected that Mrs. Isabella Beecher Hooker will be present.—*Wisconsin State Journal*, October 14, 1889.

They Said It with Cement

Poets said it with words, composers said it with songs, and artists like Fred Smith said it with cement. They seldom thought of themselves as artists, but they poured out their feelings for Wisconsin with imaginative and massive folk sculptures that decorate the rural landscape.

Of all the Wisconsin people who toted bags of cement for art, Fred Smith was the most prolific. In the northwoods town of Phillips, he created more than two hundred huge figures of animals and people: moose, fish, lions, owls, pioneers, soldiers, angels, kings and queens. For features and details he used broken beer bottles and glass insulator knobs.

Fred's figures don't just stand there like statues. Four of them are drinking beer and celebrating their double wedding. Others are riding around on horses. Various activities enliven the scene. Fred remembered his friends, as well as people from history and local folklore.

It is an amazing output for one person, especially considering that Fred didn't get started until age sixty-three. Folks in the town of Phillips thought Fred had really gone 'round the bend when, in 1950, this fantastical world began to appear in the pine grove next to his tavern. In recent years, scholarship has recognized the work of this artistic ex-lumberjack who could neither read nor write. Fred Smith's Concrete Park has been the subject of journal articles and television documentaries around the world.

Similar goings-on had occurred in the southern part of Wisconsin a few years earlier. Paul Bunyan, Uncle Sam, Snow White and the Seven Dwarfs, Neptune, and assorted Vikings, mountaineers, lions, elephants, and peacocks were rising up in front of Nicholas Englebert's small farm just outside of Hollandale. These too were made of cement and decorated with glass marbles, broken crockery, and seashells. As if Englebert had extra glass-and-plaster batter left over one day, the exterior of his frame house acquired a façade to match the sculpture.

For Engelbert, it began at age fifty with a broken ankle. To pass the time while recuperating, he fashioned a large cement vase festooned with fragments of colored glass and china. Some forty figures followed over the next twenty years.

An immigrant from Austria-Hungary, Englebert appreciated his good life here and thought of his wonderland as a loving tribute to America. Two Madison artists tell the rest of his story in a half-hour documentary film that preserves Engelbert's work. Though some pieces have deteriorated, much of the collection can still be seen at the quiet, wooded farmstead on Highway 39.

In both mass and message, the Dickeyville Grotto in the southwest corner of the state is the weightiest of Wisconsin's cement parks. No whimsical creatures cavort here. Instead, there are awesome altars and shrines labeled with straightforward commands—FAITH, PEACE, CHASTITY, MILDNESS, LONG SUFFERING, PATIENCE, FORTITUDE—and encrusted with glassware, pottery, geological specimens, fossils, Indian relics, fancy dishware, figurines, and hornets' nests.

This is the work of Father Mathias Wernerus, who, in the 1920s, saw his work as "God's wonderful material collected from all parts of the world. . . . Future generations will still enjoy the fruit of our labor and will bless the man that conceived and built this thing." He was right. Thousands of people from all over the world visit the Dickeyville Grotto every year.

The "Religion in Stone" and "Patriotism in Stone" areas inside the gates of Holy Ghost Park account for two of the forces behind Father Wernerus' productivity. But apparently there was more to it. In his own cryptic words, "The main reason why it was done, I could not reveal. The

last day will tell you more about that."

Up in Monroe County, Paul and Matilda Wegner shared Father Wernerus's religious faith and love of adopted country, though they expressed it on a smaller scale.

The centerpiece of their work is the Glass Church and its surrounding prayer garden, a glittering scene that has been the setting for many weddings. The Wegners also built a steamship, an anniversary cake, a stringed harp, an American flag—thirty sculptures in all that touch on the life they built here after leaving Germany.

For fifty years the Wegners operated a garage and automobile business in Bangor. Then, in the 1930s, they retired to their farm a few miles southwest of Cataract and took up their unusual hobby. All the pieces were made of reinforced poured concrete, and they sparkled with pieces of china and glass inlaid every half-inch in intricate patterns. On Sunday afternoons, cars lined up for miles.

By the 1980s, time and the elements had damaged and dulled the pieces. Fortunately the Kohler Foundation came to the rescue with funds, as it had for Fred Smith's Concrete Park. The Wegners' work was carefully restored and entrusted to Monroe County to manage and maintain as a public park.

Another example of these energetic, self-taught, late-blooming artists emerged in the 1950s. Herman Rusch discovered his medium to be glass and cement at age seventy-one, and proceeded to spread his whimsical dinosaurs, flamingos, polar bears, and snakes over several acres of land south of Cochrane, near the Mississippi River. He also surrounded them with ornamental spires and gates and enclosed them in a spectacular arching fence. His work has been highly praised for its sense of design and wit, but Herman seemed not to take himself too seriously. According to the inscription on a bust of himself, creating this wondrous world was just "a good way to kill old-age boredom." ❁   —D.C.

Scrumptious Cheese-Apple Bars

1-3/4 cups flour
1 cup brown sugar
1 teaspoon cinnamon
1/2 cup butter (softened)
1 cup chopped walnuts
1 8-ounce package cream
    cheese (softened)

2 tablespoons cream
    (may use milk)
1 egg, beaten
1/4 cup sugar
1/2 teaspoon vanilla
4 cups baking apples,
    pared and sliced

Combine flour, brown sugar, and cinnamon. Cut in butter until mixture resembles coarse crumbs. Add nuts. Reserve 1-3/4 cups crumbs. Press remaining mixture in bottom of a greased 9x13 baking pan. Beat cream cheese and cream together until smooth. Mix in egg, sugar, and vanilla. Spread over crust. Top with apples and sprinkle with reserved crumbs. Bake at 350° F. 30 minutes. Serve warm or cold. Leftovers should be refrigerated. Serves 12-16.

—Mrs. Lynn Ireland, Oconomowoc

Uncle Woody *Says*

Instant Camping Gear Boxes. Cardboard beer cases, of the type that hold twenty-four returnable beer bottles, make sturdy containers for items of camping equipment. The boxes are extra strong and they're usually waxed to enable them to withstand dampness or rain.

A 1753 Recipe for Quail

Get quails, truss them, and stuff their bellies with beef-suet and sweet herbs chopped together. Put quail on a small spit and baste with water and salt until they grow warm. Afterwards, baste with butter and dredge with flour.

Then continue cooking. For sauce, dissolve an anchovy in gravy, into which put two or three shallots, sliced and boiled. Add juice of two or three Seville oranges and one lemon. Dish quail in sauce and garnish with lemon peel and grated manchet. Serve them up hot!

OCTOBER IN THE GARDEN

Highlights:
❀ *Plant spring-flowering bulbs*
❀ *Put the garden to bed*
❀ *Clean and sharpen garden tools*
❀ *Sow perennials outdoors*

There is a time in mid-October, when the first really hard frosts fall over the state, and when the first snowfalls come to the north, when the Wisconsin gardener decides that it's really time to hang up the old spade and hoe and call it another season.

Of course, we put off this moment just as long as we possibly can. We gardeners are a tenacious lot, loath to give up all those plants we worked so hard on for the last five months. We want to nurse along every last tomato, keep on picking those crisp little broccoli heads, keep that beautiful head of cabbage in the ground for just another few days. The really dedicated gardener will be shoveling snow with one hand, while mulching carrots with the other.

The tender crops are first to go. Beans, melons, cucumbers, squash, corn, peppers, eggplants, sweet potatoes, tomatoes, okra—all succumb early to the first frosty breaths of autumn.

More hardy—more *Wisconsiny*, if you will—are cabbage, Brussels sprouts, kale, turnips, rutabagas, kohlrabi, collards, broccoli, horseradish, spinach, beets, and parsnips. The leafy members of this group can take some quite hard frosts without injury, while the root members can stay right in the ground through November, if they are mulched to keep the ground from freezing.

Do you want to plant your peas early next year? If so, then start to

prepare now. Choose a good planting area, then dig up the soil and spade in some manure and cover the patch with a thick hay mulch. Early next spring, that patch will thaw out more quickly than the surrounding ground, and you can plant the peas two or three weeks earlier than you could otherwise.

There are more October chores. Give evergreens a thorough watering before the ground freezes hard. They need much more moisture than do deciduous trees to survive the winter.

Think ahead to spring and plant all spring-flowering bulbs—tulips, daffodils, hyacinths, crocus, etc.— anytime up until the ground freezes hard. Choose different varieties that bloom at different times, for a succession of bloom that will take you from late March clear up to the flowering of the first summer annuals.

Now also is time to put the vegetable and annual gardens to bed, after frost has claimed all. Remove all garden debris, till under spent plants (or remove them to the compost pile), and turn the soil, leaving it rough over the winter. This will expose insects to the elements and to birds, allow water to enter the soil, and encourage organic matter to decay as it should. You may incorporate leaves into the soil, but be sure to shred them first, or they will be slow to decompose.

During the last half of the month, sow seed, outdoors, of oriental poppy, Iceland poppy, gas plant, primula, scabiosa, phlox, viola, pansy, and penstemon.

Make the last cutting of the lawn, then take your lawnmower in to be cleaned and serviced—to avoid the rush next spring. Also clean and sharpen all your garden tools and put them away for next year.

Pray for the Packers.✿
—J.M.

OCTOBER RECIPE

Cranberry Kissed Wisconsin Apple Salad

1 1-lb. can strained cranberries
1-1/2 cups water
1 6-ounce package cherry gelatin
3 cups shredded, peeled Wisconsin apples
Shredded lettuce
1 red Wisconsin apple, sliced and dipped in lemon juice
1 green or yellow Wisconsin apple, sliced and dipped
      in lemon juice
Topping
1 3-ounce package cream cheese
3/4 cup miniature marshmallows
1/2 cup whipping cream

Heat cranberries with water. Sprinkle the gelatin over the cranberries and stir until dissolved. Let mixture cool until it mounds slightly when dropped from spoon. Fold in shredded apples. Turn into a mold and refrigerate overnight.

Prepare topping: Put all three ingredients in a small covered bowl. Place in refrigerator overnight. Whip. Frost the salad. Line plate with the shredded lettuce and unmold the salad over the lettuce. Arrange the apple slices around the salad. Serves 6.

—*Margaret Zickert, Deerfield*

Years Ago . . .

SUN PRAIRIE—Henry C. Kuehn, secretary of the Arrow club of Pigeon Fanciers of Milwaukee, came up from that city last Saturday evening with about twenty-five homing pigeons belonging to different members of the club, which he liberated from their baskets at the Exchange Hotel on the following morning at 8:10 for a flight home. The birds circled about in the air for a few moments and struck a bee line for their lofts, sixty-nine miles away, where the first bird arrived at 9:43 o'clock AM and the others some few seconds later. The Arrow club is the largest pigeon flying club in this country.—*Wisconsin State Journal*, October 4, 1889.

1 *Fabulous* Firsts

Lollipops were first manufactured by the Racine Confectioners' Machinery Company in 1908. The company had a machine that could produce 40 lollipops a minute.

Cemetery
Stephen M. Miller

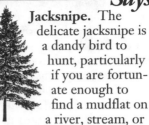

Bats hunt over a half moon
burning in a pool of water.
My dog snorts and a rabbit
    breaks
from the shadow of tombstone.
The animals run over Indian
    mounds,
up the neck of the goose,
down the tail of the lizard.
The dog returns to the pool
and his tongue slaps water.

Walking under the street lights
    of town
we step into the pool of a
    woman's voice,
Should I go?
Old man Delton answers
No. I will.
He bends behind a broom
and in the chalk of his face
his eyes burn like candles.

Uncle Woody Says

Jacksnipe. The delicate jacksnipe is a dandy bird to hunt, particularly if you are fortunate enough to find a mudflat on a river, stream, or lake where these birds elect to congregate during the early autumn. They are difficult to bag because they fly in an erratic, zig-zag pattern. Many a hunter has spent nine or ten shotshells without cutting a feather. But when you finally do kill a pair or two of these delectable birds, there's good dining in store. Draw and pluck the birds. Fry in butter over a low flame, garnishing with salt and pepper. When hunting jacksnipe, use the smallest shot size that you can find.

Uncle Woody Says

Instant Camping Gear Boxes. Cardboard beer cases, of the type that hold 24 returnable beer bottles, make sturdy containers for items of camping equipment. The boxes are extra strong and they're usually waxed to enable them to withstand dampness or rain.

Horseradish Sense

If you want to save root cuttings for next year's crop, do it while you harvest roots in late fall. Cut the best-looking lateral roots, those nearer the top of the main root. Make a straight cut, close to the main root, and then slant-cut the far end. Tie the cuttings in bunches and pack them in moist sand, as you would carrots for storage. Store the bunches in a root cellar where the temperature is close to 32 degrees F., and keep the sand just moist enough to prevent the roots from drying out. If you have no root cellar, you may pack them in sand, in a wooden box, and bury the box two feet under ground, outdoors. The roots will be in good shape for planting when spring rolls around. (And the two-foot hole you dug will be serve as an underground vegetable storage vault for years to come.) ❀

Years Ago . . .

MADISON—No law enacted by the last legislature has caused more discussion than chapter 519 of the laws of 1889. Section 5 provides that, "as part of the elementary education of children, reading, writing, arithmetic, and United States history shall be taught in the English language." Objection has been made particularly to the requirement that the instruction shall be given in the English language. The law places no obstacle in the way of teaching or learning other languages than the English. In our schools are taught Latin, Greek, Norse, French, and German, and they may legally continue to be taught. It merely asks that every boy and girl in this state, whom the flag of the nation protects, be able to read its history in the language of the country over which it waves.— *Wisconsin State Journal*, October 28, 1889.

OCTOBER RECIPE

Leftover Mashed Potato Soup

2   cups leftover mashed potatoes
4   Tbls. butter
1   cup chopped onion
1   quart whole milk
chopped parsley or chives
salt and pepper to taste

Melt the butter in a saucepan. Chop the onion and saute until limp (do not brown). Add the potatoes and stir well. Add the milk, salt, and pepper. Heat while stirring, just to the boiling point. Sprinkle parsley or chives over top and serve immediately. Don't tell anyone the potatoes were left over.

The Last Lighthouse

In September of 1883, the U.S. Lighthouse Service issued the following notice to Great Lakes Mariners:

"Notice is hereby given that on and after October 10, 1883, a fixed white light of the fourth order varied by red flashes of intervals of one minute will be shown from the lighthouse recently erected at Sherwood Point, south side of entrance into Sturgeon Bay from Green Bay Wisconsin."

The lighthouse, built atop a limestone bluff in Door County, is just south of the 45th Parallel — halfway between the Equator and the North Pole. The site was so remote in 1883 that the 40,000 bricks and other construction materials used in the lighthouse arrived by ship. It took 18 carpenters and bricklayers three months to build the lighthouse, which looked just like a red brick schoolhouse with a square tower tacked on one end.

Sherwood Point's light had a Fresnel lens and burned mineral oil. Developed in Paris, the Fresnel lens consists of a series of prisms surrounding the central light. The cut-glass prisms — dozens of them — concentrate and magnify the light. Both the lamp and lens revolved on a table that was driven by a complex clockwork mechanism. The red flash was produced when the rotating light beam passed behind a stationary red glass panel mounted outside the lens. Sherwood Point's light was displayed for the first time on October 10, 1883. The lighthouse keeper was Captain Henry Stanley, who was transferred to Sherwood Point from the Eagle Bluff Light (now in Peninsula State Park), where he had been stationed since 1868.

The lighthouse was closed in winter, so Captain Stanley's first season was barely two months long. On December 27, a Sturgeon Bay newspaper announced that, "Captain Stanley, keeper of the Sherwood Point Light,

...sed his glim on the morning of the 20th inst." The closing date was ...bitrarily chosen by the keeper, and was generally the time when Green ...ay was covered with ice as far as he could see.

The lighthouse opened each year when the ice breakup on Green Bay allowed ships to move, in some years as early as March, in others, as late as May. One of Captain Stanley's first tasks each season was to retrieve the Sherwood Point boathouse, ways, and landing pier from wherever the ice had pushed them, and to set them back into position.

The keepers' lives at early Great Lakes lighthouses were tedious, difficult, and sometimes dangerous. The Lighthouse Service records are filled with accounts of heroic rescues performed both by lightkeepers and members of their families.

Lighthouses were most often built at remote and lonely spots, and lucky was the keeper who could have his family with him. Supplies were delivered by the ships known as lighthouse tenders, which were completely at the mercy of the whims of weather.

At Sherwood Point, supplies were brought ashore from the tender in a small boat, then packed a half-mile through the woods to the lighthouse. Fresh fruits and vegetables came from the garden that Captain Stanley and his wife planted, and fresh meat came from the wild game that Stanley bagged in the nearby woods. They kept a cow and chicken for milk and eggs.

The lightkeepers were required to keep the lighthouse clean and the grounds in order, and to do all painting and minor repairs by themselves. Above all, they had to keep the light in a constant state of readiness.

The clockwork mechanism that drove the Sherwood Point light apparently gave keeper Stanley no end of trouble. On numerous occasions, the lighthouse tenders brought mechanics to overhaul the device. And just as often, it failed as soon as the mechanic left, leaving Captain Stanley to spend the night in the tower beside his light, tinkering with the clockwork. Stanley struggled with the device until 1898, when a new lamp and lens were installed.

Day or night, the keepers maintained a sharp lookout for fog, and switched on a fog signal at the first sign of diminished visibility. Sherwood Point's first fog signal was a mechanical bell run by another clockwork mechanism (poor Stanley!) that struck it twelve times a minute. It was later replaced by fog horns driven by compressed air.

William Cochems, Captain Stanley's assistant, became Sherwood Point's principal keeper upon Stanley's death. Cochems' wife, Minnie, who was Stanley's niece, served as her husband's assistant for 30 years, until her death. A small stone marker in a grove of trees near the lighthouse honors her memory. It reads: "In memory of Minnie

Cochems, Assistant Lightkeeper, 1898-1928."

Indoor plumbing did not come to Sherwood Point until 1945, although the world of electronics arrived in the late 1930s, when the lighthouse became the control station for a remotely operated light on Peshtigo Reef, nine miles out in Green Bay. The light on the reef was turned on and off by a clock, but if fog rolled in or the clock failed, the Sherwood Point keeper could send radio signals that controlled both the remote light and fog signal.

The Lighthouse Service was merged with the Coast Guard in 1939, and all U.S. lighthouses came under control of the military. Civilian keepers, however, were

allowed to remain at their posts until retirement (the last of them, stationed in New York, did not retire until the late 1980s).

In the 1960s, the Coast Guard began to equip its lighthouses with automatic equipment that required only routine visits by maintenance crews. Manned lighthouses on the Great Lakes soon became a rarity.

By the spring of 1983, Sherwood Point had become the last manned U.S. lighthouse on the Great Lakes. But after a few brief months of publicity and glory, it too fell victim to progress, ironically, in the year the lighthouse celebrated its centennial.

The end was announced in an impersonal Coast Guard notice to mariners:

> "SHERWOOD POINT LIGHT (LL 2480) FOG SIGNAL AND RADIO BEACON SECURED."

Long since electrified, Sherwood Point light continues to blink its warning to Green Bay mariners, just as it has for over a century; but the lightkeepers are gone—gone not from just this old red brick building on the shores of Green Bay, but from all of the hundreds of lighthouses spread across all five Great Lakes, where thousands of men and women faithfully kept their lights burning through long, lonely nights for 165 years.

The era ended at 8:58 A.M. on August 27, 1983, when the last manned U.S. lighthouse on the Great Lakes was closed.✤   —D.D.

Years Ago . . .

Lincoln in Beloit

JANESVILLE—On Saturday it was ascertained by some of our citizens that Hon. A. Lincoln, the Illinois orator, would address the people of Beloit on Saturday afternoon, and Mr. Tallman of this city volunteered to proceed to that place with his carriage and endeavor to induce him to address the people of Janesville in the evening. . . .

The courtroom hall was well filled with ladies and gentlemen. When Mr. Lincoln made his appearance he was greeted with cheers and was introduced to the people by Dr. Treat, the president of the republican club. Many present saw Mr. Lincoln for the first time, and as his person is tall, lean and wiry, his complexion dark, his physiognomy homely, and his phrenological developments being peculiar, he attracted much attention. His style of oratory is plain and unpretending, and his gesticulations sometimes awkward. He has studied in no school of declamation, and it is apparent at once that we have homespun, backwoods Abe Lincoln just as nature made him, without any attempts at oratorical flourish or preparation. . . . While Mr. Lincoln was laying down his propositions and preparing the way for his speech, most people no doubt thought that Abe Lincoln was not much ahead of common orators, after all; but when he came to making his points tell and to drive home his logical conclusions, the evidence of his profound thought was apparent, while his powers of satire and wit flashed brilliantly and rather startling the audience by their unexpectedness.

Whatever unfavorable opinion any person in the audience may at first have formed of Mr. Lincoln's ability as an orator soon vanishes, and the power of the high order of intellect which he undoubtedly possesses makes itself felt, not only while the speech is being delivered but afterwards. His speeches are not easily forgotten, and we doubt not that all his audience who heard him through still remember his points and will do so for many a day; and that they still have a vivid recollection of that tall gaunt form, stooping over towards his hearers, his countenance full of humor or frowning with scorn as he lays bare to the gaze of the audience the ridiculous positions of Douglas or wither with his pungent sarcasm the false positions of the believers in popular sovereignty. No one can forget Mr. Lincoln, his manner or his logic. You are *compelled* to revolve his ideas over and over in your mind, whether you will or not. . . . Mr. Lincoln's address was principally in relation to slavery.—*Janesville Gazette*, October 4, 1859.

The Seasons

The seasons occur because the earth is tilted 23 1/2 degrees off its vertical axis. As the earth revolves around the sun, its axis always points in the same direction in space. When the North Pole is tipped toward the sun, the northern hemisphere has summer and it is winter in the southern hemisphere.

The sun is farthest north at the summer solstice, about June 21, which marks the first day of summer. Then the sun is directly over the Tropic of Cancer (23 1/2 degrees north of the equator). Daylight hours are longest in the northern hemisphere and nights are the shortest of any time of year. The North Pole is in the middle of its annual period of six months of daylight and the South Pole is in the middle of its six months of darkness.

The winter solstice, about December 21, marks the first day of winter in the northern hemisphere. The North Pole is tipped farthest away from the sun, which is now directly over the Tropic of Capricorn (23 1/2 degrees south of the equator). It is now summer in the southern hemisphere, dark at the North Pole, and daylight at the South Pole.

In the northern hemisphere, the vernal equinox, about March 21, and the autumnal equinox, about September 21, mark the first day of spring and first day of autumn, respectively. On these two days, the tilt of the earth is sideways with respect to the sun, and both hemispheres get exactly the same amount of sunshine. The days and nights are of equal length everywhere on earth. ❀   —D.D.

The First 'Cheese Days'...

MONROE—No fire alarm interrupted Monroe firemen and their helpers in the manufacture of 26,500 Swiss cheese sandwiches last evening, and the task went off like clockwork, thanks to splendid organization and the installation of mechanical speed-up devices. In the afternoon 7,500 limburger sandwiches were manufactured. All were distributed free by noon today.

The Badger-Brodhead cheese company plant was the scene of the great sandwich-making bee, the likes of which has probably never been seen before anywhere.

Long lineups of men faced each other across an endless belt conveyor on which piles of bread and Swiss cheese slices kept moving. Wax paper bags were at the side of the belt. Speedy hands grabbed two slices of bread and a piece of cheese, clapping the latter between the former and putting the sandwich into the sack, bending the sack shut and tossing it on the conveyor. As piles of bags increased the piles of bread and cheese decreased until near the end of the belt practically nothing but sacks was left and these were scooped off and packed into great cardboard cartons, ready for distributing today.—*Monroe Evening Times*, October 2, 1935.

NOVEMBER

When air gets light,
The glass falls low,
Batten down tight,
For the winds will blow.

— *Old Sailor's proverb*

The eleventh month brings the infamous Gales of November to the Great Lakes. These fierce storms develop rapidly and produce strong winds and mountainous seas. The worst storm in the history of inland navigation ravaged the lakes November 7-11, 1913. November brings clouds to Wisconsin, and frequently winter weather, as the storm tracks take on the cold season patterns. Thanksgiving Day commemorates the harvest of the Plymouth Colony in 1621. George Washington proclaimed a national day of thanks for November 26, 1789; President Abraham Lincoln revived the custom in 1863. Not until 1941 did Congress officially set the holiday for the fourth Thursday of the month.❀

November Weather History

MADISON

Day	Record High		Record Low		Record Precip.		Average High/Low
1	77	1933	15	1873	2.30	1971	52/32
2	74	1938	11	1951	1.22	1961	52/31
3	76	1964	11	1951	1.50	1935	51/31
4	70	1975	8	1951	1.21	1959	51/31
5	67	1975,78	0	1951	1.07	1882	50/30
6	71	1916	7	1951	2.09	1885	49/30
7	76	1915	13	1959	1.12	1891	49/29
8	68	1915	9	1976	1.19	1932	48/29
9	70	1931	14	1925	1.22	1942	48/29
10	67	1930	10	1979	0.98	1974	47/28
11	70	1964	9	1979	1.02	1903	46/28
12	64	1964	7	1911,86	1.21	1879	46/27
13	68	1909	2	1986	0.96	1951	45/27
14	71	1971	2	1959	1.04	1956	45/27
15	66	1953	5	1959	0.75	1964	44/26
16	70	1953	2	1959	1.97	1961	44/26
17	69	1971	-1	1959	1.60	1931	43/25
18	69	1953	3	1872	1.02	1957	42/25
19	70	1930	3	1914	1.38	1934	42/25
20	64	1930	5	1914	0.93	1907	41/24
21	67	1913	-7	1880	1.94	1934	41/24
22	64	1913	0	1929	1.20	1963	40/23
23	63	1931	-5	1950	1.60	1874	40/23
24	62	1931	-5	1884	0.77	1908	39/23
25	62	1908	-2	1950	0.90	1952	39/22
26	64	1914	-5	1976	1.05	1988	39/22
27	64	1909	-7	1887	1.06	1879	38/21
28	59	1960	-14	1887	1.02	1987	38/21
29	60	1975	-11	1875	0.67	1975	37/21
30	59	1962	-4	1929	1.34	1928	37/20

NOVEMBER

November Weather History

LA CROSSE

Day	Record High		Record Low		Average High/Low
1	80	1933	15	1951	52/34
2	75	1958	11	1951	51/34
3	75	1978	13	1951	51/33
4	67	1978	7	1951	50/33
5	71	1924	1	1951	49/32
6	71	1916	-1	1951	49/32
7	75	1915	12	1956	48/31
8	69	1931	12	1976	47/31
9	69	1931	13	1921	47/30
10	67	1930	10	1979	46/30
11	70	1964	4	1986	45/30
12	67	1902	5	1986	45/29
13	67	1902	2	1986	44/29
14	68	1964	1	1916	44/28
15	64	1960	3	1940	43/28
16	70	1953	2	1959	43/27
17	70	1953	0	1959	42/27
18	68	1953	0	1891	41/26
19	73	1930	2	1914	41/26
20	72	1897	-3	1872	40/25
21	65	1913	-9	1880	40/25
22	59	1963	-1	1929	39/24
23	61	1931	-4	1950	39/24
24	62	1931	-10	1950	38/23
25	60	1896	-10	1880	38/23
26	65	1914	-9	1977	37/23
27	63	1909	-13	1872	37/22
28	57	1960	-19	1887	36/22
29	55	1941	-21	1875	36/21
30	62	1922	-14	1947	35/21

The normal average precipitation for La Crosse in November is 1.50 inches. The wettest November was in 1876 when 7.24 inches was recorded; the driest was in 1976 when only a trace of precipitation was received.

The Greatest Storm

Early November of 1913 brought Indian Summer to the upper Great Lakes. On Thursday, November 6, temperatures climbed into the 80s over northern Lake Huron and eastern Lake Superior. Seas were glassy-calm under a peculiar copper-colored sky.

But while sailors on eastern Lake Superior worked without shirts, a chill southwest wind brought small craft warnings to the western lake. Not even the forecasters realized it, but the worst storm in the history of inland navigation was warming up in the wings.

On Friday, with a low pressure system pushing eastward from the Canadian prairies, and another charging northward over Minnesota, storm warnings were posted for Lake Superior. But in those days before radio communications, when Great Lakes sailors had for 250 years made their own forecasts by the look of the sky, the rise and fall of a barometer, and a feeling in their bones, official government forecasts and warnings often went unheeded.

And so the *James Carruthers*, Canada's newest and largest lakes freighter, the *William Nottingham*, *L.C. Waldo*, *Turret Chief*, and *Leafield* all went about their business on Lake Superior.

Friday evening the two storm systems merged and all hell broke loose on the big lake. The Lake Superior waves climbed higher than most men had ever seen and snow fell in a blinding curtain. The wind shifted unexpectedly to the northwest, trapping ships along the southern shore.

A monster wave raked the *L.C. Waldo*, destroying her wheelhouse and smashing the rudder. Helpless, she swept onto the rocks of Michigan's

Keweenaw Peninsula, where she was joined a short time later by the *T* Chief. The *William Nottingham* went ashore on Parisianne Shoal, r Whitefish Bay, and three crewmen died attempting to launch a small bo

On Saturday, November 8, the *Leafield* crashed into the bluffs a Angus Island, off Fort William, Ontario (now Thunder Bay). As the storm reached Lake Michigan, the ancient tug *James H. Martin* left the barge *Plymouth* with a crew of seven in the lee of Little Gull Island, in the passage between Lake Michigan and Green Bay, and ran for shelter.

The storm ravaged Lake Michigan all day Saturday and Sunday. Snow fell cotton-thick, temperatures plunged, and waves were higher than anyone could remember. Twenty-foot seas demolished Milwaukee's new $300,000 breakwater in a matter of hours.

On Lake Superior, where the storm still raged, Captain James Owens took the big *Henry B. Smith* out of Marquette, Michigan, at 6 P.M. Sunday. Those watching were horrified as the *Smith*, with 11,000 tons of iron ore, moved out of the harbor with her crew of 26 struggling frantically to close 32 open hatch covers. On the open lake the *Smith* rolled obscenely in the mammoth seas and after 20 minutes faded from view in the snow and spume-filled skies.

While warnings were posted, the storm had not reached Lake Huron when darkness fell on Saturday, and several ships entered the lake.

From the north came the *James Carruthers*, after a rollicking passage on Superior, the 440-foot *Hydrus*, and the *Wexford*, loaded with 96,000 bushels of wheat.

Steaming northward from the St. Clair River in the southern lake was the *John A. McGean*, the 524-foot *Charles S. Price*, the *Argus* (a sister ship to the *Hydrus*), the 250-foot package freighter *Regina*, and the *H.A. Hawgood*.

At mid-morning Sunday, the combined Minnesota-Canadian lows were joined by a third storm system moving unexpectedly north from the Gulf of Mexico.

The *Hawgood* had just turned about to run back to the St. Clair River when Lake Huron exploded in a boiling white froth. Temperatures plummeted and each wave coated ships with a deadly layer of ice. Eighty mile-per-hour winds ran counter to the 30-foot waves they churned up, screaming so loudly a skipper could not hear his own distress whistle. And with it came snow so thick that a sailor could not see the bow of his ship from the pilot house.

As the *Hawgood* struggled southward, she met the upbound *Charles S. Price* off Harbor Beach, Michigan, and 15 miles farther south, the *Regina*. Both ships were fighting a losing battle with the storm. No one knows just what desperate struggles took place on that most terrible of all November days, although one final moment was witnessed. During a lull in the snow Sunday afternoon, the skipper of the *George C. Crawford* saw *rgus*, her bow and stern lifted high on separate waves with the cargo-vy midsection unsupported. "The *Argus* just appeared to crumple like eggshell and then disappeared," he later reported. The hurricane struck ake Erie late Sunday morning with peak winds of 80 miles per hour that dropped to 60 and blew for nine straight hours. Twenty-two inches of snow smothered Cleveland and a region as far west as the Chicago suburbs. Marinas and small boats were smashed to kindling, utility lines fell, rail and highway traffic ground to a halt. Late Sunday, or perhaps Monday, the 80-foot U.S. *Lightship No. 82*, anchored on station near Buffalo, New York, disappeared.

Forewarned before communications failed, Lake Ontario shipping remained in port and suffered no losses as the weakening storm moved out over the Atlantic.

Finally, it was over. For more than 100 miles the Canadian beaches of Lake Huron were littered with boxes, barrels, smashed lifeboats, shattered hatch covers — and bodies. There were scores of bodies.

It took weeks to determine the final toll, and it was devastating. Lost with all hands — more than 300 sailors — were the *Leafield, Henry B. Smith, Plymouth, Lightship No. 82, Wexford, James Carruthers, Argus, Hydrus, Regina, Charles S. Price, Isaac M. Scott*, and *John A. McGean*. In all, 19 ships were totally destroyed and 20 more were stranded. The value of vessels and cargos lost ran to more than $10 million with millions more in shoreside property damage.

On Monday, November 10, the big *Charles S. Price* was found floating upside down in lower Lake Huron, with 100 feet of her bow showing above water. It was the first time in Great Lakes history that a fully-loaded ore carrier had been capsized.

On Lake Huron's Canadian shore, the bodies of crew from the *Argus* and *Hydrus*, those sister ships bound for opposite ends of the lake, floated ashore together.

And when officials went to Canada to identify bodies recovered from the *Charles S. Price*, it was discovered that 12 *Price* sailors wore life preservers marked *Regina*. Crewmen from the two vessels floated ashore together, some with their arms entwined around each other. But no *Regina* sailor wore a *Price* life preserver.

The mystery remains unsolved to this day. Did the two ships somehow come together in the storm and men passed from one vessel to the other, seizing whatever life preservers were available? Or were the life preservers thrown to *Price* crewmen struggling in the water? If so, what of the *Hawgood*'s report of having seen the two ships 15 miles apart, and at a time that was likely to have been just before the end came for both?

Only Lake Huron knows, and she has kept the secret for more than 75 years.❀   —D.D.

Excuses for a November Party

15 Georgia O'Keeffe Day

Recognized as one of the leading artists of our time, Georgia O'Keeffe grew up on a farm near Sun Prairie. Many of her paintings depict the flowers, clouds, bones, and desert hills and cliffs of the Southwest that came to be her home. But it was in Wisconsin that she drew her first pictures, had her first art lessons, declared her intention to grow up to be an artist. In 1977 she was awarded the Presidential Medal of Honor for her contributions "to the quality of American life." Born November 15, 1887, she lived to the age of 98.

18 Escape to Wisconsin

The magician Harry Houdini, who grew up in Appleton, was an escape artist who amazed the public by escaping from paper bags, plate glass boxes, packing boxes, zinc-lined piano boxes,

prison cells, iron cages, and burglar-proof safes. On November 18, 1917, he released himself from a straitjacket while suspended by his heels 40 feet over Broadway in New York. In his earlier days, he made a 10,000-pound elephant, with a blue ribbon around her neck, disappear.

Tailgate Party

With just three minutes of play remaining, Wisconsin began an 80-yard drive that finally subdued a stubborn Minnesota team 14-9 and won the Badgers a trip to the 1963 Rose Bowl. (On New Year's Day, however, despite a 23-point fourth-quarter rally, Wisconsin lost to Southern California 42-37.)

Thanksgiving

In 1939, Wisconsin had two Thanksgiving days. Because the last Thursday of November fell on the last day of the month, President Roosevelt moved Thanksgiving to November 23 to give the merchants across the country an extra week of Christmas sales. Governor Julius P. Heil, who disagreed with FDR on most subjects, said that in Wisconsin Thanksgiving would be on November 30. Schools, banks, stores, offices, and families had to choose which day to observe Thanksgiving. Some chose the 23rd, some chose the 30th, and some chose both.

Venison Delights

Mention deer hunting to Joseph Hinrichs and he immediately has visions of sumptuous venison stew or moist pot roast.

When Hinrichs is not working as a professional chef in Madison, he is likely to be hunting deer with a bow or gun near his home in Mount Horeb.

"Deer hunting is a tradition in our family. During the gun season I've hunted from the same stand since 1970," he said.

It was on the same farm where he hunts today that he shot an eight-point buck on the last day of his first deer season. He calls it beginner's luck, but there is no luck involved in what he does with the venison afterward.

He removes the hide from the deer as soon as possible so the meat doesn't spoil. When the deer is dressed, and again before cooking, he makes sure all fat and connective tissue are removed.

"When I cook the venison, I never cook it so the meat is more done than medium, and it usually is rare to medium. Venison takes on a different flavor when it is cooked too long and it becomes dry," he said.

He also recommends that venison not be allowed to sit between the time it is cooked and served. Keeping the meat in a moist heat—like a pressure cooker, crock pot, or Dutch oven—keeps it from drying out.

Although he has most of his venison cut into traditional cuts of meat, he will mix some with beef, grind it into hamburger, and use it in chili, meat loaf, and goulash.

His favorite recipes are venison stew, pot roast, and venison stir fry.

Two of those recipes are included here for other cooks who also registered a deer this year.

And, yes, those who did not register a deer can still use these recipes, but will have to settle for beef rather than venison. ❀ —*T.E.*

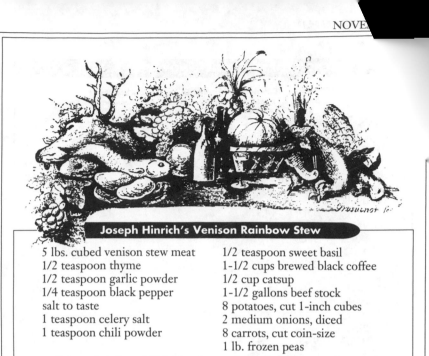

Joseph Hinrich's Venison Rainbow Stew

5 lbs. cubed venison stew meat
1/2 teaspoon thyme
1/2 teaspoon garlic powder
1/4 teaspoon black pepper
salt to taste
1 teaspoon celery salt
1 teaspoon chili powder

1/2 teaspoon sweet basil
1-1/2 cups brewed black coffee
1/2 cup catsup
1-1/2 gallons beef stock
8 potatoes, cut 1-inch cubes
2 medium onions, diced
8 carrots, cut coin-size
1 lb. frozen peas

Cut venison into 3/4-inch cubes and dust with flour and seasoning salt. Then brown in a large roasting pan. Add beef stock, coffee, catsup, onions and all the above seasoning. Bring to a boil. Reduce the heat and simmer for two hours or until the meat is tender. Add more liquid if necessary to maintain the volume at 1-1/2 gallons. Add the potatoes and carrots and cook until tender. Add frozen peas last and thicken with a butter roux (roux is equal parts of melted butter and flour formed to a cookie dough-like consistency). Serve over baking powder biscuits. This serves eight to ten cold, wet, hungry hunters.

Joseph Hinrich's Oriental Venison Stir Fry

2-3 lbs. venison steak cut julienne
    in 1/4" thick strips, 1-1/2"
    long
3 cups beef or chicken stock
1 cup soy sauce
teriyaki sauce to taste
1/4 teaspoon ground pepper
1 clove fine minced garlic
1/2 teaspoon ground sage

1/2 teaspoon sweet basil
8 oz. button mushrooms
1 green pepper cut in julienne strips
1 red pepper cut in julienne strips
3 cups celery or bok choy,
    cut diagonally
1-1/2-oz. can sliced water chestnuts
2 packages frozen snow pea pods
2 bunches green onions, cut diagonally
cornstarch for thickening sauce

In a pan, heat the stock, soy sauce, teriyaki sauce and spices. Bring to a boil and thicken with cornstarch. In a wok or large, heavy skillet, stir fry the venison steak until medium rare. Remove and put in a covered bowl. Place all the vegetables in the wok and stir fry until crisp-tender. Add hot, thickened sauce and meat to vegetables. Serve over a bed of wild rice blend.

ELECTION FOR PRESIDENT — NOVEMBER 8, 1988

County	Bush/ Quayle REP	Dukakis/ Bentsen DEM	Warren/ Mickells IND	Duke/ Parker IND	LaRouche/ Freeman IND	Paul/ Marrou IND	Fulani/ Dattner IND	Scatter
ADAMS total: 6,883	3,258	3,598	6	4	7	8	2	0
ASHLAND total: 7,489	2,926	4,526	2	7	7	10	4	7
BARRON total: 17,579	8,527	8,951	11	12	16	45	8	9
BAYFIELD total: 7,471	3,095	4,323	6	2	12	12	8	13
BROWN total: 85,953	43,625	41,788	106	104	82	196	52	0
BUFFALO total: 6,322	2,783	3,481	2	12	6	23	6	9
BURNETT total: 6,483	2,884	3,537	7	11	8	11	7	18
CALUMET total: 14,712	8,107	6,481	10	51	32	21	6	4
CHIPPEWA total: 21,367	9,757	11,447	17	28	31	53	21	13
CLARK total: 13,058	6,296	6,642	10	30	28	19	11	22
COLUMBIA total: 19,766	10,475	9,132	17	24	22	45	15	36
CRAWFORD total: 6,912	3,238	3,608	4	4	8	22	9	19
DANE total: 176,158	69,143	105,414	196	135	117	543	386	224
DODGE total: 29,950	17,003	12,663	51	93	37	66	14	23
DOOR total: 12,430	6,907	5,425	16	24	21	20	9	8
DOUGLAS total: 20,468	6,440	13,907	20	16	12	34	20	19
DUNN total: 16,625	7,273	9,205	26	23	19	37	11	31
EAU CLAIRE total: 39,023	17,664	21,150	57	37	36	60	19	0
FLORENCE total: 2,147	1,106	1,018	2	1	8	4	3	5
FOND DU LAC total: 38,193	21,985	15,887	75	56	63	86	23	18
FOREST total: 4,013	1,845	2,142	4	4	5	4	5	4
GRANT total: 19,620	10,049	9,421	21	17	19	44	9	40
GREEN total: 11,908	6,636	5,153	17	35	20	41	6	0
GREEN LAKE total: 8,299	5,205	3,033	7	20	7	21	6	0

ELECTION FOR PRESIDENT — NOVEMBER 8, 1988

County	Bush/ Quayle REP	Dukakis/ Bentsen DEM	Warren/ Mickells IND	Duke/ Parker IND	LaRouche/ Freeman IND	Paul/ Marrou IND	Fulani/ Dattner IND	Scatter
IOWA total: 8,575	4,240	4,268	5	3	5	13	14	27
IRON total: 3,717	1,599	2,090	10	5	2	5	4	2
JACKSON total: 7,523	3,555	3,924	3	11	8	11	5	6
JEFFERSON total: 26,361	14,309	11,816	42	46	32	74	23	19
JUNEAU total: 8,667	4,869	3,734	12	14	11	18	4	5
KENOSHA total: 52,149	21,661	30,089	70	83	68	120	38	20
KEWAUNEE total: 9,191	4,330	4,786	6	30	16	8	3	12
LA CROSSE total: 44,111	21,548	22,204	44	57	51	100	62	45
LAFAYETTE total: 7,235	3,665	3,521	5	5	14	15	5	5
LANGLADE total: 9,201	4,884	4,254	9	8	13	16	2	15
LINCOLN total: 11,185	5,257	5,819	22	25	16	33	6	7
MANITOWOC total: 36,025	16,020	19,680	40	113	47	63	24	38
MARATHON total: 49,543	24,482	24,658	69	74	77	125	36	22
MARINETTE total: 17,791	9,637	8,030	16	26	16	26	13	27
MARQUETTE total: 5,573	3,059	2,463	5	11	9	15	5	6
MENOMINEE total: 1,422	381	1,028	5	0	2	0	1	5
MILWAUKEE total: 440,300	168,363	268,287	567	481	332	1,082	433	751
MONROE total: 13,591	7,073	6,437	13	13	12	29	8	6
OCONTO total: 13,733	7,084	6,549	18	17	19	23	6	17
ONEIDA total: 15,670	8,130	7,414	12	21	22	55	16	0
OUTAGAMIE total: 61,304	33,113	27,771	67	135	54	103	35	26
OZAUKEE total: 35,852	22,899	12,661	32	55	31	107	27	40
PEPIN total: 3,255	1,311	1,906	13	1	6	8	3	7
PIERCE total: 14,831	6,045	8,659	11	20	14	33	7	42

ELECTION FOR PRESIDENT — NOVEMBER 8, 1988

County	Bush/ Quayle REP	Dukakis/ Bentsen DEM	Warren/ Mickells IND	Duke/ Parker IND	LaRouche/ Freeman IND	Paul/ Marrou IND	Fulani/ Dattner IND	Scatter
POLK total: 16,022	6,866	8,981	22	27	24	43	12	47
PORTAGE total: 28,542	12,057	16,317	29	23	27	48	34	7
PRICE total: 7,516	3,450	3,987	2	17	23	12	6	19
RACINE total: 76,631	36,342	39,631	155	149	74	213	67	0
RICHLAND total: 7,718	4,026	3,643	4	4	8	16	7	10
ROCK total: 58,227	28,178	29,576	81	90	45	158	60	39
RUSK total: 7,017	3,063	3,888	6	10	14	18	5	13
ST CROIX total: 21,549	9,960	11,392	21	35	42	62	21	16
SAUK total: 18,699	10,225	8,324	32	29	22	35	20	12
SAWYER total: 6,545	3,260	3,231	4	12	4	20	5	9
SHAWANO total: 15,162	8,362	6,587	11	27	32	21	7	115
SHEBOYGAN total: 47,234	23,471	23,429	41	63	52	86	35	57
TAYLOR total: 8,113	4,254	3,785	5	15	19	15	7	13
TREMPEALEAU total: 11,183	4,902	6,212	5	19	8	16	13	8
VERNON total: 11,102	5,226	5,754	13	17	21	35	12	24
VILAS total: 9,730	5,842	3,781	6	26	22	21	24	8
WALWORTH total: 30,711	18,259	12,203	38	37	42	91	15	26
WASHBURN total: 6,521	3,074	3,393	3	10	11	13	2	15
WASHINGTON total: 40,575	24,328	15,907	53	83	36	109	23	36
WAUKESHA total: 148,935	90,467	57,598	108	129	125	402	64	42
WAUPACA total: 18,784	11,559	7,078	14	43	25	30	8	27
WAUSHARA total: 8,567	4,953	3,535	7	21	15	18	4	14
WINNEBAGO total: 64,039	35,085	28,508	71	110	71	116	42	36
WOOD total: 32,856	16,549	16,074	57	56	40	52	20	8
TOTAL: 2,191,612	**1,047,499**	**1,126,794**	**2,574**	**3,056**	**2,302**	**5,157**	**1,953**	**2,273**

WISCONSIN VOTE IN PRESIDENTIAL ELECTIONS — 1848-1988

1848
Lewis Cass (D)	15,001
Zachary Taylor (W)	13,747
Martin Van Buren (FS)	10,418

1852
Franklin Pierce (D)	33,658
Winfield Scott (W)	22,210
John P. Hale (FS)	8,814

1856
John C. Fremont (R)	66,090
James Buchanan (D)	62,843
Millard Fillmore (A)	579

1860
Abraham Lincoln (R)	86,113
Stephen A. Douglas (D)	65,021
John C. Breckinridge (SoD)	888
John Bell (CU)	161

1864
Abraham Lincoln (R)	83,458
George B. McClellan (D)	65,884

1868
Ulysses S. Grant (R)	108,857
Horatio Seymour (D)	84,707

1872
Ulysses S. Grant (R)	104,994
Horace Greeley (D & LR)	86,477
Charles O'Conor (D)	834

1876
Rutherford B. Hayes (R)	130,668
Samuel J. Tilden (D)	123,927
Peter Cooper (G)	1,509
Green Clay Smith (Proh)	27

1880
James A. Garfield (R)	144,398
Winfield S. Hancock (D)	114,644
James B. Weaver (G)	7,986
John W. Phelps (A)	91
Neal Dow (Proh)	68

1884
James G. Blaine (R)	161,157
Grover Cleveland (D)	146,477
John P. St. John (Proh)	7,656
Benjamin F. Butler (G)	4,598

1888
Benjamin Harrison (R)	176,553
Grover Cleveland (D)	155,232
Clinton B. Fisk (Proh)	14,277
Alson J. Streeter (UL)	8,552

1892
Grover Cleveland (D)	177,325
Benjamin Harrison (R)	171,101
John Bidwell (Proh)	13,136
James B. Weaver (Peo)	10,019

1896
William McKinley (R)	268,135
William J. Bryan (D)	165,523
Joshua Levering (Proh)	7,507
John M. Palmer (ND)	4,584
Charles H. Matchett (SL)	1,314
Charles E. Bentley (Nat)	346

1900
William McKinley (R)	265,760
William J. Bryan (D)	159,163
John G. Wooley (Proh)	10,027
Eugene V. Debs (SD)	7,048
Joseph F. Malloney (SL)	503

1904
Theodore Roosevelt (R)	280,164
Alton B. Parker (D)	124,107
Eugene V. Debs (SD)	28,220
Silas C. Swallow (Proh)	9,770
Thomas E. Watson (Peo)	530
Charles H. Corregan (SL)	223

WISCONSIN VOTE IN PRESIDENTIAL ELECTIONS — 1848-1988

1908
William H. Taft (R)	247,747
William J. Bryan (D)	166,632
Eugene V. Debs (SD)	28,164
Eugene W. Chafin (Proh)	11,564
August Gillhaus (SL)	314

1912
Woodrow Wilson (D)	164,230
William H. Taft (R)	130,596
Theodore Roosevelt (Prog)	62,448
Eugene V. Debs (SD)	33,476
Eugene W. Chafin (Proh)	8,584
Arthur E. Reimer (SL)	632

1916
Charles E. Hughes (R)	220,822
Woodrow Wilson (D)	191,363
Allan Benson (Soc)	27,631
J. Frank Hanly (Proh)	7,318

1920
Warren G. Harding (R)	498,576
James M. Cox (D)	113,422
Eugene V. Debs (Soc)	80,635
Aaron S. Watkins (Proh)	8,647

1924
Robert M. La Follette (Prog)	453,678
Calvin Coolidge (R)	311,614
John W. Davis (D)	68,096
William Z. Foster (Workers)	3,834
Herman P. Faris (Proh)	2,918

1928
Herbert Hoover (R)	544,205
Alfred E. Smith (D)	450,259
Norman Thomas (Soc)	18,213
William F. Varney (Proh)	2,245
William Z. Foster (Workers)	1,528
Verne L. Reynolds (SL)	381

1932
Franklin D. Roosevelt (D)	707,410
Herbert Hoover (R)	347,741
Norman Thomas (Soc)	53,379
William Z. Foster (Com)	3,112
William D. Upshaw (Proh)	2,672
Verne L. Reynolds (SL)	494

1936
Franklin D. Roosevelt (D)	802,984
Alfred M. Landon (R)	380,828
William Lemke (U)	60,297
Norman Thomas (Soc)	10,626
Earl Browder (Com)	2,197

David L. Calvin (Proh)	1,071
John W. Aiken (SL)	557

1940
Franklin D. Roosevelt (D)	704,821
Wendell Willkie (R)	679,206
Norman Thomas (Soc)	15,071
Earl Browder (Com)	2,394
Roger Babson (Proh)	2,148
John W. Aiken (SL)	1,882

1944
Thomas Dewey (R)	674,532
Franklin D. Roosevelt (D)	650,413
Norman Thomas (Soc)	13,205
Edward Teichert (Ind)	1,002

1948
Harry S Truman (D)	647,310
Thomas Dewey (R)	590,959
Henry Wallace (PP)	25,282
Norman Thomas (Soc)	12,547
Edward Teichert (Ind)	399
Farrell Dobbs (ISW)	303

1952
Dwight D. Eisenhower (R)	979,744
Adlai E. Stevenson (D)	622,175
Vincent Hallinan (IP)	2,174
Farrell Dobbs (ISW)	1,350
Darlington Hoopes (IS)	1,157
Eric Hass (ISL)	770

1956
Dwight D. Eisenhower (R)	954,844
Adlai E. Stevenson (D)	586,768
T. Coleman Andrews (Ind Con)	6,918
Darlington Hoopes (Ind Soc)	754
Eric Hass (Ind SL)	710
Farrell Dobbs (Ind SW)	564

1960
Richard M. Nixon (R)	895,175

WISCONSIN VOTE IN PRESIDENTIAL ELECTIONS — 1848-1988

John F. Kennedy (D)	830,805
Farrell Dobbs (Ind SW)	1,792
Eric Hass (Ind SL)	1,310

1964

Lyndon B. Johnson (D)	1,050,424
Barry M. Goldwater (R)	638,495
Clifton DeBerry (Ind SW)	1,692
Eric Hass (Ind SL)	1,204

1968

Richard M. Nixon (R)	809,997
Hubert H. Humphrey (D)	748,804
George C. Wallace (Ind A)	127,835
Henning A. Blomen (Ind SL)	1,338
Fred. W. Halstead (Ind SW)	1,222

1972

Richard M. Nixon (R)	989,430
George S. McGovern (D)	810,174
John G. Schmitz (A)	47,525
Benjamin M. Spock (Ind Peo)	2,701
Louis Fisher (Ind SL)	998
Gus Hall (Ind Com)	663
Evelyn Reed (Ind SW)	506

1976

Jimmy Carter (D)	1,040,232
Gerald R. Ford (R)	1,004,987
Eugene J. McCarthy (Ind)	34,943
Lester Maddox (A)	8,552
Frank P. Zeidler (Ind Soc)	4,298
Roger L. MacBride (Ind Lib)	3,814
Peter Camejo (Ind SW)	1,691
Margaret Wright (Ind Peo)	943
Gus Hall (Ind Com)	749
Lyndon LaRouche (Ind USL)	738
Jules Levin (Ind SL)	389

1980

Ronald Reagan (R)	1,088,845
Jimmy Carter (D)	981,584
John Anderson (Ind)	160,657
Ed Clark (Ind Lib)	29,135
Barry Commoner (Ind Cit)	7,767
John Rarick (Ind Con)	1,519
David McReynolds (Ind Soc)	808
Gus Hall (Ind Com)	772
Deidre Griswold (Ind WW)	414
Clifton DeBerry (Ind SW)	383

1984

Ronald Reagan (R)	1,198,800
Walter F. Mondale (D)	995,847
David Bergland (Lib)	4,884
Bob Richards (Con)	3,864

Lyndon LaRouche (Ind)	3,791
Sonia Johnson (Ind Cit)	1,456
Dennis L. Serrette (Ind WIA)	1,007
Larry Holmes (Ind WW)	619
Gus Hall (Ind Com)	597
Melvin T. Mason (Ind SW)	445

1988

Michael Dukakis (D)	1,126,794
George Bush (R)	1,047,499
R. Paul (Ind)	5,157
D. Duke (Ind)	3,056
J. Warren (Ind)	2,574
Lyndon LaRouche (Ind)	2,302
L. Fulani (Ind)	1,953

ABBREVIATIONS

A - American (Know-Nothing)
Cit - Citizens
Com - Communist
Con - Constitution
CU - Constitutional Union
D - Democrat
FS - Free Soil
G - Greenback
Ind - Independent
IP - Ind. Progressive
IS - Ind. Socialist
ISL - Ind. Socialist Labor
ISW - Ind. Socialist Worker
Lib - Libertarian
LR - Liberal Republican
Nat - National
ND - National Democrat
Peo - People's (Populist)
PP - People's Progressive
Prog - Progressive
Proh - Prohibition
R - Republican
SD - Social Democrat
Soc - Socialist
SL - Socialist Labor
SW - Socialist Worker
SoD - Southern Democrat
U - Union
UL - Union Labor
USL - U.S. Labor
W - Whig
WIA - Wis. Independent Alliance
WW - Workers World

NOTE: Candidates whose party affiliation is listed as independent with a party designation appeared on the Wisconsin ballot identified as an "independent."

Source: Wisconsin Blue Book

NOVEMBER IN THE GARDEN

Highlights:
- ❀ *Protect roses for the winter*
- ❀ *Dig hole for living Christmas tree*
- ❀ *Pot up amaryllis for holiday bloom*
- ❀ *Water evergreens for winter survival*

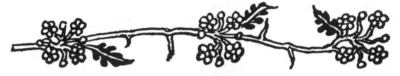

As the earth makes its annual trip around the sun, a slight tilt on its axis sends all life forms, flora and fauna, into a tizzy of activity. Autumn is at hand, and winter is poised on the backyard fence, ready to take command. Earthworms burrow deeply into the soil to escape the frost line. Humans cut and stack firewood, cauk doorframes, and stock larders. And birds—many of them, anyway—pack their bags and fly to warmer climates.

It doesn't seem fair that the smallest birds have to fly the farthest, but it's true. Robins generally fly to Florida or the Gulf Coast, where there are still plenty of insects and earthworms to eat. Phoebes and flycatchers go farther, down to Mexico and Central America for their preferred cuisine. But the tiny ruby-throated hummingbird must go farther than any—all the way to the tropical rain forests of South America. Of all the hummingbird species in the world, the ruby-throated is the only one who chose Wisconsin for its summer home. We wish her well on her arduous journey, and already look forward to her return next spring.

The gardener's November is relaxed, a brief respite between the autumn harvest and the busy holiday season. But there are still chores to keep one out of the house on a nice Saturday afternoon.

Roses should be protected when the plants are completely dormant. The plastic foam cones are good, but not fully trustworthy in a really cold winter. Much better, albeit more work, is the famous "Minnesota tip." In this method, the soil is loosened around the base of the plant, a trench is dug, leading from the plant base away in any direction, and the entire plant is then tipped over and covered with soil for the winter.

Evergreens need soil moisture throughout the winter, and this month is your last chance to provide that moisture. Especially if the autumn has been dry, give every specimen plant a very thorough, slow soaking, lasting at least four hours. The importance of this chore cannot be overstressed.

If you have amaryllis bulbs resting in your basement, repot them into fresh soil and bring them up during the first week in the month, if you want them to bloom during the holidays. Now is also the time to buy and start new amaryllis bulbs.

Do not mulch with leaves that pack down into a dense carpet when wet. Instead, shred them. If you don't have a shredder, use a rotary lawn mower. Catch them in your bagger or blow them against a fence or garage wall.

If frost killed your chrysanthemums before they had a chance to bloom, you probably have a variety unsuited to this climate. And if you receive a pot of blooming chrysanthemums for Thanksgiving, give them bright light, cool temperatures, and plenty of water for longest bloom.

Clean out your windowboxes and replace summer plants with evergreen boughs and berries. They will stay green over the holiday season, at least.

Pray for the Packers.❀

—J.M.

Wood Measure

To ascertain the contents or number of cords in a given pile of wood — Multiply the length by the width, and that product by the height, which will give you the number of cubic feet. Divide that product by 128, and the quotient will be the number of cords. A pile of wood 4 feet wide, and 4 feet high, and 8 feet long, contains 1 "cord"; and a "cord foot" is l foot in length of such a pile.❧

—*Farmer's and Mechanics Manual, 1869*

Uncle Woody *Says*

Whitetails Aplenty. If you enjoy watching deer, drive around on the rural, back roads during dawn and evening hours. These are the times that deer are feeding in fields, along woodland edges, Find an area where there's little traffic and drive slowly.

NOVEMBER RECIPE

Cranberry Fiber-Full Fruit Salad

Dressing:
6 tablespoons orange juice
3 tablespoons salad oil
2 teaspoons honey
1 teaspoon grated orange peel
1/2-teaspoon salt
1/4-teaspoon freshly ground pepper

Salad:
1 large red apple, cored and diced
1 large pear, cored and diced
1-1/2 cups cranberries, coarsely chopped
3 tablespoons golden raisins
2 tablespoons sugar
6 cups spinach, coarsely chopped
1/2 small red onion, finely chopped
2 tablespoons sliced almonds
2 medium oranges, peeled and sectioned
2 tablespoons pumpkin or sunflower seeds

In a medium bowl combine apple and pear with 1/4 cup dressing. Cover and refrigerate 1 to 2 hours. Combine cranberries with raisins and sugar. Set aside 2 hours. Just before serving, toss spinach and onion with remaining dressing. Arrange on platter or dish. With slotted spoon arrange apple and pear in center. Surround with cranberry and raisin mixture. Add oranges. Sprinkle with nuts and seeds.

—*Mary Jean Hlavac, McFarland*

A Brush with Death

Armistice Day brings back memories for many Wisconsin duck hunters.

They remember November 11, 1940, when the wind howled, bringing blinding sleet and Arctic temperatures.

With the winds came the ducks, searching for secluded water and shelter. Hunters sensed that the hunting would be good and were in the marshes. It was a day that ducks died, but so did some hunters.

"That was the closest that I ever came to 'cashing in the chips,'" said Earl Loyster of Madison. Loyster was hunting on Lake Maria in Green Lake County the day the big storm hit. He now smiles as he tells about his flirt with death. But he wasn't smiling on that day.

Loyster, 28 years old at the time, was employed by the Milwaukee Public Museum. A year later he joined the Wisconsin Conservation Department. He retired as Southern District wildlife staff specialist for the Department of Natural Resources in 1974.

On the morning of that November day in 1940, Loyster drove from Milwaukee to Lake Maria in a drizzling, warm rain. He launched his duck boat from the Hein farm on the lake's north side and proceeded to hunt ducks from a small blind he had constructed out of burlap. "Towards midday the wind started blowing and it got worse, much worse," Loyster said. "I figured that it would calm down as the afternoon went on, but it didn't. It became difficult to see as the wind drove snow and sleet horizontally.

"But, with the wind came ducks. I saw flocks of 150 to 300 ducks in the air. There were flocks all over that day and a mixture of all species, such as mallards, teal, and ringnecks. They were in big flocks and had it not been for the weather, the limit of 10 birds would have been easy to get. It was a phenomenal day for waterfowling," Loyster said.

Loyster estimated that within a

wo-hour period, the temperature dropped about 60 degrees and the wind was blowing at speeds of 70 miles per hour with gusts up to 90.

"I decided to lay down in the boat and wait out the storm, but suddenly the wind took hold of the chicken-wire blind surrounding my boat and blew it away. With that, the wind quickly blew my boat to shore as the waves filled it with water.

"I was wet and cold and realized that I had to find shelter. I decided to walk to the Ernest Weber farm which was nearby. The walking was extremely difficult as the wind and snow blew so hard that I could hardly see where I was going. It eventually blew me over and I crawled up the hill towards the farmhouse. My clothes were covered with ice by that time," Loyster said.

Along the way, he abandoned his gun and shells. Once at the boundary of the farmyard, he lunged forward and lay resting just inside the fence.

"I knew that I had to get into the house, but I literally could not move." At that moment a bit of luck happened, as the gale ripped part of the metal roof off the nearby barn. Mr. Weber heard the noise from inside the farmhouse and came out to investigate.

"I had to do something to attract his attention so I yelled as loud as I could," he said. "He heard me, but couldn't see me because the sleet was so thick. He came in my direction and only when he got to within a few feet did he finally see me." Mr. Weber dragged Loyster into the farmhouse, where he and Mrs. Weber peeled off the icy clothing and warmed him in a hot bath.

"The next day my hands were all puffy, but I was glad to be alive. I looked outside to find the temperature well below freezing and dressed warmly to retrieve some of my things. The lake was frozen, though not solid, and I found my gun and shells near the boat. Further along the lake edge I jumped a mallard, but when I pulled the trigger to shoot, my gun was frozen tight and didn't shoot."

Loyster went back to the Weber farm, where he laid the gun near the radiator to thaw out.

"I was in the kitchen a few minutes later when suddenly the gun went off in the other room. The heat thawed the mechanism, releasing the firing pin and sending a charge of shot across the room. The shot disintegrated a wooden rocking chair. Fortunately nobody was in the room and the Webers told me not the worry about the rocker."

The radio reported that the roads were coated with ice and many telephone lines were down the day after the storm. He wasn't able to leave until the second day after the storm. Even then, Loyster's first trip was into Markesan to replace the rocking chair.❧   —T.E.

Solitude

by Ella Wheeler Wilcox
(born near Madison, 1855)

Laugh, and the world laughs with you;
    Weep, and you weep alone;
For the sad old earth must borrow its mirth,
    But has trouble enough of its own.
Sing, and the hills will answer;
    Sigh, it is lost on the air;
The echoes bound to a joyful sound,
    But shrink from voicing care.

Rejoice, and men will seek you;
    Grieve, and they turn and go;
They want full measure of all your pleasure,
    But they do not need your woe.
Be glad, and your friends are many;
    Be sad, and you lose them all—
There are none to decline your nectared
      wine,
    But alone you must drink life's gall.

Feast, and your halls are crowded;
    Fast, and the world goes by.
Succeed and give, and it helps you live,
    But no man can help you die.
There is room in the halls of pleasure
    For a large and lordly train,
But one by one we must all file on
    Through the narrow aisles of pain.

Wild Turkeys in Wisconsin

Governor William Bradford, his Plymouth colonists, and their wild turkeys won't be at our Thanksgiving dinner, but some distant offspring of those first wild turkeys certainly will be featured.

Our modern day wild turkey was shot May 2 in Crawford County and has been in the deep freeze for this special Thanksgiving Day.

It will be roasted along with one of its domestic brethren, for the one 18-pounder just won't feed the whole clan. The gobbler will be accompanied with my aunt's 24-hour fruit salad, my wife Linda's special stuffing, mashed potatoes, and followed with Mom's homemade pumpkin pie.

Our surroundings will be much more comfortable than that first Thanksgiving. It was September of 1620, as schoolchildren well know, when the *Mayflower* set out for America with its 120 passengers and sighted land in November. That first winter was tragic, as about half the pilgrims perished.

But the following spring the Indians showed the survivors how to plant corn "when the oak leaves are as big as mouse-ears." And plant they did, and celebrated their bountiful harvest with the Indians who brought deer and wild turkeys for the feast.

At that time wild turkeys filled the woods surrounding the first colonies. In Wisconsin, the earliest record of wild turkeys was in 1670 when the Jesuit Allouez noted turkeys in the Lake Winnebago area. Later records indicate that turkeys were abundant south of a line from Green Bay to Prairie du Chien. The largest concentration of turkeys was most likely in southwestern Wisconsin. During the early 1800's, flocks of from 10 to 40 wild turkeys were seen frequently in forests along the Grant River. In 1856, wild turkeys sold for 25 cents apiece around Lancaster.

By 1860, turkey sightings were rare, and the last turkey noted was near Darlington in May of 1881. Where they once were found over the southern half of the state, settlement, clearing of forests, unregulated hunting, and the introduction of domestic fowl, which brought with them many diseases, all led to the demise of the wild turkey population.

Between 1954 and 1957, the Wisconsin Conservation Department, predecessor to today's much larger Department of Natural Resources (DNR), released 827 turkeys in the Meadow Valley Wildlife Area and Necedah National Wildlife Refuge. The birds were purchased from a game farm in Pennsylvania, the progeny of domestic pen-reared hens and wild, free-ranging gobblers.

Although this part-wild strain of birds seemed to be adapting to their new home, a disease outbreak killed hundreds of birds. A severe winter combined with a poor corn crop took its toll the following year and nearly eliminated the flock. Since then, the Meadow Valley flock has increased slowly in numbers.

As Wisconsin's forests matured, wildlife biologists realized that good turkey habitat existed in the southwestern counties. The hardwood forests provided acorns, small streams provided open water, rolling hills provided south-facing slopes, and agricultural crops provided excellent brood habitat and winter food.

In 1974, the DNR began the successful turkey reintroduction program when it traded 135 live-trapped ruffed grouse for 45 live-trapped wild turkeys from Missouri. The birds were trapped by the Missouri Conservation Department, and the first group of 20 hens and nine gobblers were released in Vernon County on a cold winter day in 1976.

Turkey populations have since been established along the Mississippi River from Buffalo down to Grant counties, and inland to Richland, Sauk, and Iowa counties. Currently, Wisconsin has a flock of about 20,000 to 30,000 wild turkeys.

The glimpse of young "jake" turkeys noiselessly walking through a forest or of an old Tom displaying his bronze finery, strutting and gobbling, is a sight that nobody can forget.

So, pass the gravy and the stuffing. Spoon out some veggies and add a hot buttered bun alongside the plate. But, then please pass that wild turkey my way, while I lift a glass of wine to toast that grand old bird, and the fact that he once again struts across Wisconsin ridge tops, fills the woods with excited gobbling, and is part of our traditional Thanksgiving.❀
                                                                              —*T.E.*

DECEMBER

What freezings I have felt,
what dark days seen!
What old December's bareness
every where.

— *Shakespeare, Sonnet 97*

December brings the official start of winter.
The sun sinks lower and lower on the horizon
for the first three weeks of the month. At the
winter solstice, on or about the 21st, the direct
rays of the sun fall on the Tropic of Capricorn
(23 1/2 degrees south of the equator), which is
the southernmost point in its annual journey.
The solstice brings the shortest day and the
longest night of the year, with about 16 hours of
darkness in Wisconsin. December is the cloudi-
est month. In the northern Great Lakes region,
the sun will shine only about 25 percent of the
time. December is also the snowiest month in
Wisconsin. White Christmases occur about 60
percent of the time. ❋

December Weather History

MADISON

Day	Record High		Record Low		Record Precip.		Average High/Low
1	62	1970	-11	1893	1.73	1985	36/20
2	62	1982	-12	1886	1.58	1982	36/19
3	61	1951	-12	1940	0.92	1932	35/19
4	59	1961	-15	1886	0.97	1973	35/18
5	60	1960	-15	1871	1.16	1982	35/18
6	53	1897,1988	-11	1972	1.32	1884	34/18
7	60	1916	-15	1972	1.17	1967	34/17
8	60	1946	-16	1876	0.82	1966	33/17
9	60	1946	-22	1876	0.73	1879	33/17
10	55	1911	-16	1919	1.34	1970	33/16
11	59	1946	-17	1972,76	1.02	1869	32/16
12	53	1968	-10	1962	0.96	1909	32/15
13	57	1975	-17	1903	1.09	1928	31/15
14	59	1975	-17	1901	1.04	1891	31/15
15	51	1957	-16	1901	1.57	1971	31/14
16	57	1959	-18	1876	0.55	1879	30/14
17	54	1939	-13	1972	0.44	1896	30/14
18	53	1923	-20	1884	0.57	1957	30/13
19	53	1918	-25	1983	0.76	1987	29/13
20	62	1877	-17	1963	0.80	1882	29/13
21	58	1877	-22	1872	0.85	1887	29/12
22	54	1875	-17	1983	1.18	1869	28/12
23	58	1877	-21	1983	0.64	1941	28/11
24	60	1889	-28	1872	1.01	1979	28/11
25	56	1982	-15	1983	0.67	1876	28/11
26	50	1936	-22	1962	1.07	1888	27/11
27	50	1946	-26	1886	2.54	1904	27/10
28	62	1984	-21	1924	0.79	1987	27/10
29	54	1984	-21	1880	0.93	1914	26/10
30	54	1936	-16	1887	1.65	1884	26/9
31	55	1955	-16	1967	0.85	1876	26/9

DECEMBER

December Weather History

LA CROSSE

Day	Record High		Record Low		Average High/Low
1	60	1962	-12	1893	35/20
2	64	1982	-10	1940	35/20
3	61	1961	-19	1940	34/19
4	61	1961	-7	1950	34/19
5	60	1975	-5	1880	33/18
6	55	1939	-16	1972	33/18
7	57	1916	-20	1882	32/18
8	55	1946	-16	1876	32/17
9	53	1939	-24	1876	32/17
10	56	1979	-18	1919	31/16
11	56	1949	-11	1936	31/16
12	57	1968	-13	1958	30/15
13	56	1891	-23	1901	30/15
14	50	1894	-23	1901	30/15
15	52	1923	-23	1901	29/14
16	58	1959	-21	1932	29/14
17	52	1895	-19	1985	29/13
18	54	1923	-26	1983	28/13
19	51	1923	-30	1983	28/12
20	54	1894	-24	1983	28/12
21	60	1877	-29	1872	27/12
22	58	1877	-23	1983	27/11
23	59	1877	-28	1872	27/11
24	61	1889	-37	1872	26/10
25	55	1936	-26	1879	26/10
26	54	1936	-24	1914	26/10
27	51	1936	-23	1880	25/9
28	60	1984	-25	1880	25/9
29	46	1908	-22	1880	25/9
30	55	1875	-18	1946	24/8
31	59	1965	-24	1946	24/8

The normal average precipitation for La Crosse in December is 1.07 inches. The wettest December was in 1875 when 3.43 inches was recorded; the driest was in 1943 when only 0.01 was received.

Body Heat
GEORGE VUKELICH

When you live up in the north country in winter, you just naturally keep track of things, because you could wind up freezing your buns if you don't.

So you come to know when the ice on the lakes is strong enough to support you without a snowmobile, then with a snowmobile, and then, eventually, with a whole snowmobile club.

Three Lakes, Wis., is just full of folks who keep track of such things. They know when certain things are supposed to happen, and if those things don't happen on schedule they get antsy. Well, the lakes froze over pretty much on schedule this year, but the Christmas creche over at St. Theresa's that's usually set up by this time *wasn't*.

Folks got to talking about it, especially those who go to Mass and were eyewitnesses. the eyewitnesses took it upon themselves to spread the truth into every nook and cranny of Oneida County, including the American Legion Bar.

The other night Gene Stepshinski was just about to close when Doc came in from a call in the country. They were sitting there, having "a toddy for the body," as Doc puts it, when Father Himmelsbach came in, looking, as Gene says, like a rabbit that just found out beagles weren't family.

Gene got out the brandy, poured a shot and asked him what was wrong. Father Himmelsbach knocked back the brandy and said:

"I can't find *Jesus*."

"God," Doc said. "That's like your pilot telling you he can't find O'Hare."

"The baby Jesus got lost," Father Himmelsbach said. "That's why the creche isn't up. I've been looking for a week."

"What you gotta do," Doc said, "is ask St. Anthony. If St. Anthony can't find Jesus, we're all in trouble."

"Everybody else is there," Father Himmelsbach said. "Mary, Joseph, the shepherds, the kings, the animals, the camels. Even the crib is there, but baby Jesus is missing."

"Listen," Gene said. "We'll lock up here and go have a look-see."

"Sure, Father," Doc said. "What could we lose?"

Father Himmelsbach didn't think that was so funny.

The church was warm and cozy, the heat clunking through the pipes like little animals scuttling in the darkness. Father Himmelsbach turned on the sanctuary lights and there it was: the manger at Bethlehem. It looked like a disaster area. Beneath the blue spruce branches, the carved

wooden figures were scattered about. The boxes and tissue paper looked like windblown debris. Doc offered his professional opinion right away.

"You could say it was vandals," he said.

Gene began lining up the figures in the traditional arrangement, two lines radiating outward from the stable, with the manger in the center.

"Yeah," Doc said, "you notice right away the crib is empty."

Gene backed up and stood there, arms akimbo. Then he began tapping his lips with the forefinger of his right hand. He does that just before he climbs into a trout stream, too.

"I just looked *everywhere*," Father Himmelsbach said. "You can't replace pieces like that anymore. You need an old-time carver."

"You know," Doc said, "the last time I was in a sanctuary I was getting married. And before that I was serving Mass. Back in the old days, before Rome changed all that and turned you guys around."

Gene looked as wooden as the figures he was staring at.

Father Himmelsbach scratched his head.

"We could skip the whole thing," he said, "but there'd be hell to pay. Another tradition shot. A guitar Mass for the old-timers."

"It all comes back to me, like riding a bicycle," Doc said. "Once you learn, you never forget. *Confiteor Deo omnipotenti, beate Mariae semper virgini, beato Michaeli archangelo, beato Johanni Bapistae, sanctis apostolis Petro et Paulo.* Didn't the Jesuits say that if they had the child for the first seven years of life, they had the child forever?

"It's just amazing how you get imprinted," he said. "I haven't said a Latin prayer since I was a little boy, and there it is. It's all right there. I confess to almighty God, to blessed Mary ever virgin, to blessed Michael the archangel, to blessed John the Baptist, to the holy apostles Peter and Paul. The part I liked best was *mea culpa*, *mea culpa*, *mea maxima culpa:* through my fault, through my fault, through my most *grievous* fault. *Maxima*. To the max. Good time to try that one, Father."

Gene suddenly slapped his hands together, and it sounded like a pistol shot in the empty church. He leaped to the creche and began moving the wooden figures.

"We're talking about a cold night," he said. "Right? We're talking about a baby in a stable—a newborn baby, right? Now, who in his right mind is not gonna be concerned for the kid in the cold? The night wind and the chill and the drafts?

"We're talking *body heat*," Gene said. "These are folks who know all about cold nights and heat loss. We're talking survivors."

He moved the figures with a gentle touch, nudging them to make room for the others who huddled tightly around the creche, not only to worship, but to keep a little baby alive on a cold winter's night.

"You wrap the baby so you can barely see anything sticking out," Gene said. "Insulate him. Pile straw around him, over him. You get his mom right over him, and you get the sheep and the donkeys right up close so they're radiating heat like Coleman stoves. You get one row of shepherds up close, then another, another and another. You got a windbreak that won't quit. All you can see from out here is their backs. But you *know* a baby is in there. You take it on *faith*."

That's the way it is this Christmas in Three Lakes. Everybody crowding in, keeping the cold world off the Little One. When you think about it, that's the way it *should* be. ❀

Excuses for a December Party

Holiday Open House

Frank Lloyd Wright, who was born in Richland Center, was a rare American genius whose innovative designs changed American architecture permanently, especially its residences. As a finishing touch to one of his houses, he carved over the fireplace: "The reality of the house is order/ The blessing of the house is community/The glory of the house is hospitality/The crown of the house is godliness." His ideas owed much to his communion with the southern Wisconsin countryside and his use of native materials. Wright's work expressed his philosophy that land, nature, buildings and furnishings should be treated as one.

Ethnic Festival

Wisconsin has been called a living ethnological museum for its variety of people of different nationalities. First the French, then Teutonic, Scandinavian, and Slavic groups have contributed dress, diet, and customs to the cultural mix. The most recent addition are the Hmong people of Southeast Asia, thousands of whom have settled in Eau Claire, La Crosse, Madison, and Sheboygan. They are admired particularly for their rich heritage of art needlework.

Sing-along

Wisconsin song-writers offer much material to choose from.

From the nineteenth century: "After the Ball," the leading sob ballad of the 1890, by Milwaukee banjo teacher Charles K. Harris; such songs of sentiment as "I Love You Truly" and "O Promise Me," by Carrie Jacobs-Bond, of Janesville; the tender "Silver Threads Among the Gold," by Eben E. Rexford, of Shiocton; and such hymns of the hereafter as "In the Sweet Bye and Bye," by Samuel F. Bennett and Joseph P. Webster, of Elkhorn. Today, Peter and Lou Berryman write from the heart too, but with more humor. Their songbooks cover the subjects of Wisconsin weather and people— "Weyauwega Moon," "Pour Me More Polka," "The February March," "Why Am I Painting the Living Room," "Who Put the Si in Siberia?" . . .

31 Super Bowl Warmup

On December 31, 1967, Bart Starr's touchdown with 13 seconds remaining gave the Green Bay Packers a 21-17 win over the Dallas Cowboys for its third straight NFL title and a trip to Super Bowl I.

Although it was 13 degrees below zero at Lambeau Field that day—48 degrees below with the wind chill factor—50,861 fans packed the stadium. TV commentator Frank Gifford quipped, "Excuse me while I take a bite of my coffee."

The Christmas Tree Ship

Of an estimated 6,000 to 8,000 maritime disasters in the 300 years of navigation on the Great Lakes, few have captured the imagination like the disappearance of the Christmas Tree Ship in a 1912 Lake Michigan gale.

The 123-foot, three-masted schooner *Rouse Simmons* was built in Milwaukee in 1868. She was owned and skippered by Captain Herman Schunemann, of Chicago, who kept the schooner eking out a profit in an era when steam and propellers were sounding the death knell for sailing ships.

Each November Schunemann took the *Simmons* to Thompson Harbor, Michigan, near Manistique, on Lake Michigan's north shore, and filled her to the limit with Christmas trees. He then took his piney load to Chicago, where he tied up in the Chicago River at the Clark Street Bridge and, with the help of his wife and daughters, sold the trees directly from the ship. It was the one cargo that each year assured Schunemann of a good profit.

By 1912, the *Rouse Simmons* was well past her prime. Sailors' scuttlebutt had it that the rats abandoned her that summer — a sure sign a ship was doomed, but Captain Schunemann sailed the entire season and took her to Thompson Harbor in November.

It had been a good year for Christmas trees, and there were perhaps 35,000 waiting on the dock when the *Rouse Simmons* arrived. The crewmen tied the trees in bundles and jammed them into every nook and cranny of the ship. Captain Schunemann even added a deck load, piling hundreds of trees on the deck and lashing them down as best possible. When the last was aboard, the *Rouse Simmons* sat low in the water, a veritable mountain of fragrant green trees from bowsprit to stern.

The schooner set sail for Chicago on Thursday, November 21, with Lake Michigan's notorious autumn weather brewing thick and worsening. The skipper of the schooner *Butcher Boy* saw her depart and told his crew, "I wouldn't go out in this storm for all the trees the *Mauritania* could carry." He later told a reporter, "There was a heavy head sea running. Later there was sudden nasty weather, about the most sudden I remember."

The Christmas Tree Ship's course took her southerly down cucumber-shaped Lake Michigan, past the treacherous island and shoal-studded passage between Green Bay and Lake Michigan, and along the thumb of Wisconsin's Door Peninsula. No one knows just what happened, but the scenario is easily imagined.

The winds reached 60 miles per hour as they howled through the *Rouse Simmons'* tattered rigging. The old ship groaned and shuddered in protest as the massive gray-green waves battered her tired hull and swept through her piney deck load. Some of the trees were washed overboard, or perhaps jettisoned by her frightened crew. The schooner's yawl boat was swept away.

The "sudden nasty weather" the *Butcher Boy*'s master reported probably caught the Christmas Tree Ship off the Door Peninsula, bringing with it a blinding blanket of snow and a terrifying drop in temperature.

Each wave that boarded the vessel now left a thin coat of ice that thickened with each succeeding sea. Water seeped around the canvas-covered hatches, and the hold began to flood. The lower rigging and sails grew rigid, and the trees left on deck turned white with ice. Waterlogged and growing top heavy, the *Rouse Simmons* began ever-so-slowly to settle.

At 3 P.M. on Saturday, November 23, a lookout at the Kewaunee Life Saving Station spotted a three-masted schooner—presumably the *Rouse Simmons*—ice-encrusted and flying distress signals, pounding southward before a northwest gale.

The schooner was too far off shore, and the seas were too rough for Kewaunee's small surfboat, and the station commander hurried to the harbor to find a tug to go to her aid. None were available. Heavy snow then began to fall and the *Rouse Simmons* was lost to view behind a veil of white. The Two Rivers Life Saving Station, 30 miles to the south, was alerted and a power lifeboat rushed to the scene. But despite an extensive search, there was no sign of the vessel. The Christmas Tree Ship was missing.

A series of fierce gales lashed Lake Michigan in the days after the schooner disappeared, and bundles of Christmas trees began to come ashore on western beaches. A yawl boat, identical to that carried by the *Simmons*, was found tossing in the waves off Kewaunee, but there were no markings to prove its origin. Commercial fishermen from Two Rivers began to lift bits of evergreen in their nets.

After three weeks, the *Rouse Simmons* was given up for lost. Captain Schunemann's wife and daughters moored a schooner at the *Simmons*' old slip and filled it with trees shipped to Chicago by rail. Demand was overwhelming.

The following spring, Two Rivers fishermen found their nets clogged with trees, and it was assumed the Christmas Tree Ship's final resting place lay somewhere off that port. Twelve years after the vessel disappeared, a wallet belonging to Captain Herman Schunemann was raised in a fish tug's nets, and the Christmas Tree Ship became part of Great Lakes folklore. The story's final chapter was written on Halloween of 1970,

when a team of scuba divers stumbled across the schooner's remains in 180 feet of water.

The Christmas Tree Ship lies about eight miles off the Wisconsin shore between Kewaunee and Two Rivers, sitting upright and very close to level. The bow points roughly west-southwest. The deckload of Christmas trees is mostly gone. There are a few on the bottom of the lake off to one side of the ship, but most of the Christmas trees that remain are in the *Rouse Simmons'* hold. Lake Michigan's cold water acts as a preservative, and many of the trees still retain their needles.

Divers report there is still a large amount of debris on the *Rouse Simmons'* deck, which is unusual, because debris normally floats away or is blown off by the rush of compressed air when a ship sinks.

There is much speculation about the *Rouse Simmons'* last hours— a feeling that rigging and parts of the masts collapsed under the weight of the ice that built up and fell across the rear deck. As the waves boarded the ship, the theory goes, the debris would have frozen to the deck and cabin, which would have kept it from floating away when the ship sank. Then the ice melted, which accounts for the large amounts of debris on deck.

To date, the remains of the *Rouse Simmons* have not been seriously scavenged or vandalized, an increasingly common practice that gives Great Lakes shipwreck divers much concern.

Most divers view the Christmas Tree Ship as special, a symbol of the maritime way of life on the Great Lakes. Hers is a classic tale of iron men and wooden ships struggling against the sea, and she represents all the men and all the ships "gone down to the sea." ❀   —*D.D.*

Wisconsin's 72 Counties

Wisconsin's 72 counties were created by the legislature and named by their people. The names reflect history, for they represent U.S. Presidents; military and political figures; adventurers and trail blazers; Indian tribes; natural phenomena; Indian words and French words for phenomena; as well as a wife, a battlefield, and an animal that once roamed here.

ADAMS
Created: 1848
County seat: Friendship ZIP: 53934
Population: 15,099   Rank in State: 61
Land area (sq. mi.): 648 Rank in State: 43
Water area (sq. mi.): 5
Per capita income: $5,082
Notable natural feature: Roche a Cri, a sandstone butte rising 300 feet above surrounding plain

ASHLAND
Created: 1860
County seat: Ashland   ZIP: 54806
Other places: Gingles, Mellen
Population: 16,734   Rank in State: 57
Land area (sq. mi.): 1,048
Rank in State: 11
Water area (sq. mi.): 12
Per capita income: $5,712
Notable natural feature: Apostle Islands

BARRON
Created: 1859
County seat: Barron   ZIP: 54812
Other places: Cumberland, Rice Lake
Population: 40,732   Rank in State: 30
Land area (sq. mi.): 865 Rank in State: 23
Water area (sq. mi): 29
Per capita income: $6,187
Notable natural feature: lakes and rolling landscape

BAYFIELD
Created: 1845
County seat: Washburn   ZIP: 54891
Other places: Bayfield, Cable
Population: 14,118 Rank in State: 64
Land area (sq. mi.): 1,462 Rank in State: 2
Water area (sq. mi.): 37.7
Per capita income: $5,702
Notable natural feature: Apostle Islands National Lakeshore

BROWN
Created: 1818
County seat: Green Bay   ZIP: 54305
Other places: Allouez, De Pere
Population: 187,471 Rank in State: 4
Land area (sq. mi.): 524 Rank in State: 56
Water area (sq. mi.): 3
Per capita income: $9,484
Notable natural features: Fox River and Green Bay

BUFFALO
Created: 1853
County seat: Alma ZIP: 54610
Other places: Fountain City, Mondovi
Population: 14,253 Rank in State: 62
Land area (sq. mi.): 699 Rank in State: 42
Water area (sq. mi.): 13
Per capita income: $5,852
Notable natural feature: bluffs and cliffs along the Mississippi River

BURNETT
Created: 1856
County seat: Meenon
Mailing address: Siren, WI 54872
Other places: Grantsburg, Wood River
Population: 12,893 Rank in State: 66
Land area (sq. mi.): 818 Rank in State: 28
Water area (sq. mi.): 54
Per capita income: $5,248
Notable natural features: 318 lakes, 5 rivers, many streams

CALUMET
Created: 1836
County seat: Chilton ZIP: 53014
Other places: Brillion, New Holstein
Population: 33,514 Rank in State: 36
Land area (sq. mi.): 326 Rank in State: 68
Water area (sq. mi.): 0.6
Per capita income: $7,993
Notable natural feature: Lake Winnebago beaches

CHIPPEWA
Created: 1845
County seat: Chippewa Falls ZIP: 54729
Other places: Bloomer, Lafayette
Population: 53,886 Rank in State: 23
Land area (sq. mi.): 1,017
Rank in State: 12
Water area (sq. mi.): 34
Per capita income: $6,325
Notable natural feature: pure water from deep springs

CLARK
Created: 1853
County seat: Neillsville ZIP: 54456
Other places: Loyal, Thorp
Population: 32,613 Rank in State: 38
Land area (sq. mi.): 1,218 Rank in State: 7
Water area (sq. mi.): 6
Per capita income: $4,976
Notable natural feature: dairyland (fourth in U.S. milk production)

COLUMBIA
Created: 1846
County seat: Portage ZIP: 53901
Other places: Columbus, Lodi
Population: 43,902 Rank in State: 28
Land area (sq. mi.): 771 Rank in State: 34
Water area (sq. mi.): 36
Per capita income: $7,746
Notable natural features: Wisconsin River and Lake Wisconsin

CRAWFORD
Created: 1818
County seat: Prairie du Chien ZIP: 53821
Other places: Gays Mills, Soldiers Grove
Population: 16,527 Rank in State: 58
Land area (sq. mi.): 566 Rank in State: 52
Water area (sq. mi.): 12
Per capita income: $5,131
Notable natural feature: largest caverns, at Kickapoo Indian Caverns

DANE
Created: 1836
County seat: Madison ZIP: 53709
Other places: Middleton, Sun Prairie
Population: 341,262
Rank in State: 2
Land area (sq. mi.): 1,205 Rank in State: 8
Water area (sq. mi.): 36
Per capita income: $10,367
Notable natural features: Yahara River valley and its chain of lakes

DODGE
Created: 1836
County seat: Juneau ZIP: 53039
Other places: Beaver Dam, Horicon
Population: 76,631 Rank in State: 17
Land area (sq. mi.): 887 Rank in State: 21
Water area (sq. mi.): 24
Per capita income: $7,529
Notable natural feature: 21,000-acre Horicon National Wildlife Refuge

DOOR
Created: 1851
County seat: Sturgeon Bay ZIP: 54235
Other places: Egg Harbor, Sevastapol
Population: 26,342 Rank in State: 44
Land area (sq. mi.): 492 Rank in State: 58
Water area (sq. mi.): 5
Per capita income: $7,823
Notable natural features: islands and peninsula extending into Green Bay and Lake Michigan

DOUGLAS
Created: 1854
County seat: Superior ZIP: 54880
Other places: Parkland, Solon Springs
Population: 42,403 Rank in State: 29
Land area (sq. mi.): 1,305 Rank in State: 4
Water area (sq. mi.): 34
Per capita income: $6,473
Notable natural feature: waterfalls on the Amnicon River; Big Manitou Falls, Wisconsin's highest (165 ft.)

DUNN
Created: 1854
County seat: Menomonie ZIP: 54751
Other places: Colfax, Tainter
Population: 35,482 Rank in State: 34
Land area (sq. mi.): 853 Rank in State: 26
Water area (sq. mi.): 10
Per capita income: $5,323
Notable natural feature: Red Cedar River

EAU CLAIRE
Created: 1856
County seat: Eau Claire ZIP: 54701
Other places: Altoona, Washington
Population: 83,694 Rank in State: 15
Land area (sq. mi.): 638 Rank in State: 45
Water area (sq. mi.): 7
Per capita income: $7,437
Notable natural features: Chippewa and Eau Claire rivers

FLORENCE
Created: 1881
County seat: Florence   ZIP: 54121
Other places: Aurora, Fern
Population: 4,344   Rank in State: 71
Land area (sq. mi.): 486   Rank in State: 59
Water area (sq. mi.): 13
Per capita income: $6,628
Notable natural feature: wilderness—
forests, rivers, rapids, waterfalls

FOND DU LAC
Created: 1836
County seat: Fond du Lac
ZIP: 54935
Other places: Friendship, Ripon
Population: 90,417   Rank in State: 13
Land area (sq. mi.): 725   Rank in State: 39
Water area (sq. mi.): 3
Per capita income: $8,139
Notable natural feature: glacial land forms
and landscapes at Ice Age National
Scientific Reserve

FOREST
Created: 1885
County seat: Crandon   ZIP: 54520
Other places: Laona, Wabeno
Population: 9,327   Rank in State: 68
Land area (sq. mi.): 1,011
Rank in State: 13
Water area (sq. mi.): 38
Per capita income: $4,391
Notable natural feature: Nicolet National
Forest (651,000 acres)

GRANT
Created: 1836
County seat: Lancaster   ZIP: 53813
Other places: Boscobel, Platteville
Population: 51,795   Rank in State: 24
Land area (sq. mi.): 1,144
Rank in State: 9
Water area (sq. mi.): 17
Per capita income: $5,631
Notable natural feature: confluence of
Wisconsin and Mississippi rivers

GREEN
Created: 1836
County seat: Monroe   ZIP: 53566
Other places: Brodhead, New Glarus
Population: 30,464   Rank in State: 40
Land area (sq. mi.): 583   Rank in State: 50
Water area (sq. mi.): 2
Per capita income: $7,857

Notable natural features: Sugar River and
trout streams

GREEN LAKE
Created: 1858
County seat: Green Lake   ZIP: 54941
Other places: Berlin, Princeton
Population: 18,958   Rank in State: 52
Land area (sq. mi.): 357   Rank in State: 65
Water area (sq. mi.): 28
Per capita income: $6,774
Notable natural feature: Green Lake,
Wisconsin's deepest (236 feet)

IOWA
Created: 1829
County seat: Dodgeville   ZIP: 53533
Other places: Arena, Mineral Point
Population: 20,280   Rank in State: 47
Land area (sq. mi.): 760   Rank in State: 35
Water area (sq. mi.): 11
Per capita income: $5,895
Notable natural feature: highest point in
southern Wisconsin at Blue Mound State
Park

IRON
Created: 1893
County seat: Hurley   ZIP: 54534
Other places: Mercer, Montreal
Population: 6,421   Rank in State: 70
Land area (sq. mi.): 751   Rank in State: 37
Water area (sq. mi.): 48
Per capita income: $4,761
Notable natural feature: 78-foot Saxon
Falls on Montreal River

JACKSON
Created: 1853
County seat: Black River Falls ZIP: 54615
Other places: Adams, Brockway
Population: 16,771 Rank in State: 56
Land area (sq. mi.): 998 Rank in State: 15
Water area (sq. mi.): 9
Per capita income: $5,204
Notable natural feature: Black River State
Forest

JEFFERSON
Created: 1836
County seat: Jefferson   ZIP: 53549
Other places: Fort Atkinson, Watertown
Population: 66,901 Rank in State: 21
Land area (sq. mi.): 562 Rank in State: 53
Water area: 27
Per capita income: $7,900

Notable natural feature: Lake Koshkonong and wildlife area

JUNEAU
Created: 1856
County seat: Mauston   ZIP: 53948
Other places: Elroy, New Lisbon
Population: 21,861 Rank in State: 46
Land area (sq. mi.): 774 Rank in State: 33
Water area (sq. mi.): 74
Per capita income: $5,772
Notable natural features: 44,000-acre
Necedah National Wildlife Refuge; rock
formations at Mill Bluff State Park

KENOSHA
Created: 1850
County seat: Kenosha   ZIP: 53140
Other places: Pleasant Prairie, Somers
Population: 121,236 Rank in State: 9
Land area (sq. mi.): 273 Rank in State: 69
Water area (sq. mi.): 6
Per capita income: $8,887
Notable natural feature: Lake Michigan
shoreline

KEWAUNEE
Created: 1852
County seat: Kewaunee   ZIP: 54216
Other places: Algoma, Luxemburg
Population: 20,103 Rank in State: 49
Land area (sq. mi.): 343 Rank in State: 66
Water area (sq. mi.): 1
Per capita income: $6,748
Notable natural feature: trout and salmon
from streams and Lake Michigan

LA CROSSE
Created: 1851
County seat: La Crosse   ZIP: 54601
Other places: Onalaska, Shelby
Population: 96,648 Rank in State: 12
Land area (sq. mi.): 457 Rank in State: 60
Water area (sq. mi.): 3
Per capita income: $8,039
Notable natural features: Mississippi
River; bluffs; panoramic views

LAFAYETTE
Created: 1846
County seat: Darlington   ZIP: 53530
Other places: Shullsburg, Wiota
Population: 17,111 Rank in State: 55
Land area (sq. mi.): 634 Rank in State: 46
Water area (sq. mi.): 2

Per capita income: $5,121
Notable natural feature: vestiges of lead
mines

LANGLADE
Created: 1879
County seat: Antigo   ZIP: 54409
Other places: Elcho, Rolling
Population: 20,215 Rank in State: 48
Land area (sq. mi.): 873 Rank in State: 24
Water area (sq. mi.): 17
Per capita income: $5,656
Notable natural feature: wilderness—
forests, streams, lakes

LINCOLN
Created: 1874
County seat: Merrill   ZIP: 54452
Other places: Bradley, Tomahawk
Population: 26,755 Rank in State: 42
Land area (sq. mi.): 886 Rank in State: 22
Water area (sq. mi.): 23
Per capita income: $6,773
Notable natural features: 70 percent
woodlands, lakes, trout streams,

MANITOWOC
Created: 1836
County seat: Manitowoc   ZIP: 54229
Other places: Kiel, Two Rivers
Population: 82,697 Rank in State: 16
Land area (sq. mi.): 594 Rank in State: 48
Water area (sq. mi.): 4
Per capita income: $7,629
Notable natural features: six-mile long
sand beach and 2,800 wooded acres at
Point Beach State Forest

MARATHON
Created: 1850
County seat: Wausau   ZIP: 54401
Other places: Mosinee, Weston
Population: 112,094 Rank in State: 10
Land area (sq. mi.): 1,559 Rank in State: 1
Water area (sq. mi.): 47
Per capita income: $8,075
Notable natural features: Rib Mountain;
gorge along Eau Claire River

MARINETTE
Created: 1879
County seat: Marinette   ZIP: 54143
Other places: Niagara, Peshtigo
Population: 40,647 Rank in State: 31
Land area (sq. mi.): 1,395 Rank in State: 3
Water area (sq. mi.): 26

Per capita income: $6,866
Notable natural features: rivers, waterfalls, wild blueberries

MARQUETTE
Created: 1836
County seat: Montello ZIP: 53949
Other places: Oxford, Westfield
Population: 12,615 Rank in State: 67
Land area (sq. mi.): 454 Rank in State: 61
Water area (sq. mi.): 9
Per capita income: $5,388
Notable natural features: Observatory Hill; rolling wooded hills

MENOMINEE
Created: 1961
County seat: Keshena ZIP: 54135
Population: 3,947 Rank in State: 72
Land area (sq. mi.): 359 Rank in State: 64
Water area (sq. mi.): 6
Per capita income: $1,081
Notable natural features: Wolf River; wilderness

MILWAUKEE
Created: 1834
County seat: Milwaukee ZIP: 53233
Other places: Cudahy, West Allis
Population: 935,757 Rank in State: 1
Land area (sq. mi.): 241 Rank in State: 70
Water area (sq. mi.): 1
Per capita income: $9,655
Notable natural feature: Lake Michigan shoreline

MONROE
Created: 1854
County seat: Sparta ZIP: 54656
Other places: Fort McCoy, Tomah
Population: 36,517 Rank in State: 33
Land area (sq. mi.): 904 Rank in State: 19
Water area (sq. mi.): 6
Per capita income: $6,330
Notable natural feature: mesas and buttes

OCONTO
Created: 1851
County seat: Oconto ZIP: 54153
Other places: Gillett, Oconto Falls
Population: 30,390 Rank in State: 41
Land area (sq. mi.): 1,002
Rank in State: 14
Water area (sq. mi.): 20
Per capita income: $6,244
Notable natural features: forests, lakes, trout streams

ONEIDA
Created: 1885
County seat: Rhinelander ZIP: 54501
Other places: Minocqua, Pelican
Population: 32,523 Rank in State: 39
Land area (sq. mi.): 1,130
Rank in State: 10
Water area (sq. mi.): 116
Per capita income: $7,011
Notable natural feature: hundreds of lakes

OUTAGAMIE
Created: 1851
County seat: Appleton ZIP: 54911
Other places: Kaukauna, Grand Chute
Population: 135,910 Rank in State: 8
Land area (sq. mi.): 642 Rank in State: 44
Water area (sq. mi.): 4
Per capita income: $9,410
Notable natural feature: Fox River

OZAUKEE
Created: 1853
County seat: Port Washington
ZIP: 53012
Other places: Cedarburg, Mequon
Population: 67,779 Rank in State: 20
Land area (sq. mi.): 235 Rank in State: 71
Water area (sq. mi.): 2
Per capita income: $13,395
Notable natural feature: Lake Michigan beaches and harbors

PEPIN
Created: 1858
County seat: Durand ZIP: 54736
Other places: Pepin, Stockholm
Population: 7,359 Rank in State: 69
Land area (sq. mi.): 231 Rank in State: 72
Water area (sq. mi.): 5
Per capita income: $5,140
Notable natural features: Lake Pepin; bluffs along the Mississippi River; Maiden Rock

PIERCE
Created: 1853
County seat: Ellsworth ZIP: 54011
Other places: Prescott, River Falls
Population: 32,617 Rank in State: 37
Land area (sq. mi.): 576 Rank in State: 51
Water area (sq. mi.): 1
Per capita income: $7,338
Notable natural feature: Crystal Cave, a three-level cave at Spring Valley

POLK
Created: 1853
County seat: Balsam Lake ZIP: 54810
Other places: Amery, St. Croix Falls
Population: 34,837 Rank in State: 35
Land area (sq. mi.): 919 Rank in State: 17
Water area (sq. mi.): 36
Per capita income: $6,595
Notable natural feature: Old Man of the Dalles rock formation along St. Croix River

PORTAGE
Created: 1836
County Seat: Stevens Point ZIP: 54481
Other places: Hull, Plover
Population: 61,256 Rank in State: 22
Land area (sq. mi.): 810
Rank in State: 30
Water area (sq. mi.):10
Per capita income: $7,259
Notable natural feature: sandy central plains

PRICE
Created: 1879
County Seat: Phillips ZIP: 54555
Other places: Park Falls, Prentice
Population: 16,374 Rank in State: 59
Land area (sq. mi.): 28 Rank in State: 5
Water area (sq. mi.): 28
Per capita income: $6,445
Notable natural features: Chequamegon National Forest, Flambeau State Forest

RACINE
Created: 1836
County seat: Racine ZIP: 53403
Other places: Burlington, Sturtevant
Population: 169,373 Rank in State: 5
Land area (sq. mi.): 334
Rank in State: 67
Water area (sq. mi.): 7
Per capita income: $9,820
Notable natural feature: Lake Michigan shoreline

RICHLAND
Created: 1842
County seat: Richland Center
ZIP: 53581
Other places: Gotham, Lone Rock
Population: 17,355 Rank in State: 54
Land area (sq. mi.): 585 Rank in State: 49
Water area (sq. mi.): 8
Per capita income: $5,610

Notable natural feature: rock formations— Elephant Trunk Rock, Steamboat Rock, Rock Bridge

ROCK
Created: 1836
County seat: Janesville ZIP: 53545
Other places: Beloit, Edgerton
Population: 139,078 Rank in State: 6
Land area (sq. mi.): 724 Rank in State: 40
Water area (sq. mi.): 6
Per capita income: $9,241
Notable natural feature: Rock River

RUSK
Created: 1901
County seat: Ladysmith ZIP: 54848
Other places: Flambeau, Weyerhaeuser
Population: 15,644 Rank in State: 60
Land area (sq. mi.): 913 Rank in State: 18
Water area (sq. mi.): 17
Per capita income: $5,035
Notable natural features: forests, Chippewa and Flambeau rivers

ST. CROIX
Created: 1840
County seat: Hudson ZIP: 54016
Other places: Glenwood City, New Richmond
Population: 47,247 Rank in State: 25
Land area (sq. mi.): 723 Rank in State: 41
Water area (sq. mi.): 12
Per capita income: $9,361
Notable natural features: St. Croix River, wooded bluffs

SAUK
Created: 1840
County seat: Baraboo ZIP: 53913
Other places: Prairie du Sac, Spring Green
Population: 45,613 Rank in State: 26
Land area (sq. mi.): 838 Rank in State: 27
Water area (sq. mi.): 20
Per capita income: $7,066
Notable natural features: rock formations and glacial features at Devil's Lake State Park; Baraboo Range

SAWYER
Created: 1883
County seat: Hayward ZIP: 54843
Other places: Radisson, Winter
Population: 13,652 Rank in State: 65
Land area (sq. mi.): 1,255 Rank in State: 6
Water area (sq. mi.): 93

Per capita income: $4,905
Notable natural features: Flambeau River
State Forest; Meteor Hill (1,801 ft.)

SHAWANO
Created: 1853
County seat: Shawano ZIP: 54166
Other places: Bonduel, Wittenberg
Population: 36,646 Rank in State: 32
Land area (sq. mi.): 897 Rank in State: 20
Water area (sq. mi.): 18
Per capita income: $6,097
Notable natural features: 40 percent forest,
50 lakes

SHEBOYGAN
Created: 1836
County seat: Sheboygan
 ZIP: 53081
Other places: Plymouth, Sheboygan Falls
Population: 102,503 Rank in State: 11
Land area (sq. mi.): 515 Rank in State: 57
Water area (sq. mi.): 24
Per capita income: $8,955
Notable natural feature: lake dunes at
Kohler Park Dunes

TAYLOR
Created: 1875
County seat: Medford ZIP: 54451
Other places: Gilman, Rib Lake
Population: 19,387 Rank in State: 51
Land area (sq. mi.): 975 Rank in State: 16
Water area (sq. mi.): 12
Per capita income: $5,671
Notable natural feature: Chequamegon
National Forest

TREMPEALEAU
Created: 1854
County seat: Whitehall ZIP: 54773
Other places: Arcadia, Osseo
Population: 26,521 Rank in State: 43
Land area (sq. mi.): 736 Rank in State: 38
Water area (sq. mi.): 2
Per capita income: $5,623
Notable natural feature: Brady's Bluff
Prairie, a dry prairie 460 feet above the
Mississippi River

VERNON
Created: 1851
County seat: Viroqua ZIP: 54665
Other places: Hillsboro, Westby
Population: 26,082 Rank in State: 45
Land area (sq. mi.): 808 Rank in State: 31

Water area (sq. mi.): 1
Per capita income: $5,408
Notable natural features: Driftless Area;
Ocooch Mountains; Kickapoo River

VILAS
Created: 1893
County seat: Eagle River ZIP: 54521
Other places: Arbor Vitae, Lac du Flam-
beau
Population: 17,635 Rank in State: 53
Land area (sq. mi.): 867
Rank in State: 25
Water area (sq. mi.): 148
Per capita income: $6,039
Notable natural features: hundreds of
lakes; Muskellunge Hill (1,845 feet)

WALWORTH
Created: 1836
County seat: Elkhorn ZIP: 53121
Other places: Lake Geneva, Whitewater
Population: 73,091 Rank in State: 19
Lake area (sq. mi.): 556 Rank in State: 54
Water area (sq. mi.): 21
Per capita income: $8,265
Notable natural feature: Kettle Moraine
State Forest

WASHBURN
Created: 1883
County seat: Shell Lake ZIP: 54871
Other places: Minong, Spooner
Population: 14,209 Rank in State: 63
Land area (sq. mi.): 815 Rank in State: 29
Water area (sq. mi.): 50
Per capita income: $5,357
Notable natural features: Namekegon and
Yellow rivers, numerous lakes

WASHINGTON
Created: 1836
County seat: West Bend
 ZIP: 53095
Other places: Germantown, Hartford
Population: 87,783 Rank in State: 14
Land area (sq. mi.): 431 Rank in State: 63
Water area (sq. mi.): 6
Per capita income: $10,229
Notable natural features: lakes and crop-
lands

WAUKESHA
Created: 1846
County seat: Waukesha ZIP: 53188
Other places: Brookfield, New Berlin

Population: 288,150 Rank in State: 3
Land area (sq. mi.): 554 Rank in State: 55
Water area (sq. mi.): 25
Per capita income: $12,411
Notable natural features: Kettle Moraine
State Forest; spring and mineral waters

WAUPACA
Created: 1851
County seat: Waupaca
ZIP: 54981
Other places: Clintonville, Weyauwega
Population: 44,949 Rank in State: 27
Land area (sq. mi.): 754 Rank in State: 36
Water area (sq. mi.): 14
Per capita income: $7,055
Notable natural feature: chain of 22
spring-fed interconnected lakes

WAUSHARA
Created: 1851
County seat: Wautoma
ZIP: 54982
Other places: Plainfield, Wild Rose
Population: 20,002 Rank in State: 50
Land area (sq. mi.): 628 Rank in State: 47
Water area (sq. mi.): 8
Per capita income: $5,739
Notable natural features: small lakes and
ponds, woods

WINNEBAGO
Created: 1840
County seat: Oshkosh
ZIP: 54901
Other places: Menasha, Neenah
Population: 137,914 Rank in State: 7
Land area (sq. mi.): 449 Rank in State: 62
Water area (sq. mi.): 256
Per capita income: $9,540
Notable natural feature: largest lake,
Winnebago (215 square miles)

WOOD
Created: 1856
County seat: Wisconsin Rapids
ZIP: 54494
Other places: Marshfield, Nekoosa
Population: 75,806 Rank in State: 18
Land area (sq. mi.): 801 Rank in State: 32
Water area (sq. mi.): 11
Per capita income: $8,775
Notable natural features: diverse wildlife
areas; Wisconsin River, rapids

Source:
Wisconsin Blue Book 1987-1988

Population:
Wisconsin Department of Administration, Demographic Services Center, Official Population Estimates for 1986, as of January 1, 1986.

Ranking:
Legislative Reference Bureau based on 1986 population estimates.

Land and Water Area:
Department of Natural Resources, December 1986.
Water area figures have been converted from acres to sq. mi., for comparison with land area. For reporting purposes, DNR assigns the acreage of lakes spanning two or more counties to the county containing the majority of acreage. Counties were not ranked for watery-ness because DNR does not include the Great Lakes and the Mississippi River in its acreage. Thus, for example, Door County, which is surrounded by water, appears to be virtually arid in this accounting.

Per Capita Income:
Wisconsin Department of Revenue, Division of Research and Analysis, April 1987.

Fifty-One Things You Should Know about Wisconsin

Memorize these Wisconsin tidbits and never lack for party conversation

1. "On, Wisconsin!" was written in 1909. Its composer, William Purdy, intended to enter it in a Minnesota football song contest. A friend talked him into giving it to UW. It became the state song in 1959, with these lyrics prescribed by law (sec. 1.10, Wisconsin Statutes):

> *On, Wisconsin! On, Wisconsin!*
> *Grand old badger state!*
> *We, thy loyal sons and daughters*
> *Hail thee, good and great.*
> *On, Wisconsin! On, Wisconsin!*
> *Champion of the right*
> *Forward, our motto*
> *God will give thee might!*

Paul McCartney now owns the rights to "On Wisconsin!"

2. Wisconsin's highest point is Timm's Hill in Price County. It soars to a majestic 1,951.8 feet.

3. There are 108,000 miles of roads in Wisconsin.

4. Green Bay is known as the Toilet Paper Capital of the world.

5. At one million acres, Marathon County is Wisconsin's largest. It is larger than Rhode Island.

6. In 1634, the French explorer Jean Nicolet was the first European to Escape to Wisconsin. He was

looking for the Northwest Passage. He found Green Bay.

7. Mrs. Dena Smith, a Republican elected State Treasurer in 1960, was the first woman to hold statewide elective office in Wisconsin.

8. Artifically colored oleomargarine was outlawed in Wisconsin until 1967.

9. Two Wisconsinites have won the Nobel prize: in 1958, Prof. Joshua Lederberg, UW geneticist, won the prize for medicine; in 1975, Dr. Howard Temin, UW oncology researcher, shared the prize in Physiology-Medicine.

10. Wisconsin Pulitzer Prize winners include: Zona Gale (1921) for her play *Miss Lulu Bett*; Hamlin Garland (1922) for his biography *A Daughter of the Middle Border*; Edna Ferber (1925) for her novel *So Big*; and Thornton Wilder (1938) for his play *Our Town*.

11. The first mental hospital in Wisconsin was the Mendota State Hospital for the Insane, which opened in 1860.

12. Wisconsin's founding fathers were men of few words. The state motto "Forward" was chosen in 1851. Rejected mottos included "Onward", "Upward" and "Excelsior."

13. The first civilian hospital in Wisconsin was St. John's Infirmary, which opened in Milwaukee in 1848. It refused to accept patients who had contagious diseases.

14. The American water spaniel is the Wisconsin state dog. The breed was developed by Dr. Fred Pfeifer in New London in the 1920s. It is the only breed of dog developed in Wisconsin, one of only five breeds developed in the United States.

15. The highest waterfall in Wisconsin is 165-foot Big Manitou Falls in Pattison State Park near Superior. It is the fourth highest waterfall east of the Rockies.

16. America's first hydroelectric dam was built on the Fox River near Appleton in 1882.

17. The first house in the United States to be wired for electricity was in Appleton.

18. In 1946, Sheboygan became the first community in Wisconsin to fluoridate its water.

19. America's first kindergarten was begun by German immigrant Margarethe Schurz in Watertown in 1856.

20. The first auto race in history took place in 1878. Two steam-powered cars raced from Green Bay to Madison. One finished the

course in 33 hours and collected a $5000 prize. The other broke down enroute.

21. The oldest continually operating radio station in the world is WHA in Madison, which began sending out signals in 1917. In keeping with its public radio format, it produced the first music appreciation progam shortly thereafter.

22. Alvan Earle Bovay presided over the first meeting of a new political party in the Ripon schoolhouse in 1854. He thought the disaffected Whigs, Democrats, and Free Soilers should call themselves Republicans because "it is a good name... with charm and prestige."

23. Wisconsin was the first state to begin assigning numbers to highways. Before 1917, there were no uniform highway marking systems, anywhere.

24. The sole remaining covered bridge in Wisconsin is an 1876 structure spanning Cedar Creek, three miles north of Cedarburg.

25. Dr. Erastus Wolcott performed the world's first kidney removal operation at St. Mary's Hospital (formerly St. John's Infirmary) in Milwaukee on June 4, 1861.

26. Governor Louis Harvey is the only Wisconsin governor to die in a war. Soon after his 1862 inauguration, he led a relief contingent to help Wisconsin units that had taken heavy losses at the Battle of Shiloh. He fell into the Tennessee River and drowned.

27. Carroll College, which

opened its doors on September 8, 1846, with a faculty of two and a student body of five, is Wisconsin's oldest college.

28. The Gideons, the Bible-in-every-hotel-room organization, began in Boscobel in 1898.

29. Poplar native Major Richard Bong shot down 40 enemy aircraft in air combat during World War II, becoming America's all-time leading air ace.

30. The first Christian Science Church in America was built in 1886 in Oconto.

31. In 1936, Oneida County adopted the first rural zoning ordinance in the United States.

32. The world's first electric trolley began operation in Appleton in 1886.

33. On October 8, 1871, the most disastrous forest fire in American history destroyed the entire city of Peshtigo and claimed more than 800 lives.

34. Terry Anne Meeuwsen, a DePere girl, was Miss America 1973. She is the only Miss Wisconsin ever to win the title.

35. The Green Bay Packers won the Super Bowl in 1967 and 1968.

36. The Milwaukee Braves won the World Series in 1957.

37. The Milwaukee Brewers lost the 1982 World Series to the St. Louis Cardinals.

38. Speedskater Eric Heiden was the only American ever to win five gold medals in a Winter Olympics.

39. Wisconsin is the only state in which sphagnum moss is harvested commercially.

40. John Heisman, for whom football's Heisman Trophy is named, played and coached football in the late 19th and early 20th centuries, inventing in the course of his career such current standards as the forward pass, the center snap, and the "hike" signal for starting a play. He died in 1936, and is buried in Forest Home Cemetery in Rhinelander.

41. Almost one third of Americans live within 500 miles of Wisconsin.

42. Wisconsin was the birthplace of more than a hundred circuses. Twenty six had their winter quarters at Delavan between 1847 and 1894. The Ringling Brothers Circus began in Baraboo in 1884.

43. The University of Wisconsin was the first to begin correspondence courses.

44. The *Green Bay Intelligencer*, established in 1833, was Wisconsin's first newspaper.

45. In 1853, Wisconsin became the first state to abolish capital punishment.

46. The H.H. Bennett Photo Studio of Wisconsin Dells is the oldest photo studio in the United States in continuous existence.

47. There are 11 Indian reser-

vations in Wisconsin governed by the Chippewa, Menominee, Oneida, Potawatomi, Stockbridge-Munsee and Winnebago tribes.

48. The largest experimental aviation event in the world is the Experimental Aircraft Association fly-in held each August in Oshkosh. During that event, Oshkosh's Wittman Field becomes the busiest airport in the country.

49. There are 72 counties, 189 cities, 393 villages and 1266 towns in Wisconsin — a total of 1920 separate local government units.

50. Primary and secondary education is the state's largest public employer. The state's 427 school districts employ more than 110,000 teachers.

51. The American Birkebeiner, the largest cross country ski race in the United States, brings more than 5000 competitors to Cable each February for the 55 kilometer race.
—K.V.

The Pleasures of Parsnips

Parsnips are one of the tastiest of all vegetables, and yet many people don't understand this humble root. They harvest it at the wrong time, find that it is bland-tasting, and then never plant it again.

The truth is that parsnips should not be harvested virtually until winter has set in. They are a real Wisconsin crop! You start them from seed sown into the open garden in early spring, then wait for many months, at least until a month after the first heavy autumn frosts, before you even begin to harvest. Throw a deep hay mulch over the parsnip row and you may continue to harvest roots well into winter. Then resume harvesting as soon as you can dig into the soil in spring. But be sure to harvest all roots before new leaves begin to sprout in April, because after that the roots begin to lose quality quickly. You will sow seeds for next year's crop just as you are harvesting the last of the current crop.❀

1 Fabulous Firsts

The first time that the gross receipts for a football game exceeded $1 million was on December 31, 1961, in Green Bay. On that day the Green Bay Packers defeated the New York Giants 37-0 for the National Football League championship. There were 39,029 spectators, and the paid attendance totaled $1,013,792. Each of the Packers received $5,195.44, and each of the Giants received $3,339.99.

Christmas is here:
Winds whistle shrill,
Icy and chill.
Little care we;
Little we fear,
Weather without,
Sheltered about
The Mahogany Tree.

—*William Makepeace Thackeray*

DECEMBER IN THE GARDEN

Highlights:
❊ *Give houseplants a rest*
❊ *Buy the living Christmas tree*
❊ *Buy blooming cyclamen now*
❊ *Check vegetables stored in root cellar*

December is devoted to the hustle and bustle of holiday preparations. It is also "last chance" time for many Wisconsin gardeners. Last chance before the ground freezes hard to water evergreens for the winter. Last chance to mulch parsnips—and, in warmer sections, carrots, too—so that we can harvest them for another month or more. Last chance to mulch perennial beds before the holidays consume all our time. Even last chance to plant trees and shrubs before the ground becomes totally unworkable.

All the nation yearns for a white Christmas, but here in Wisconsin we actually have one—well, most years, anyway. In the state's northern tier, a white Christmas is virtually assured. In the La Crosse area the chances are about 8 in 10. And in the southern and eastern sections, snow is on the ground at Christmas 6 to 8 years out of every 10.

You can't predict a season's snowfall with great accuracy, but you can make an educated guess. One weather study found that summer weather patterns are, much more often than not, carried over to winter. In five of every six instances, a summer drought meant scant snowfall the following winter—and a wet summer meant lots of snow to follow. In a just world, it should be the other way around, but—in gardening as in life and poker—we must play the hand we are dealt.

The purpose of a winter mulch is not to keep the ground warm but to keep it cold. It is not the cold that injures hardy plants but the heaving of the soil caused by alternate freezes and thaws. It is the purpose of the mulch to prevent that heaving. A good snow cover is the best winter mulch. But if Ma Nature doesn't cooperate, we must pitch in with shredded leaves, pine boughs, spoiled hay, straw, or other organic materials.

This is the month to set up your bird feeding station, before the heavy snows fly. Be sure to keep the birds' food supply constant through the winter, because your feathered friends quickly become dependent on your largess.

Most houseplants stop growing now, as days grow short and often are cloudy, greatly reducing light intensity. This begins a needed rest period for houseplants. Cooperate by withholding fertilizer and reducing water, until new plant growth begins early next spring.

Spend a little time in your basement to check vegetables and fruits stored in the root cellar. Remove any that show the slightest signs of decay. Also check the dahlias and other tender bulbs. Keep them just moist enough to prevent desiccation, but dry enough to prevent rot. Beginning gardeners usually keep them too moist. Gladiolus bulbs should be kept in a cool, dark, well-ventilated place.

Buy your living Christmas tree anytime during the month, and treat

it as you would a prize houseplant until it is ready to go to its permanent outdoor location after Christmas.

Blooming gift plants received for holiday show will perform longest if they are given bright light, cool temperatures, and plenty of water. Cyclamen is among the most beautiful of all, and will keep on blooming well into April if given proper care.

If you want geraniums to bloom as winter houseplants, give them the brightest window in the house and plenty of warmth. They will bloom best if kept slightly potbound and a little dry.❀　—*J.M.*

ANSWERS TO PUZZLES

CROSSWORD, page 40.

R¹	O²	B³	I⁴	N⁵		S⁶	O⁷	B⁸	S⁹			G¹⁰	O¹¹	D¹²
E¹³	R	A	S	E		O¹⁴	R	A	L			O¹⁵	L	E
D¹⁶	I	C	T	A			S¹⁷	H	A	W¹⁸		L¹⁹	D	E
	T²⁰	H	O	R	N²¹	T²²	O	N	W	I	L	D²³	E	R
		M²⁴	E	A	N			L²⁵	E	A				
D²⁶	I²⁷		L²⁸	E	A	D		P²⁹	A³⁰	C	E	M		
E³¹	B³²	E	N			A³³	L	D	O		E³⁴	B³⁵	B³⁶	
W³⁷	I	L	L	I³⁸	A³⁹	M⁴⁰	P	R	O	X	M⁴¹	I	R	E
Y⁴²	S	L		C⁴³	N	E	T			O⁴⁴	R	A	N	
	S⁴⁵	A⁴⁶	I	N	T		I⁴⁷	P⁴⁸	S⁴⁹	O		T⁵⁰	D	
	W⁵¹	I	N			S⁵²	L	O	T					
G⁵³	E⁵⁴	O	R	G	I⁵⁵	A⁵⁶	O	K	E	E	F⁵⁷	F⁵⁸	E⁵⁹	
A⁶⁰	A	R		S⁶¹	O	W	N			L⁶²	A	U	R	A⁶³
I⁶⁴	S	T		W⁶⁵	O	O	D⁶⁶			L⁶⁷	I	M	I	T
N⁶⁸	T	H		A⁶⁹	L	F	A			A⁷⁰	L	I	C	E

ENTERTAINERS, page 54 (bottom)
1-D; 2-E; 3-A; 4-F; 5-C; 6-B.

TV STARS, page 54 (top)
1-D; 2-F; 3-H; 4-J; 5-I; 6-B; 7-A; 8-E; 9-C; 10-G.

JUMBLE PUZZLE, page 121
Jumbles: TAXES PENNY LOBBY BUTTER SMUGGLE
Answer: (The) BLUEBONNET PLAGUE

Ye · end · of · ye · story